REVIEWS FOR NICOLA PIERCE

Titanic: True Stories of Her Passengers, Crew and Legacy
'A delightful book and a valuable resource in the *Titanic* canon' RTE.ie

Spirit of the Titanic
'Gripping, exciting and unimaginably shattering' *The Guardian*

O'Connell Street: The History and Life of Dublin's Iconic Street
'A fascinating tour of the street.' *The Irish Times* reviewing Nicola Pierce on RTÉ TV's *Nationwide*

Chasing Ghosts
'A fascinating story about Arctic exploration, full of historical detail. Perfect for readers with adventure in their hearts' *Irish Independent*

Kings of the Boyne
'Compelling and reveals ... how all great historical events are shaped by the actions of those caught up in them, from king to foot soldier.' *Books for Keeps*

Behind the Walls
'History as it really happened with its gritty depiction of the terror-struck city of Derry in 1689 ... a vivid evocation of life in a city under siege' *parentsintouch.co.uk*

City of Fate
'Historical fiction at its best'
The Guardian

NICOLA PIERCE is an author of historical books, including *Titanic: True Stories of Her Passengers, Crew and Legacy* and *O'Connell Street: The History and Life of Dublin's Iconic Street*. She published her first novel, *Spirit of the Titanic*, to rave reviews, and her second novel, *City of Fate*, transports the reader deep into the Russian city of Stalingrad during the Second World War. Her *Behind the Walls*, set in the besieged city of Derry in 1689, was followed by *Kings of the Boyne*, also set in seventeenth-century Ireland during a defining moment in history. Nicola then delved deep into the story of explorer Francis Crozier and the Sir John Franklin Arctic North West Passage expedition, in her haunting novel *Chasing Ghosts*, and took the reader to Australia during the Great Famine in nineteenth-century Ireland with *In Between Worlds*, a novel of the journey of the Famine girls to the New World.

To read more about Nicola, go to nicolapiercewriter.com.

for my husband

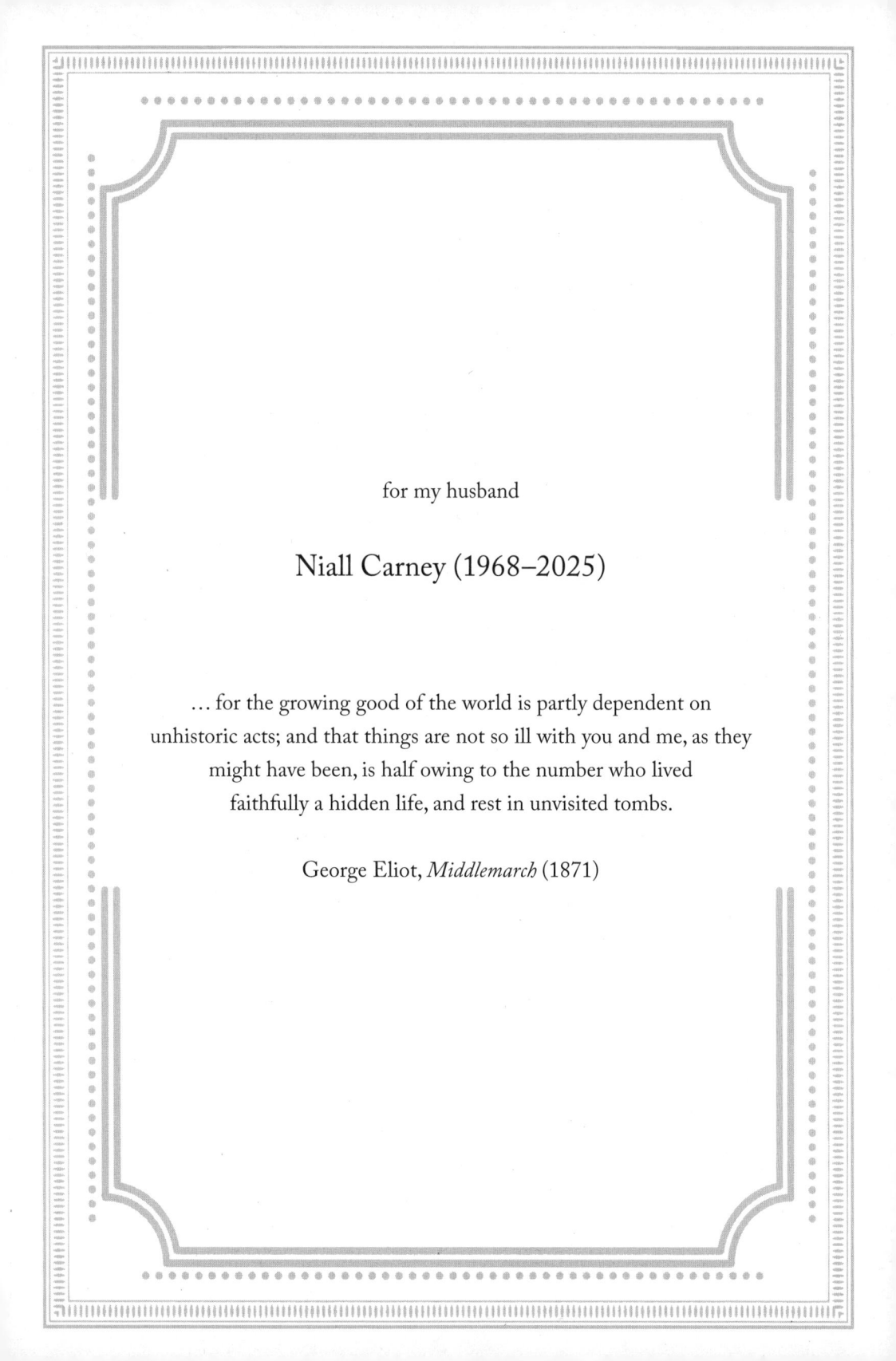

Niall Carney (1968–2025)

… for the growing good of the world is partly dependent on unhistoric acts; and that things are not so ill with you and me, as they might have been, is half owing to the number who lived faithfully a hidden life, and rest in unvisited tombs.

George Eliot, *Middlemarch* (1871)

ACKNOWLEDGMENTS

I was in the middle of my Annette Carson chapter when my husband was diagnosed with terminal cancer. I want to thank my friend, writer and biographer Eleanor Fitzsimons, for her tremendous help with researching Annette, and, also, for reading my Constance Wilde chapter. Eleanor wrote about Constance in her bestselling *Wilde's Women: How Oscar Wilde was Shaped by the Women He Knew*. Eleanor's passion for research was infectious and helped reignite mine after Niall died.

I also have to thank Rottingdean historians Mike Mole and Mike Laslett who provided me with pertinent information and images in relation to Annette Carson.

Thanks to Michael Smith who kindly read my chapter on Emily Shackleton. I recommend his books on Irish polar explorers, Ernest Shackleton, Francis Crozier and Tom Crean.

Thanks to writer and editor Rachel Pierce for being my first reader and for sending me that wonderful *Middlemarch* quote which reminded me why I was writing this book.

I am so very grateful to Beatrice Behan's daughter Blanaid who took the time to talk to me about her mother and shared photographs of her mother's paintings. Thanks also to historian Ciarán MacGonigal, writer Donal Fallon, Paolo Viscardi and Nigel Monahan from the Natural Museum of Ireland, Colin Kelleher from the National Botanic Gardens, Susan Dolan from the RHA Gallery, along with botanist and writer Doctor Declan Doogue for providing information for my Beatrice chapter.

Susan Houlden, my longtime editor, and Emma Byrne, artist and designer, were obliged to put together the list of images and then source all the pictures, a job that ordinarily is the writer's responsibility. However, following Niall's funeral, I was temporarily unable to work and needed their help as I have never needed it before.

The manuscript benefited hugely from Susan's expertise and, as always, I relied on her enthusiasm and curiosity for the subject matter. A few weeks before Niall died, Emma took the time to send him all her ideas for the cover. He favoured two, and Emma produced a beautiful cover that incorporates his preferences.

Niall was my greatest champion and supporter. Just like the wives inside this book, Niall provided me with everything I ever needed to chase my dreams. This book is here today because of him.

First published 2025 by The O'Brien Press Ltd.,
12 Terenure Road East, Rathgar, Dublin 6, Ireland.
Tel: +353 1 4923333 E-mail: books@obrien.ie. Website: obrien.ie
The O'Brien Press is a member of Publishing Ireland.

ISBN: 978-1-78849-477-9

Copyright for text © Nicola Pierce 2025

The moral rights of the author have been asserted.
Copyright for typesetting, editing, layout, design © The O'Brien Press Ltd.
Cover and inside design by Emma Byrne.
End paper images: (front from top left) Mary O'Connell, Alamy; Sinéad de Valera, Alamy; Margaret Clarke, Bridgeman Images; (back from top left) Charlotte Shaw, Bridgeman Images; Constance Wilde and son, Alamy; Emily Shackleton, Alamy.

All rights reserved. No part of this publication may be reproduced or utilised in any form or by any means, electronic or mechanical, including for text and data mining, training artificial intelligence systems, photocopying, recording or in any information storage and retrieval system, without permission in writing from the publisher.

2 4 6 7 5 3 1
26 28 27 25

Printed and bound by Drukarnia Skleniarz, Poland.
The paper in this book is produced using pulp from managed forests.

To the best of our knowledge, this book complies in full with the requirements of the General Product Safety Regulation (GPSR). For further information and help with any safety queries, please contact us at productsafety@obrien.ie

Published in
DUBLIN
UNESCO
City of Literature

Great Irish books
O'BRIEN
obrien.ie

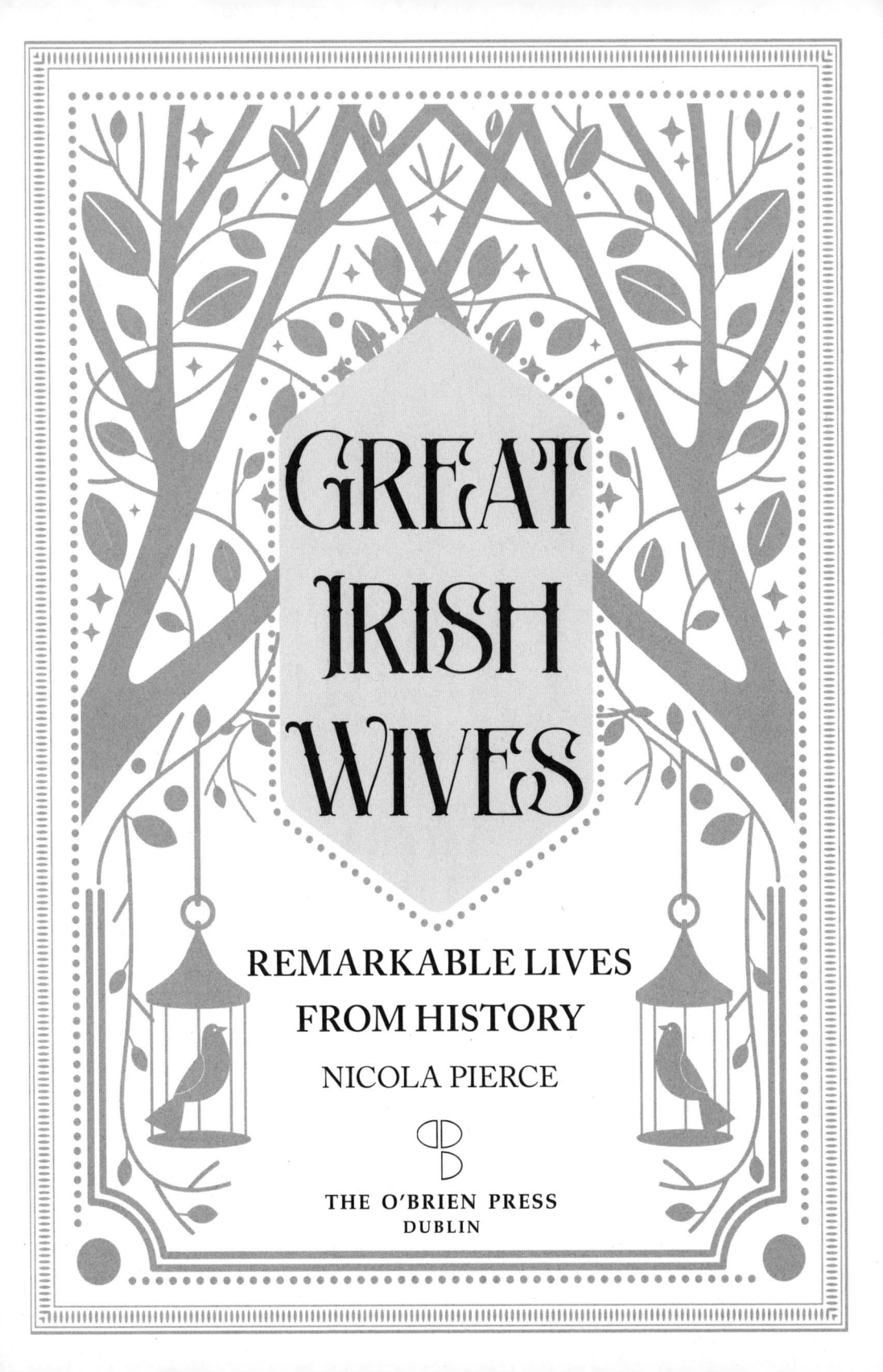

GREAT IRISH WIVES

REMARKABLE LIVES FROM HISTORY

NICOLA PIERCE

THE O'BRIEN PRESS
DUBLIN

Table of Contents

Author's Note		Page 11
1	Matilda Tone	15
2	Mary O'Connell	41
3	Constance Wilde	65
4	Charlotte Shaw	93
5	Emily Shackleton	117
6	Annette Carson	143
7	Sinéad de Valera	165
8	Margaret Clarke	189
9	Georgie 'George' Yeats	209
10	Beatrice Behan	239
Further Reading		263
Index		269

AUTHOR'S NOTE

In 1973, English couple Maurice and Maralyn Bailey set sail for New Zealand on their boat *Auralyn* but were forced to abandon her after colliding with a whale and ended up adrift on a tiny life raft for a total of 118 days until their rescue by a Korean ship, by which point the Baileys were in bad shape, needing help to stand, wash and put on clean clothes. In her book about the couple, Sophie Elmhurst describes Maralyn crawling toward their possessions to dig out her comb. Returning to her husband's side, Maralyn began to comb his hair and stroked his face. This simple gesture stunned the crew, who had been at sea for two years, and convinced the captain that it was the wife's tenderness that had kept the couple alive. In the weeks that followed, 1970s media attempted to make the story Maurice's, with some newspapers not bothering to mention Maralyn by name. Perhaps Maurice was ahead of his time when he openly praised his wife's discipline and self-mastery, it was she who took charge after their boat sank and, ultimately, it was her strength that saved them.

Just like my history of O'Connell Street, this book is the result of an idea that bubbled up during a sleepless night and I began it just before my fourth wedding anniversary. Previously, I had written about the likes of Daniel O'Connell, William Butler Yeats and George Bernard Shaw, without knowing or even considering if they were married at all.

I decided to choose ten wives because of their husbands – the barristers and politicians, the activists, the playwrights, the artist and the polar explorer – realising that I knew next to nothing about these women.

Perhaps my biggest challenge in writing about the women was the husbands. From time to time, they got in my way, their outsized personalities matching their extraordinary ambitions and achievements. It was a blessing when the wife wrote letters or kept a journal. For instance, Mary O'Connell's letters to Daniel allow us to bypass her husband's celebrity and appreciate his flaws and foibles. Meanwhile, the most elusive of the women was Edward Carson's first wife Annette, as the only words of hers in print are her brief response to identifying the young man who robbed her purse.

Each woman was remarkable in her own way. One could argue that Constance Wilde's achievements, as a writer and fashion icon, were on a par with her husband's while Charlotte Shaw literally rescued her husband from poverty before setting him on the road to stardom, discreetly providing him with subjects to write about and the security to do so without interruption.

In becoming a wife, Sinéad de Valera gave up two careers; she was an award-winning teacher whose work on the stage had impressed the likes of William Butler Yeats and George Moore. For the bulk of her children's childhood, she parented alone, keeping them safe during the Easter Rising, the War of Independence, the Civil War and the Spanish flu. In later years, she dedicated herself to writing.

By the time I finished this book, I was a widow, just like Matilda Tone, Emily Shackleton, Margaret Clarke, George Yeats and Beatrice Behan, and I found myself in awe of these women all over again. Each had had to soldier on, looking after children, maintaining homes and paying bills whilst ensuring that her husband's legacy flourished.

Matilda Tone edited Theobald Wolfe's diaries, while Emily Shackleton approached Ernest's publishers about producing a sanctioned biography and chose his biographer wisely – both women taking control of their husbands' stories.

Margaret Clarke kept Harry's studios in production whilst fulfilling commissions for her own artwork and taking care of her three young children. George Yeats was publicly vilified for not bringing William's body back from France for a big funeral. However, it later transpired that she was fulfilling his wishes to avoid such pomp and ceremony in Ireland. For the next thirty years, she made herself available to visiting students and teachers who wished to know more about her husband's work and jokingly referred to the summer months as her 'American Season'.

Several biographers believe that had Brendan Behan not married Beatrice, he might not have written anything after *The Quare Fellow*. Newly widowed Beatrice had to keep calm when all manner of strangers, from taximen to drinking buddies, turned up at her door claiming to be owed money by Brendan. In fact, his death left her in financial straits, with a young baby, forcing her to rent out half her home to pay his income tax bill.

These women prioritised their husbands' passions and demons over their own, with only one, Charlotte Shaw, remaining childless. Each wife provided her husband with a home, where he was not only loved and supported, but also sheltered, in mind and body, from mounting pressures brought on by his chosen vocation. And while some of the husbands yearned for more, in rejecting their partners, those women who had freed them to chase their dreams, Oscar Wilde, Ernest Shackleton and Brendan Behan displayed chronic self-doubt.

The ten husbands have one thing in common: they married well. In truth, the more I unveiled about each wife, the more it became impossible to imagine their husbands' careers without them.

Matilda Witherington Tone

CHAPTER ONE

MATILDA TONE (1769-1849)

Wife of Theobald Wolfe Tone, United Irishman

'Scarcely any of the incidents in this tale are imaginary ...' So begins Irish writer and activist Rosamond Jacob's (1888–1960) author's note for her 1957 novel, *The Rebel's Wife*. Jacob had turned her biography of Matilda Tone into a novel when the biography had failed to garner any interest from publishers. She added in two fictional scenes (at least), highlighting these for the reader. The book was reviewed in the *Galway Observer* on Saturday, 28 June 1958, as 'a fascinating book in the form of a novel ... which is based entirely on fact'. A brief outline of the story is provided: that it will shed light on Martha Witherington's marriage to Ireland's first republican, Theobald Wolfe Tone, and how bravely she overcame misfortune after his death. The book opens on Dublin's Grafton Street, in the spring of 1785, when fifteen-year-old Matilda's days as Martha Witherington were numbered.

Martha lived at number 69 (number 68 in Marianne Elliott's biography of Wolfe Tone) on the right-hand side of Grafton Street, looking towards St Stephen's Green from College Green.

In 1986, Terry de Valera (1922–2007) gave a talk to the Royal Dublin Society about the historic importance of Grafton Street. He relates how his mother, Sinéad, always lamented that one of Dublin's principal thoroughfares was called after a foreigner, the first Duke of Grafton (1663–1690), Henry Fitzroy, an illegitimate son of King Charles II (1630–1685). She felt the name should have been changed to Wolfe Tone Street, no doubt thinking of Sackville Street being finally renamed after Daniel O'Connell, the Irish political leader, in May 1924. However, perhaps a more suitable name for Grafton Street might have been Matilda Tone Street.

Martha was the eldest daughter of merchant William Witherington (1737–1802) and his wife Catherine (1741–1797), who lived with her widowed father, the wealthy Reverend Edward Fanning (1709?–1791). The reverend doted on Martha, his favourite grandchild, little knowing that she was soon to break all their hearts.

According to Jacob's novel, Reverend Fanning had just one problem with Martha and that was her habit of sitting in the window. The family lived over her father's shop and so had a prime view of the comings and goings of the busy street below. From the beginning, Grafton Street was a mixture of residences and businesses with men like William Witherington preferring to reside in apartments above their shops. In her book, Rosamund Jacob mentions places like George Draper's haberdashery and John Parker's bookshop. In fact, there were several bookshops in and around the street which would have been particularly convenient for students attending Trinity College.

In a 2004 essay, Máire Kennedy writes of Patrick Byrne's bookshop at 108 Grafton Street, a favourite of politicians and academics, which was to host meetings of the Society of United Irishmen (formed to press for peaceful reform and fairer representation) after its founding in 1791.

And so it was, on a spring day in 1785, that Martha was sitting in her window, when the society's future founder, Theobald Wolfe Tone (1763–1798), who was studying law, at his father's behest, in Trinity College, is believed to have been making his way to Byrne's bookshop on Grafton Street and happened to look up as he passed by number 69. In that same moment that the twenty-one-year-old law student caught sight of her, she saw him, and both, it seems, were instantly impressed. In his journal, Tone describes how, following that first encounter, he would traipse up Grafton Street every day, after lectures, to catch a glimpse of the beautiful girl who so intrigued him. Over the next few weeks, 'a mutual affection', nurtured solely by longing looks, sprang up between them without a single word being exchanged. He thought her 'as beautiful as an angel' and sought to reduce the distance from the street to the apartment framed by that window; in short, he needed a way inside the family home.

As a penniless student, Tone knew that he had nothing to offer the girl's parents. His own parents were now living in reduced circumstances on a small farm in Blackhall, near Clane, in County Kildare. Previously, his father Peter ($d.$1805) had been a prosperous builder of luxury coaches and owned some property, thereby allowing the Tones to employ servants. Everything changed in the late 1770s when Peter's business went under.

A lover of theatre and Shakespeare, Tone had found in Martha Witherington at her Grafton Street window his own Juliet and balcony. He came up with a plan, which he did not relish, to befriend Martha's older brother Edward, whom he knew from college. One wonders if Edward ever read Wolfe Tone's journal in later years and saw himself described as 'a most egregious coxcomb', a conceited and foolish person. Initially, Edward was likely flattered at being singled out by the popular Tone and proudly brought him home to meet the family. After that, there were musical evenings at number 69, where Edward played the violin accompanied by Tone on the flute and, in this way, Tone and Martha 'grew more passionately fond of each other' in full view of the unsuspecting Witheringtons and Martha's grandfather, Reverend Fanning.

Both their birthdays fell in June, Martha turned sixteen and Tone twenty two. Typically, Tone did not ask for permission to propose to Martha, who typically immediately said yes. A few weeks later, on the morning of 21 July 1785, the couple snuck off to St Ann's church in Dawson Street and were pronounced man and wife. Presumably Martha brooked no argument when Tone suggested that they escape for a few days' holiday to allow her family to get over their shock. By the time they returned to Grafton Street, Martha's family had made their peace with Tone, though it would not last. But, for the time being, all was well, and the Witheringtons helped the newlyweds find nearby lodgings, for which Reverend Fanning provided the rent.

Martha underwent a complete name change. Not only did she become Mrs Tone, but her husband preferred that she be called Matilda. Historian Marianne Elliott is disdainful of his choice as Matilda was the name of a character in John Home's play *Douglas*, starring Tone's previous crush, the married actress Eliza Martin, whom he had loved for two years, mostly at a distance. In an essay about Matilda, Nancy J Curtin explains that Home's Matilda is the beautiful wife of a brave fallen hero, who remarries after his death, though her second husband understands that her heart belongs to his predecessor, her only true love. Martha could not have known that this was the future that also awaited her. In any case, Martha insisted that everyone call her Matilda, and one can imagine deep sighs in the Witherington household.

With a wife to keep, Tone determined to get his degree as quickly as possible, while Matilda set about learning how to keep house. A few short months later, Reverend Fanning declared he would no longer assist his granddaughter by paying the couple's rent. Tone blamed Matilda's brother Edward for this further souring of relations, believing that his brother-in-law was jealous of his grandfather's attachment to Matilda and, furthermore, could not abide the growing friendship between Tone and Reverend Fanning. Edward might well have realised that Tone had only ever seen him as a pawn in his pursuit of his sister.

We can only guess at sixteen-year-old Matilda's feelings about losing her family along with her grandfather's financial support. The only one to stay in touch with her was her younger sister Kate. This must have been even more hurtful when Matilda discovered that she was pregnant. Glean what you may from the fact that when Matilda sat down in old age to write her memoir, she made no mention of this part of her life.

Marriage seems to have motivated Tone to study, as previously he had not been the most diligent of students. All he had ever wanted in his life was to be a soldier, but his father had insisted that he attend Trinity College and get himself a degree. A couple of months after their elopement, Tone received the college's highest honour when he was made auditor of the College Historical Society.

Meanwhile Matilda's world, though free of accolades, was undoubtedly sustained by her love for her husband and visits from Kate. Being disowned by her family left Matilda and Tone virtually penniless and, with a baby on the way, they exchanged Dublin for Kildare and moved in with Tone's parents.

For Tone, this entailed a lot of travel until he graduated from Trinity College in February 1786, while Matilda found herself launched into a family that quickly proved much friendlier than her own. Her in-laws may well have hoped that the marriage would quash Tone's earlier ambitions about soldiering and travelling the world. Apart from Peter and Margaret Tone, Matilda also met fourteen-year-old Matthew, six-year-old Mary, three-year-old Arthur and one-year-old Fanny. One more child would be added with the birth of Matilda and Tone's daughter, Maria, who proved a delight to all.

However, a few months later, the first of many tragedies was to strike the young family.

On the evening of 17 October 1786 (or 16 October according to Marianne Elliott), Tone was out in the yard and found himself surrounded by six armed men whose faces were blackened with soot. He was quickly bound up, put under the guard of one of the robbers and then obliged to watch the other five, with pistols cocked, enter the Tone house, where chaos ensued. The family and servants were tied up as the robbers proceeded to look for treasure and smash up anything that did not appeal. Tone heard it all and could only imagine what might be happening to his wife and infant, parents, sisters and brothers. The noise made baby Maria scream but mercifully one of the robbers only picked her up and placed her beside Matilda. Two long hours later, it was over. According to Tone, one of the servants managed to make her escape, presumably to get help, which sent the robbers running. He got himself to his feet, still bound up, and shuffled from window to window calling for his family in the darkness, fighting the fear that they had all been murdered.

Mercifully, no one had been hurt aside from Peter Tone who sustained a knife cut to the head. When the robbers left, the family untied themselves, crept out a back window and fled into the night until they realised that Tone was not with them. Incredibly, Matilda returned alone to find him. It was dark and she had no idea where the gang was. Furthermore, she had no idea if her husband was still alive until she reached the house and heard him calling her name. He was in awe of her courage and grateful that the robbers had left the women alone. It could have been so much worse in that respect.

Still, that night had its consequences. The robbers made off with Peter Tone's savings, medals that Tone had won in Trinity for debating, a regimental sword, jewellery, silverware and clothes. Despite the fact that two of the gang were caught a few days later, resulting in their hanging, Tone confesses that, from then on, he slept with his guns in reach, while the slightest noise sent him patrolling through the house on high alert at all hours. It was a long winter.

Meanwhile, the stolen money had been earmarked for Tone's further education in London, where he needed to go if he was to make a proper living. In January 1787, Matilda and Maria bade him goodbye as he set out for two years' study at London's Inns of Court. His father had borrowed from a rich friend and neighbour to assist his son, with little left over for anyone else. In *Rebel Wife*, Rosamond Jacob describes how Tone's letters home began to present a problem for Matilda as she witnessed Peter and Margaret Tone's increasing bitterness on hearing of their son's exciting life in London, as he made new friends and became a regular theatregoer, while his studies were hardly mentioned. Although Tone found he could earn pocket money by writing reviews, novels and political essays, he did not send a single penny home. In London, he met his brother William, who, seven years earlier, had run away from home to enlist in the East India Company, and probably reminded Tone of his youthful dreams of travelling and soldiering.

If Matilda felt neglected, she had every reason to. At some point, Tone became depressed over his financial struggles and, perhaps too, his lack of freedom as a young husband and father. Both Tone's father and Matilda wrote telling him that his father could not afford to feed Matilda and Maria for much longer. As the pressure mounted, Tone decided the only sensible thing to do was for him to become a soldier for the East India Company, telling himself that Matilda would have an easier life without him. He was ignoring the fact that his wife was living with his family, and it was indeed convenient that this desperate choice coincided with his lifelong passions and dreams. According to his diary, he wished to 'quit Europe forever, and to leave my wife and child to the mercy of her family, who might, I hoped, be kinder to her when I was removed'.

Fortunately for his wife and child, it was the wrong time of the year – September or November – to run off to sea. This, in effect, returned Tone to his senses and led him to face reality. He endeavoured to achieve enough in London to be eligible for the Irish bar and wrote to Reverend Fanning, Matilda's grandfather, who promised him £500 if he returned home to take his final exams.

What Matilda went through can be guessed from the state Tone found her in on Christmas Day 1788. She was deathly pale and underweight. Of course, she must have wondered if she would ever see him again. Perhaps over those two years she worried that he regretted their hasty marriage. And if he did, what would she do? The only family she had in the world was his. Everything depended on him and her being together, and at long last they were.

In the new year, they relocated to Dublin, where Reverend Fanning supported them with the promised £500, and Tone repaired relations with the Witheringtons. He and Matilda, and three-year-old Maria, set up home in Clarendon Street, five minutes away from Grafton Street, and Tone passed his final exams. Now qualified, he could work the Leinster circuit. Matilda must have felt that her penance of the previous two years was now rewarded. Tone was also fulfilling his father's desires though, as always, his heart lay elsewhere. A passion for politics, ignited in London, was to be further fuelled by his experiences at court.

The next three years saw Tone busy with work and family matters, in particular trying to assist his father whose turbulent relationship with his brother Jonathan over their father's estate ended in bankruptcy for Peter Tone despite Tone's effort to help him.

Matilda again suffered poor health in 1790, possibly following the birth of her first son, Richard Griffith. However, what could have been a worrying time for the family became a time of gladness when, following the doctor's advice that Matilda needed to bathe in salt water, Tone rented a small summer house in Irishtown. There, the family spent the entire summer, walking and picnicking on the sandy beaches that stretched all the way to Kingstown, what is now Dún Laoghaire. Tone's new friend Thomas Russell (1767–1803) also joined them. The pair had met a few months earlier in the House of Commons and quickly became fast friends. Tone provides a wonderful description of that summer in 1790. Meals were cooked by Matilda, him and Thomas, and they were visited by Thomas's seventy-year-old father, who Matilda 'doated' upon, Thomas's brother John along with Tone's brother William and sister Mary. There were long conversations around the table, jokes were told, poems were recited, and songs were sung, and Tone played his flute in the evenings. We only see Matilda through Tone's account, and he describes her as the life and soul of the party, thanks to her unfailing kindness and sense of humour. Who knows what she felt when Tone and Thomas began to rework an old dream of Tone's to create a military colony in the South Seas. A few letters were sent out to prominent men in London, but nothing came of their proposals.

That August, Thomas had his final dinner in Irishtown, dressed in his new uniform as an officer of the 64th Regiment of Foot, which was stationed in Belfast. This was a move that would, in time, impact the Tones as much as their friend.

With Matilda's health much improved, the Tones packed up and returned to Dublin, to new lodgings in Longford Street. Neither Matilda nor Tone could have guessed that the Irishtown summer was to be one of the few last times that they were truly at peace.

The year 1791 was a challenging one. Firstly, they lost baby Richard to an unnamed illness. Then, just as Tone's side of the family had fallen apart due to his father's rivalry with his uncle, a similar fate began to unfold for the Witherington family with Matilda's brother Edward on the warpath again. According to Tone, Edward was once more scheming to oust Matilda from their grandfather's obvious affections. While Tone was away on the law circuit, Edward encountered Matilda on the street. It is not known what passed between them, but it resulted in Edward moving to strike his sister. Tone's brother William, who was staying with Matilda, reacted immediately, demanding that Edward either apologise to Matilda or be challenged to a duel. Lacking the appetite, or courage, for a duel, Edward complied with William's demand and wrote an apology for Matilda.

According to Tone's account of the incident Edward was absolutely to blame. However, Marianne Elliott believed that both sides were guilty of obstinancy.

Whatever the truth of the matter, we do know that when Reverend Fanning died in 1791, Tone attended the reading of the will to hear that not one penny had been left to Matilda. This was yet another episode that Matilda omitted from her 1826 memoir.

But 1791 brought something to celebrate too, when Matilda gave birth to a healthy boy, William, in April 1791. In later years, she remembered the day in glowing terms: with her new baby in her arms, five-year-old Maria by her side and her husband standing over her, Matilda felt loved and much cherished.

Yet, in reality, Matilda hardly saw Tone that year as he began to pursue politics at the expense of his law practice and family life. That October, Tone along with Thomas Russell and several others founded the Society of United Irishmen in Belfast. Inspired by the French Revolution, the society wanted Ireland governed by 'an equal representation of all the people'. On Thomas's and Tone's return to Dublin, they set up a Dublin branch of the Society of United Irishmen. Around this time, Tone also accepted a job with the Catholic Committee, as agent and assistant secretary, earning £200 a year. His duties obliged him to attend meetings all over the country.

Sometime after William's birth, Tone moved his family to Kildare, to one of his Uncle Jonathan's properties which was part of the estate lost by Tone's father, Peter, in 1790. The cottage, which Tone christened Chateau Boue/Bowe (Mud House), stood on two acres of land. Tone had remained on good terms with his uncle despite the family feud. It was here that Matilda did her best to cope alone with a demanding new baby and persistent headaches.

Tone stayed in Dublin after his return from Belfast, thus obliging his wife to write and beg him to come home. He replied, telling her to wean William as the child was obviously too strong for her, and he was sorry about her headaches, but surely, she did not really wish him to leave Dublin just when things were getting interesting – 'I am sure you would not wish me to quit whilst things are in their present train' – and he was so busy. Would she not ask his sister Mary to help her? That would make him happy. Unfortunately, he declared, he had no time to ask Mary himself, 'I will leave it to you, as I am with my head, hands and heart so full of business.' And so on.

In the winter of 1791, he found unfurnished lodgings for himself in Dublin's Queen Street, a squalid area in walking distance of College Green. He spent the first two months of 1792 turning it into a home and then had Matilda send him clothes and whatever else he needed to live there for a while. She tried to fit in with his new social life, leaving the children in the country to visit him, but it did not suit her. Tone's college and childhood friends had been replaced by political ones and Matilda felt like a stranger amongst them. She rarely saw Thomas Russell as he was stationed in Belfast.

Marianne Elliott quotes a letter that Matilda sent to Thomas's sister Margaret (1752–1834) from Dublin, telling her that she was having to attend a dinner party in Kilmainham where she knew nobody and was in terror of the evening ahead. She added that she missed her old friends and declared that she had no real friends anymore. She also described trying to get Tone to visit her and the children in Kildare more often and wished he was more like Thomas who knew how to treat women. Matilda was using the letter to make her point to Tone as best she could as she knew he intended to make his own additions while she dressed for the dreaded party. And it worked. Within two weeks he had given up his Queen Street home and moved back to Kildare, where he was surprised at how much William had grown, having not seen him in a while. Of course, this did not reduce his workload, but when he was home, he busied himself with the garden. One frequent visitor to the cottage was his sister Mary, who presumably helped Matilda as Tone knew she would. At least she was a friendly face from the couple's earlier days.

The Tone family were hit by another tragedy that September when both Uncle Jonathan and Tone's sister Fanny died a week apart, from tuberculosis. One positive outcome was that Jonathan had left Tone the cottage and two acres of land. This would not be the last time that this disease would visit the family and might also explain the previous death of baby Richard. In the late eighteenth century, tuberculosis was responsible for more deaths in Ireland than any other single cause.

Matilda gave birth to another boy, Frank, on 23 June 1793, six days after her twenty-fourth birthday. The child was christened Francis Rawdon after his godfather, the second Earl of Moira (1754–1826).

One can only hope that the family enjoyed time together over the next two years as Tone grew busier and more ambitious for himself and for Ireland. It is difficult to catch sight of Matilda at this time, though she shared her husband's interest in politics and supported him in his work.

During this period Tone became increasingly inspired by the goings on in France and considered how a similar situation could be created in Ireland by organising a revolution to bring down the British and the aristocracy.

Danger arose at the end of April 1794 following the arrest of a French agent, the radical Reverend William Jackson (1737?–95), who had been on a secret mission in England and in Ireland, where he had met with prominent

United Irishmen, including Tone, to ascertain how much support would be available for a possible French invasion. Tone had been tasked with supplying Jackson with a report on the political situation in Ireland. Betrayed by a friend, Jackson was arrested for high treason. That and the seizure of his papers endangered anyone who had crossed his path. Tone escaped prison by agreeing to leave the country.

Over the following year, the Tones prepared to emigrate to America. Six hundred books were sold as well as Chateau Bowe, the only real home this young family would ever know. Tone also secured his father's permission to bring Arthur, his younger brother, and sister Mary with him, and on 20 May 1795, seven Tones headed for Belfast, from where they would sail to America.

By this stage, the French agent, Reverend Jackson, was dead. His April trial found him guilty as charged and he chose to poison himself before the state could hang him.

Up north, Matilda and Tone revelled in the warm welcome from like-minded friends like the Russells and the McCrackens. One surprise was the £1,500 that had been collected for the Tone's family's new life across the water. This was surely the sort of life Matilda might have preferred for herself, to have her husband by her side day after day and to be surrounded by people who loved and respected them both.

A final farewell party, the day before the Tones left, saw Matilda in tears, which alarmed her friends. She did not want to leave. In later years, activist Mary Ann McCracken (1770–1866) remembered the gentleness shown by Thomas Russell as he reassured both Matilda and Tone that a brighter future awaited their certain return to Ireland. One wonders if any of them believed this or if Matilda somehow sensed that this would be the last time that she and Tone would be together in Ireland, and, indeed, her last time in Ireland too. From now on, the clock was ticking. Tone had sworn to leave America as soon as he could and sail to France to raise support for a revolution in Ireland.

They boarded the *Cincinnatus*, alongside three hundred other passengers, on Saturday, 13 June 1795, for the six-week journey across the Atlantic.

The Tones shared what they had with their fellow passengers, while Tone, thanks to a gift of a medicine chest in Belfast, became the unofficial doctor and did his best to promote cleanliness on the crowded ship. Calamity befell the *Cincinnatus* in the fifth week when she was surrounded by three English warships and boarded by a naval recruiting party that spent the next two days forcing – pressing – forty-eight passengers and most of the crew into joining the British navy. This press-ganging of young men into the navy was a regular occurrence at the time and distressing for those young men who were travelling with their families and for their womenfolk now bereft of their menfolk. An attempt was made to grab Tone because he was wearing long trousers instead of the more fashionable breeches worn by gentlemen. Once more, Matilda came into her own. Just as she had set out to rescue him on the night of the robbery, years earlier, now she set out to save him once more, this time with her sister-in-law's Mary's help. They protested and screamed so much that Tone was released to them.

The following week, on Saturday, 1 August 1793, the *Cincinnatus* and her remaining passengers docked at Wilmington, Delaware, where the Tones booked into an inn run by an Irishman. They were befriended by an elderly veteran of the American War of Independence, who helped them settle in Philadelphia. Tone met up with other Irish exiles and found himself alone in his desire to return to Ireland as soon as possible.

'Never come here unless you are driven.' This was what Tone wrote to Thomas Russell a few short weeks later when he had come to detest everything about America, and we may assume that Matilda shared his feelings. His voice is the loudest, of course, thanks to his letters and journals. Matilda disliked writing letters and only did so when completely necessary. Tone regarded Philadelphians as unfriendly, ill-bred and overly taken up with making money, 'a mongrel breed, half English, half Dutch, with the worst qualities of both countries'. Moreover, the weather was scorching hot, and everything was wildly expensive.

Things were no better when they left Philadelphia for Princeton, New Jersey, and found themselves living amongst Quakers and farmers and 'ignorant Germans'. Tone and Matilda fretted over their children growing up amongst such uncultured neighbours, whilst Tone raged at the idea of his eldest daughter marrying an American. On top of all that, Tone hated America and George Washington for not siding with France in her war against Britain.

Of course, the truth may be that Tone, in particular, was simply not prepared to like America. He missed friends like Thomas Russell and wanted to return to the country that he had been forced to leave. As for Matilda's feelings about America, well, this would be where she would make her home years later. Meanwhile, this first stay was far from easy, particularly after Tone left for France. The couple had six months together before Tone's determination to rouse France into helping Ireland banish her British oppressors could no longer be ignored. His brother Arthur left America for Belfast on 10 December 1795, with instructions to let selected United Irishmen know what Tone was planning. Everyone else was to be told that he was perfectly happy in America.

Matilda and Mary spent the night of 13 December keeping Tone company until his departure at four in the morning for the two-day trip to New York, to board his ship for France. Even he professed surprise at his wife's genuine encouragement about his mission. And while we can only wonder whether Matilda's feelings were as steadfast as she displayed, the fact is that she kept something from him in case it derailed his plans. Only when he left did she sit down to write that she was pregnant once again. He received her letter the day before he left for France, on 1 January 1796.

Historian Nancy F. Curtin describes Matilda's decision not to impart her news as confirmation of her commitment to her husband's dreams and her belief in their partnership. Tone was prepared to risk his life for Ireland, but that meant his wife having to cope without a full-time husband, a co-parent, a stable and comfortable home, not to mention the loss of her blood relatives. Matilda prioritised Tone's ambitions over everything else, which is what he needed from her, but was it worth the sacrifices that she was continually making?

She lost the baby long before its summer due date. One letter arrived from Tone announcing his arrival in Paris and then all went quiet. For a detailed account of what transpired in France, one must read his journals. Because it took a while to get things organised, he sought distraction from his limbo with trips to the theatre, three bottles of wine of an evening and a visit with a 'French lover' to the Palace of Versailles, although in his published memoirs, this lover is described as 'he'. He writes that he found French women 'enchanting', superior in figure and dress to English women but 'give me Ireland … for women to make wives and mothers of'. Tone's published diaries were edited by his wife and William, his eldest son, who was determined to portray Tone as the quintessential Irish hero.

That September, Matilda confessed her sadness in a letter to Thomas Russell. He had succeeded in comforting her before she left for America and, perhaps, she was seeking his help and guidance once more. She told him that she was in poor health and found life in America with three young children difficult, but she also expressed her thanks for the financial help from their Belfast friends. She still had Mary but, of course, she missed her husband.

Finally, she received a long-awaited letter from Tone and an explanation for the months of silence. He had written to her in May, telling her to come to France, but the *Argus*, the ship carrying this letter, had been seized by the English. Now, here was her summons to France, with Tone's instructions on how to proceed should he be killed in action. The letter was written onboard the *Indomptable* before it set sail from France that December. So, it was finally happening: a fleet of French ships carrying 14,450 men were bound for Cork's Bantry Bay to raise hell for Ireland.

If the revolution succeeded, Matilda was to bring their family to Ireland and if it failed, she was to ask his friends for financial help and make her own decision between staying on in France or returning to America. If he lived but the revolution failed, he promised a life of tranquillity with her and the children in France. Well, the Bantry Bay expedition failed utterly thanks to atrocious weather off the coast of Cork preventing any ship from offloading its cargo of soldiers. They turned around and sailed back to France.

Stormy weather did not only destroy Tone's first attempt at revolution, but it also played havoc with the ship carrying Matilda and her family from America. However, their eventual arrival in Hamburg was good news for a thoroughly dejected Tone, although his relief was tinged by concern for Matilda's dubious health. In the posthumously published *Life of Theobald Wolfe Tone ... written by himself and extracted from his journals*, edited by Matilda and their son William, William Tone describes the family disembarking at the mouth of the frozen Elbe, following a rough two months at sea, before travelling in an open wagon in the bitter cold to Hamburg, where Matilda heard of the failed rebellion. Rumours swirled about what had happened, and Matilda had to steel herself against panicking. William reminds the reader that his mother was in a strange country, with a foreign language, without friends or support. She also had to conceal her identity and could only write to Paris to enquire about her husband's whereabouts.

On his return to Paris, Tone, alarmed at reading about his wife's difficulties, wrote to tell her to stay in Hamburg and keep herself warm and dry.

In his journal for January 1797, Tone describes his worry over Matilda but then is wonderfully distracted by the love story concerning his sister Mary and the Swiss passenger onboard their ship. Jean Frédéric Giauque was on his way home to Hamburg when he and Mary fell in love. He wrote to Tone, asking for his consent to marry his sister, which was gladly given.

With the failure of the Bantry Bay expedition, Matilda might have expected her husband to return to her, in readiness for that tranquil life he had promised, especially since Mary Tone was soon to marry and have her own home. Instead, Tone became an Adjutant General in the French army and was much taken up with his new post. That he missed his wife and children is evident in his journals, but there was also time for dreams of romance and adventure. For example, he visited a church in Cologne in which he thought himself alone until he spied a nun in the shadows. Despite being able to see only her mouth and chin, he was convinced that she was young and beautiful. Apparently, they stared at one another in silence for five minutes as he dreamt of rescuing her from the convent.

Matilda would not see her husband until the evening of 7 May when she and the children met up with him in Groningen in the Netherlands. They enjoyed two weeks together, travelling around Holland and Belgium, and then Tone left for Germany, whilst his family went to Paris to stay with a friend of Tone's until they found somewhere to live.

That July, Tone was set to sail with a Dutch fleet, and 15,000 men, for a second attempt to invade Ireland. Once more, he was denied due to stormy weather, with winds preventing the ships from going anywhere for the next two months.

Tone met with the new chief of the Army of England, Napoleon Bonaparte (1769–1821), in December, to discuss further invasions of Ireland but no promises were made. When Tone received orders, the following March, to join the army at Rouen, it was up to Matilda, with Matthew Tone's help, to secure cheaper lodgings. Tone had helped his brother attain a captaincy in the French army and until he was called up, Matthew stayed with Matilda and the children on the outskirts of Paris in Chaillot. Tone's letters of instructions provide an insight into Matilda's domestic life. She ensured that seven-year-old William and five-year-old Frank worked hard at their books. Apart from reading and writing, the children were to study music, and so sheet music was ordered from Holland, while Matilda was to keep the piano in tune. Furthermore, twelve-year-old Maria was to have dance lessons. It was Matilda's responsibility to accommodate all her husband's wishes as frugally as possible with the money he sent her every month. She hired a servant to help with the housework, but Matilda did all the shopping to guarantee that she spent only what she could afford. She probably also played hostess to newly arrived United Irishmen who were escaping the government's crackdown in Ireland.

Discord blossomed between Tone and fellow Irish revolutionary James Napper Tandy (1739–1803) who had arrived in Paris the previous June and saw himself leading the French forces to Ireland. Accusations that were made about Tone prioritising his own interests over Ireland's suggest jealousy regarding Tone's army appointment and contacts. Tandy had his followers, but Tone told Matilda to welcome all Irish arrivals no matter who they supported.

Meanwhile, in 1798, informers were causing serious problems in Ireland. In Dublin, a meeting to discuss an immediate uprising in March was raided by the British who had received their intelligence from Thomas Reynolds (1771–1836), the husband of Matilda's sister Harriet, which must have cut Matilda to the quick.

A few months later, news filtered through that a rebellion had finally happened in Ireland, between the end of May and beginning of June. Irishmen in France determined to sail to Ireland, but their urgency was lost in the lack of proper organisation and cash. Tone wrote to Matilda in August, apologising for being unable to send her any money.

Tone finally left France in September but not before signing documents giving Matilda Power of Attorney. Years later, she wrote that he knew he was going to die and, very likely, she too was of the same opinion. If sentenced to death, Tone had vowed to take his own life, thus robbing the British of their chance to murder him – just as Reverend William Jackson had in 1794. Tone kept his promise. He left France onboard the *Hoche*, which found itself under attack from the British navy off the coast of Donegal. Following a six-hour battle, Tone was captured on 31 October and brought to Dublin for the trial that saw him condemned to hang, just as he had expected. He slit his throat, dying by his own hand on Monday, 19 November 1798.

Of course, Matilda had to stay in France and perhaps she preferred to be spared the sight of her husband's lifeless body. In fact, she had been planning to travel to Ireland, hoping to get him out of jail on a last-minute reprieve. She chose to believe, until it was impossible not to, that Tone would survive, and that she could save him, just as she had done twice before. The news confirming his death must have been shocking no matter how much he had done to prepare her for it. He was waked for two days in the house his parents were living in, and many showed up to pay their respects. A plaster cast was taken of his face, but none of the resulting death masks reached his widow. Because the authorities wanted him buried quickly and quietly, his body was taken, with just two in attendance, to the Tone family plot in Bodenstown, where Wolfe Tone's brother Matthew had been placed seven weeks earlier, after he was hanged for his part in the rebellion. Matilda's sister Kate sent her a lock of Tone's hair. As usual, she was the only Witherington to stay in touch with Matilda. Tone had written to ask both William and Harriet to look after Matilda once he was gone, but neither complied with his wishes. Who knows if they would have acted differently had Matilda and the children returned to Ireland. She and Tone had discussed her options should the rebellion fail, and he died in action. For the time being, the only country she relied on was France.

She was twenty-nine years old, with three children under the age of thirteen, and penniless. Thanks to her husband being recognised as an honorary Frenchman and brave soldier, she received an initial lump sum of 1,200 francs and was due a pension until complications arose following political upheaval in France. The next few years would not be easy for the Tone family.

Initially, however, she must have been relieved to hear that, thanks to their father's standing, William and Frank would attend the best of schools. Until they were old enough to do this, Matilda secured lodgings nearby and had the boys attend French classes locally. She lived a quiet life and focused on her children's education, just as Tone had wanted. The only people she saw were her husband's friends. Tragically, in 1799, her small support network took a direct hit when Mary, her sister-in-law, and husband Giauque died in Santo Domingo from yellow fever. Tone's brother William, who had left Ireland in 1792, for a military life in India, sent Matilda £233 and promised to look after her financially. Unfortunately, he was also to die shortly after, in 1802, in battle.

The only surviving brother-in-law was Arthur Tone, but he avoided any family expectations by sailing to America without a word. Matilda believed he must have died until she heard, in 1812, that he was in the American navy, at which point she had no interest in re-building relations with him.

In 1802, she was visited by Thomas Russell who had spent the previous six years in Dublin's Newgate Prison. He returned to Ireland to take part in Robert Emmet's doomed rising (1778–1803) and was hanged in October 1803; a dreadful year in the life of Matilda that saw sixteen-year-old Maria, her cherished daughter, die from tuberculosis, the same disease that would kill thirteen-year-old Francis three years later. It is not hard to imagine her terror when, shortly after burying Francis, fifteen-year-old William, her sole surviving child, started coughing and showing symptoms of TB. Mercifully, he lived after she rushed him to America for its warmer climate. The trip proved a saving grace for both mother and son in that it healed William, while Matilda attributed her newly enhanced well-being to the change of scenery distracting her from her grief. This would prove to be no more than a temporary reprieve for William, although they would have another twenty-two eventful years yet. Had she lost him at this point, in 1806, she really would have been cut adrift, but she had saved him, and he became her anchor, her reason to go on living.

In 1826, prompted by reading articles about herself written by men who had never met her, fifty-seven-year-old Matilda sat down to write her memoir. She wished to tell her own story, chiefly what happened after she lost her husband and children, how she sought to uphold Tone's legacy and reputation, and champion their son William's career. It transpired that what William wanted was a place in the Cavalry School of St Germain, upending a promising academic career that might have seen him become a professor. While his mother may secretly have hoped that William kept at his books, and remained safe, she would not have ignored his unhappiness and impatience to be a man of action, like his father. Believing also that Tone should have liked for a son of his to join the French army, she set out to make it happen.

She found little support from Tone's United Irish friends in Paris who felt that William's rightful place was in the Irish Legion, if only his mother would let him go. Her fury is evident in the following letter, from 1813:

... I was extremely harassed and perplexed by advice to send him (William) into the world and even with reproaches that I kept him tied to my apron string ... Oh how ungenerous they have been to me, Good God! How did the Irish ever get the character of a generous nation? But, indeed, it is only themselves who say it ... Do the Irish think that because Tone volunteered in their service and shed his best blood in their cause and left his family destitute in a foreign country that his posterity is to be their slaves.

Strong words indeed from the wife of an Irish rebel who clearly felt that she had sacrificed enough for Ireland. As far as Matilda was concerned, the Irish Legion had nothing to offer William who enrolled in Napoleon's cavalry school in 1812. Cadets stayed in the huge castle; a chateau built in the 1300s during the reign of King Charles V (1338–1380). This was where James II (1633–1701) lived after his disastrous loss to William of Orange (1650–1702) at the 1690 Battle of the Boyne.

Matilda moved to St Germain to be near her only surviving child. From her hotel window, she watched William at his daily exercise on the castle grounds and visited him every Sunday. Glad that he was happy, she now determined to have William made a French citizen which, for her, meant going all the way to the top.

The entire direction of Matilda's life had been spawned from her habit of sitting in the window on Grafton Street, a habit she seized upon anew. Knowing that Napoleon regularly passed her hotel to hunt in the forests around St Germain, she began to keep watch for him. In fairness, she bided her time, waiting until William was distinguishing himself at school before making her approach. Her plan was simple. She would position herself at the first entrance to the forest where Napolean's horses, on their arrival from Paris, were replaced by a fresh set. However, the guard there advised her to wait outside where Napoleon had his breakfast, telling her that the horses were changed at top speed, but Matilda did not want to risk having to join a large crowd of petitioners, all vying for a moment of their emperor's time. As soon as the carriage carrying Napoleon and Josephine came to a halt in front of her at the entrance to the forest, she stepped forward, presenting the French leader with one of William's highly regarded essays and a memorial card to her husband. On realising that she was Wolfe Tone's widow, Napoleon read through both card and book and asked if she had a decent pension. This was unexpected as her only focus was William. She told Napoleon, 'That his majesty's goodness left me no personal want; that all my cares, all my interests in life were centered in my child, whom I now gave up to his majesty's service.'

She fancied that Napoleon hid a smile at her referring to her twenty-year-old son as 'my child' and he replied in kind: '*Votre enfant sera bien naturalisé*/'your child will be naturalised.'

She describes her appearance in her memoir, explaining that everyone in St Germain wondered at the identity of the woman who commanded Napoleon's full attention. Dressed in grey silk, from head to foot, with her face hidden behind a long black veil, she had some people guessing from her attire that she was a nun.

She provides an interesting insight into the emperor's manner, including his casual generosity to the poor, who begged him for coins, and also his fierce temper. When Napoleon visited William's school, he heard complaints about bad bread being served to the cadets. Demanding to see a loaf, he discovered cheap substitute ingredients, such as potato and peas, being used in place of good wheaten flour. The baker was summoned for a fiery interview and threatened with the gallows.

Matilda decided to visit Talleyrand-Périgord, Prince of Benevento (1754–1838), the controversial diplomat and statesman, who was at his holiday home in St Germain and had known Tone very well. She updated him on the last few years, including how she had managed to find William a place in the Cavalry School and how she had approached Napoleon. He told her that her priority should be William's good health and that any debt she had incurred over William's training should be considered a national debt.

After quizzing her about her pension, he asked her to bring him all her paperwork so that he could take charge of her situation. This he subsequently did, and Matilda received a full pension. For the first time since leaving Grafton Street, Matilda was financially independent and could return money she had borrowed from a friend.

According to his mother, twenty-one-year-old William became a French citizen on 4 May 1812, a few weeks before Napoleon embarked on his Russian campaign. Fortunately for William, he had to finish his schooling and missed out on that ill-fated invasion. The following January, however, William joined the 8th Chasseurs as a sub-lieutenant and was instructed to go to Gray in Franche Comté to instruct new recruits. So, the time had finally come for mother and son to part. Matilda describes the scene in her memoir. After saying goodbye to William, she sat down in a field and was overwhelmed with a desire to die. At forty-three years of age, she felt her life was over. She had no one left to live for, nothing left to do, and did not want to return to an empty house. Just then a lark flew out of the long grass and made right for her, singing out its song as it circled her head. Immediately believing that the bird was sent by Tone to rouse her spirits, Matilda felt renewed and was able to go home.

But she would not be alone forever. In July 1816, Matilda married her and Tone's friend, Scottish businessman Thomas Wilson (*d*.1824), at the British embassy in Paris. Not much is known about her second husband other than he looked after her financial affairs. Indeed, in 1949, Rosamond Jacob was obliged to enlist help from the readers of *The Scotsman* newspaper, begging for any information on Thomas – in vain, it would seem. By this stage Napoleon's reign was over. This threw William's career into disarray, and when the British government refused to allow Wolfe Tone's son and widow to return to Ireland, or England, Wilson decided that they should move to America, which they did in 1817. This must have presented mixed feelings for Matilda as it meant leaving the graves of Maria and Frank behind.

The new family settled in Georgetown, where William studied law and married Catherine Sampson (*b*.1796–1864), daughter of United Irishman Willam (1764–1836). Two years later, William showed himself yet again to be his father's son when he abandoned his books for a post in the United States army. Thomas Wilson died five years later, in 1824, making Matilda a widow once more.

One can only conclude that this second marriage had been a successful one, judging from the epitaph that Matilda had inscribed on Thomas's headstone, 'A true philanthropist. His life was consecrated to deeds of benevolence, and his wishes and endeavour all tended to the happiness, information and freedom of all kind.' Matilda, as Mrs Thomas Wilson, had surely experienced a contentedness and stability that was out of reach when married to Wolfe Tone.

In any case, Wilson's death allowed Matilda to devote herself all over again to the memory of her first husband and she and William spent the next two years preparing Tone's journals, essays and pamphlets for publication.

Nancy J Curtin highlights the timing of this project. A frivolous article in an English newspaper, describing Matilda's glamorous widowhood in Paris, provoked Matilda into action. She wanted to set the world straight about her husband, and, also, about herself. Furthermore, as news filtered through of the latest popular figure in Irish politics – Daniel O'Connell (1775–1847) – Matilda may well have desired to remind all of Wolfe Tone's sacrifices and how his ambitions for his country reflected those of O'Connell – both desiring to free the Catholics of Ireland from English rule. In publishing his papers twenty-six years after his death, William and Matilda showed Tone to be as relevant as ever he was and, thus, his spirit lived on.

Would we know Theobald Wolfe Tone today if Matilda had not initiated this project? It is an interesting question, considering that Tone's political and military life could be summed up in a paragraph or two and ultimately one might concur that he did not achieve too much of anything, albeit not for the lack of want. The two-volume *Life of Wolfe Tone* was published in 1826 and became a bestseller and, on reading this book, one can never forget him.

MATILDA TONE (1769-1849)

Matilda, with her son's help, took charge of Tone's legacy, pruning the journals of unnecessary distractions. Wolfe Tone, the honourable, fearless and selfless warrior, survives to this day, thanks largely to a wife who had, in her own way, sacrificed just as much as he did.

Matilda became a grandmother with the birth of baby Grace Georgiana in 1827 (*d.*1900) and then suffered the huge loss of William who died the following year, at the age of thirty-seven, from what his wife described as 'an intestinal disorder'. His mother survived him by another twenty-one years.

In 1849, Matilda was interviewed by Young Irelander Charles Hart (1824–1898), who was on a tour of the United States and wanted to meet the eighty-year-old widow of Wolfe Tone. He acknowledged her great age and physically weakened state, neither of which, however, diminished her lively conversation. Matilda asked after the landmarks of her childhood and first marriage, Trinity College and Grafton Street, and was most interested to hear how the wall in front of the college had been replaced by railings. She told Hart that she had spent the last thirty years longing for Ireland but could never work up the courage to visit. Ireland's problems, she felt, would continue to be compounded by the fact that the country was so small, confessing that she sometimes wished it would grow. When Hart complimented her on her strong feelings for Ireland, she replied that 'it was Tone gave it all to me'. By the time he left, Hart was newly appreciative of what Wolfe Tone had experienced for Ireland and concluded that his wife was a true heroine.

Matilda died two weeks later and was buried near her son in Georgetown until 1831 when they were both moved to Greenwood cemetery in New York.

Mary O'Connell, painting in Derrynane House, Caherdaniel, County Kerry.

CHAPTER TWO

MARY O'CONNELL (1778-1836)

Wife of Daniel O'Connell, nationalist leader

If this book is an attempt to pull the wives of Ireland's famous men out from behind their husbands' shadows, the story of Mary O'Connell shows a courtship entirely carried out in the shadows for the sake of a promised inheritance.

There is only one surviving image of Mary O'Connell; the *c.*1817 portrait by Limerick man John Gubbins that hangs today in O'Connell's Derrynane House in County Kerry. Thirty-nine-year-old Mary chooses to be shown adorned by her seventh surviving child, toddler Daniel (1816–1897), who shares his mother's blue eyes and pale, smooth skin. Mary is presenting herself in what was possibly her second favourite role, that of a doting mother, whilst the quantity and apparent quality of her jewellery, the delicate hat that crowns her perfectly round ringlets of hair, along with the billowing white dress with its fine lace sleeves surely pay homage to her role as the wife of a successful lawyer turned ambitious politician who believed in the importance of appearances. For instance, in 1809, Daniel ignored his wife's protest and bought a stately Georgian house they could ill afford in Dublin's Merrion Square, number 58, because he believed that such a grand home would enhance his reputation.

If one discerns a hint of sadness in Mary's gaze, then today's viewer should know that between 1812 and 1816 she gave birth to five children, of whom only young Daniel survived. Furthermore, those four infants were not the only ones that she lost.

Mary was born in Tralee on 25 September 1778 into a branch of the O'Connell family. The family raised their children in two different faiths. Mary and her sisters were brought up in their mother Ellen Tuohy's Catholic faith, whilst her brothers were raised in their father's Church of Ireland faith. The widowed Thomas O'Connell was a physician and father-of-three when he met and married his second wife, Ellen. They had eight children and not much else is known about Mary's childhood other than the fact of Doctor O'Connell's untimely death in 1785, a family tragedy which left Ellen and the eleven children in financial straits, the most pressing consequence being that his daughters would not have dowries, a potential impediment to making a successful marriage. This lack of dowry would sorely impact Mary's entire life after she fell in love with Daniel O'Connell, a distant cousin who was both a friend and colleague of her brother-in-law James O'Connor.

One wonders when and how Mary and Daniel first met. He was a busy young lawyer from Derrynane, in Kerry, who travelled to wherever he was needed throughout the province of Munster and would have had cause to visit Tralee. Perhaps the couple met at a social function or, maybe, Mary simply encountered him in her sister Betsey's house as he worked on a case with James. In any case, in 1800, Mary and Daniel struck up a secret correspondence, shortly after which he proposed to her. Her acceptance was, initially, for his eyes and ears only.

The reason for the secrecy was money. Daniel stood to inherit a fortune from wealthy Uncle Maurice (1728–1825), known in the family as Hunting Cap, for whom a dowry-less bride would have been unacceptable, and who was capable of punishing a wayward nephew by disinheriting him. While Daniel was determined to marry the woman he loved, he was equally determined not to forfeit the riches that would someday be his.

In Daniel's earliest surviving letter to Mary, he wrote: 'You know as well as I do how much we have at stake in keeping the business secret. I have certainly more at stake than ever I had before, or I really believe if I fail at present I shall ever have again. Secrecy is therefore a favour I earnestly beg of you.'

Of course, nothing could be achieved without Mary's full cooperation and, so, she said yes to all.

For the next two years, their mutual friend, another Daniel O'Connell, nicknamed Splinter, was charged with sending letters between the couple, but Splinter sometimes went missing just when he was needed. Also, Mary's brother Rickard grew concerned over the number of letters his unmarried sister was receiving from Splinter and felt morally obliged to open one whereupon he discovered the existence of another Daniel O'Connell entirely. We can assume that Rickard kicked up a patriarchal fuss about impropriety until Ellen, his mother, told him that she had read all the letters and found nothing untoward in them. His mother was lying out of loyalty to Daniel who had confessed all to her in a letter. Whilst appreciating being included in the secret, Ellen urged Daniel to stop writing to Mary as it was causing trouble with her brother but this he could not do. Instead, he changed tack and sent Mary an impersonal letter about a lottery ticket – and nothing else – enabling her to read it aloud without causing Rickard any discomfort.

In want of a better courier, Daniel told his friend, James, Mary's brother-in-law, about their engagement and entrusted him with sending their letters. This meant that Mary would receive letters from Daniel in an envelope addressed by James, which was well and good until one was delivered while his wife was visiting her sister. Recognising the familiar handwriting, Betsey imagined that her husband must be hiding a serious illness from her, thus forcing Mary to confess all. Now there were four who knew of the clandestine relationship. Since the whole point of all of this was to keep his uncle in the dark, it must have been worrying as the number of people who knew of the couple's attachment increased, but Daniel obviously felt it was worth the risk. In any case, it ended in marriage, albeit a secret one.

The earliest biography about Daniel, published in 1872, was by the Republican Nun of Kenmare, Sister Mary Francis Cusack (1829–1899), who dates the wedding as being Wednesday, 23 June 1802; however, it is believed that it took place on Saturday, 24 July 1802. The venue was Betsey and James O'Connor's house in Dame Street, in Dublin, with at least two of Daniel's brothers and Reverend Finn, the parish priest of Irishtown, making up the wedding party.

A few days later, Mary returned to Tralee, while Daniel continued a bachelor existence, commuting for work between Dublin, the Munster circuit and Derrynane. Those stolen days after the wedding proved fruitful when Mary discovered that she was pregnant, thus complicating an otherwise simple plan to keep quiet about the marriage until Daniel worked up the courage to tell his uncle. Impending fatherhood could not be denied unless Mary was willing to hide herself away, and then what? Also, what if there were problems with the pregnancy and a doctor needed to be called?

As the months tumbled by, Mary grew lonely for her husband but could not make any demands on him until the situation with his uncle was resolved. The fearless Daniel who would take on Britain almost single-handedly and address a million people at the Hill of Tara clearly feared one person as, in the end, Daniel had his brother John confess on his behalf to Uncle Maurice that he had married a financially insecure prospect and there was a baby on its way. The pronouncement was not well received. His uncle was outraged, but for the next year no one knew what repercussions this would have for Daniel and his inheritance. One might also wonder if some of Maurice's rage was due to having been told about the marriage so long after the fact and so close to the arrival of a baby.

Meanwhile, Mary suffered at being the cause of such trouble but chose to focus on what was more important than money in a letter to her husband: 'We will yet, love, be happy together. Depend on it.' She was doing her best to reassure herself as much as her husband as her mood dipped due to their stressful situation which, in turn, affected her well-being. Daniel wrote, urging her to look after herself. She replied, 'It was not your fortune but yourself, my dearest heart, that I married. If you were possessed of but fifty pounds a year, I would be happy.'

However, money became an immediate problem following a couple of months of solitary house hunting in Dublin, whereby Daniel had to accept that they could not yet afford one.

When their first child was born in June 1803, in a probable attempt to appease his namesake, he was called Maurice. Mary and the baby exchanged her parents' home for her in-laws' modest farmhouse in Cahersiveen. Her moving in with Daniel's parents probably coincided with her first introduction to them. Maybe Daniel worried about their reaction to his wife as a letter from his brother John tells him that Mary is welcome but that 'father disapproves of your marriage only as far as he thinks it will hurt you with your uncle.'

And for a while, Mary was happy, but it could not last. Daniel was away most of the time and as the memories of their wedding day faded, she was no closer to living with her husband. Letters continued to be the foundation on which their relationship was built and nurtured. It was only natural that a new wife and mother wanted her own home. However, an added complication was that Mary was all too aware that her in-laws would rather that Daniel had remained on good terms with Uncle Maurice, keeping his future financially secure. In a letter to Daniel, she describes her mother-in-law being somewhat cool to her but then adds that the situation has improved.

Then the news broke about Uncle Maurice's new will, in which he replaced Daniel with his brother John, who had toed the line and married, as arranged by Maurice, the wealthy heiress Miss Elizabeth Coppinger. Daniel's mother confided in Mary that Uncle Maurice 'would settle the entire of his landed property on John but would not tie himself down to settle more than ten thousand pounds on him.'

On 14 December 1803, Mary wrote to Daniel: 'Your father had a letter … from your Uncle O'Mullane mentioning your uncle [Hunting Cap], the king (as he calls him), has made a will in John's favour … in consequence of your having run counter to his wishes.'

In March 1804, Mary discovered that she was pregnant again.

The previous November, Daniel had rented a three-storey house on Upper Ormond Quay in Dublin, where husband and wife were reunited in the spring of 1804, although it meant leaving baby Maurice behind with his grandparents. It was a temporary break from the norm as a heavily pregnant Mary was eventually obliged to return to Cahirciveen to collect the baby and relocate to her parents' house in Tralee, where she had her second child, Morgan, that October or November. Daniel met his second-born the following month and brought his family back to his parents for Christmas.

Five months later, Mary was two months pregnant and travelling to Dublin, where Daniel had finally bought them a house, on Westland Row. His work obliged him to be away, more often than not, and Mary writes to him of her sadness at being apart on their third wedding anniversary in 1805. The next week saw her leaving Dublin too, returning to her in-laws where she had her first daughter, Ellen, on 12 November. There she remained until the New Year when she packed herself up with Maurice and Ellen and returned to Dublin, leaving Morgan behind with his Kerry wetnurse. This time, however, Mary had a proper assistant as she and the babies were joined by Daniel's sister Kitty.

Historian Erin Bishop established the pattern of all this leave-taking and travel. Twice a year, starting in March, Daniel spent up to two months away on the Munster circuit. During the summer break, he visited his parents for a blend of work and pleasure before going home to Dublin until the autumn term of court sessions brought him back to Munster again. Mary and Daniel wrote to each other almost every day when they were apart, and when they were together, they made the most of it, resulting, usually, in another pregnancy. Mary gave birth to their second daughter, Kate, in March 1807, in Dublin. Now that she had proper help, she did not need to travel down to Kerry or Cork to have babies, which must have been a huge relief considering the frequency of these new arrivals. Eight months after Kate's birth, Mary was pregnant again.

Of course, the problem with Mary making her home miles away from Kerry is the same problem that affects anyone who settles down far from their childhood home, which is the feeling of powerlessness and distance in the face of bad news. In 1808, Mary received word that her brother Edward was seriously ill in Tralee. This was quickly followed by hearing that Daniel's father was also unwell, having suffered 'a severe fit'. How anxiously she must have awaited her post in Dublin for updates on both O'Connells along with her husband's response to what she was going through. When it seemed that her brother was surely dying, she took to her bed for two days. Daniel wrote from Munster pleading with her to take better care of herself. Miraculously, both men improved, although Mary could not relax as, by then, she was dealing with her seriously ill housekeeper who died in April, leaving Mary six months pregnant, with four very young children and a house to look after. Daniel, as usual, was away. Luckily, help arrived in the shape of her sister Betsey.

Edward, her third son, was born in July, which made a grand total of five children under the age of seven, with the eldest, Maurice, having turned six the previous month. A few weeks later, Mary and her family set off to Tralee for their summer holiday.

The following year, 1809, brought a quick succession of tragedies beginning in January with the death of baby Edward. Erin Bishop also surmised that Mary had a miscarriage two months later and two months after that, in May, Daniel's father died. Two months later, it was July, and time for the family holiday in Tralee. Mary was once more two months pregnant and surely looking forward to a break. However, hearing that her husband had fixed his sights on a luxury townhouse in Dublin's Merrion Square spurred her into action in a frantic bid to dissuade him from buying it, writing, 'I can't tell you, love, how unhappy I am about this business … For God's sake, darling love, let me entreat of you to give up this house in the Square if it is in your power as I can see no other way for you to get out of difficulties … If you borrow this money [one thousand guineas], how will you pay it back? In short, love, I scarcely know what I write I am so unhappy about this business.'

As she was kept busy by her growing family and in providing an oasis for her husband to rest up from his daily toil, he was coming into his own as a popular Irish, Catholic politician. In the year since the 1800 Act of Union, which shifted all the ruling and administration of Ireland back to London's Westminster, Daniel had joined a Catholic Committee, alongside businessmen and landowners, and quickly rose through its ranks thanks to fiery speeches such as the one he gave at the Royal Exchange in Dublin on 13 January 1800 to rouse a nation of Catholics against the union that made his 'blood boiled' because it was killing Ireland.

He determined upon a course of action to strengthen his, and Ireland's, position and that was to win Catholic Emancipation and return the ruling of Ireland to where it belonged. Emancipation meant freedom for Irish Catholics to practise their religion, to advance themselves professionally and to be elected to represent their county in Westminster.

In 1809, it seemed that Daniel was next in line to lead the committee and maybe even Ireland herself and, therefore, the stately, Georgian-style house at 58 Merrion Square, with its ornamental railings and upmarket neighbours, appealed to him as an appropriate home for a man of his standing. Mary, knowing that their finances were hopelessly precarious, strove to make him see sense but Daniel went ahead with his plans and bought the property.

Mary made her usual mark on this new home by having a baby within its walls. Betsey, a third daughter, arrived in February 1810. And just to be sure, only ten months later, she had a second baby, John, in December. Delivering two babies in one year must have meant that 1811 was a particularly busy one for the mother of seven, but it would also be the first year since 1802 that she was not pregnant. However, in 1812 she was soon pregnant again and every year after that until 1816. Out of all these children only, Danny, the baby in the Gubbins portrait, survived.

Daniel O'Connell had two favourite stories about his wife and Sister Cusack includes them in her biography. When Mary was a little girl, her school route took her past Kerry's County jail in Tralee. The jail, which first appeared on a map in 1756, was infamous for its appalling conditions. Part of it was built over the River Lee, which provided an archway for pedestrians. Every school day saw Mary walking through the archway and every day, according to Daniel, she was confronted by the 'uncouth' gaoler Patrick Hands who made her stop and curtsey to him. Perhaps Mr Hands enjoyed having a doctor's daughter treat him like royalty. Mary would give the best curtsey she could muster. One might wonder why this tale was such a favourite of her husband's. Perhaps he recognised in the young girl the compassionate and loving woman who would, one day, cost him his uncle's fortune; after all, she could have refused to stop at all. Or was it simply because the unfortunate gaoler would come to a notorious bloody end during one of the jail's many breakouts. In August 1776, Mr Hands was murdered by prisoners who stole his money along with his ten-shilling silver shoe buckles before making their getaway.

The second story concerns Mary's grandmother, who Daniel loved to tease by pretending to complain about Mary being bad-tempered. The elderly woman always took her granddaughter's side as she exclaimed, 'Sir, you must have provoked her very much! Sir, you must yourself be quite in fault. Sir, my little girl was always the gentlest, sweetest creature born.'

We can assume that as far as Mary was concerned, family was the most important thing.

In 1812, she went to the famous spa 'Irish Bath' at Mallow. With so many pregnancies in quick succession, it is hardly surprising that she was troubled, from time to time, by bad health. She was also coping with a husband whose fame and work commitments were spiralling and taking him away from her for longer periods. Daniel began holding nationwide meetings, to promote emancipation, and summer proved a particularly busy time for outdoor gatherings. Mary read the newspapers and had, or maybe feigned, an interest in politics. Erin Bishop makes the point that she would always relate the political back to the personal. For instance, she wanted emancipation as much as the next person because it would mean that Daniel could spend more time at home. She kept up with his doings through the papers that she read with pride and, as usual, their daily letters had to substitute for meandering conversations at mealtimes, pillow talk and walks about town.

For all her political opinions, her only genuine consideration was Daniel and if anyone were giving him a hard time, be they Irish and/or Catholic, she would rage, by letter, telling Daniel to forget the whole lot of them. When people in Carlow were causing her husband problems, she wrote, 'Were I in your place, I would not go a step to the Carlow meeting and, what is more, I would give up Catholic politics and leave the nasty ungrateful lot to sink into insignificance.'

It would only be natural if she were jealous of the time and energy that Daniel allotted to 'the nasty ungrateful lot'. In another letter to her husband, she confesses that 'I much fear there is little chance for Emancipation. Everything seems to be against it and surely, while the Catholics continue to disagree among themselves, what can they expect?' It is easy to imagine a wife hoping that her husband will forget the world outside their door in preference to living contentedly with her and their children.

There was never a dull moment. In 1815, Mary must have been more than a little shocked, if not outright terrified, by her husband's new passion for duelling. It began on 24 January with John D'Esterre, a member of Dublin Corporation, taking grave offence at Daniel referring to the Corporation as being 'beggarly'. They opposed Catholic Emancipation as did D'Esterre, a Protestant from Limerick and a member of Dublin Corporation.

A paper delivered to Naas Historical Society on 9 November 1995 describes D'Esterre as a man down on his luck in every way; his marriage was falling apart, and he was on the verge of declaring himself bankrupt. So, he may have been manipulated into challenging the famous Catholic leader to a duel and how could O'Connell refuse? Now was not the time for Daniel to show weakness or cowardice; Catholic Ireland needed him to be strong in the face of adversity and he agreed to meet with D'Esterre at a designated spot.

Daniel O'Connell did not believe in using violence to achieve political gain. A visit to France in the middle of the bloody French Revolution (1789–1799) had left its mark on him for life and he would always champion words over bullets. However, a duel was different, being both a personal and a public affront. One's reputation was on the line for all to see. O'Connell undoubtedly had political enemies who would relish seeing him being revealed as a coward and/or conveniently being shot dead. And, in fact, the latter was a real possibility since D'Esterre was a former marine lieutenant who was known both for his bravery and for being an excellent shot.

But Daniel's hand was forced. According to Sister Mary Francis Cusack, who had more than a soft spot for her subject, D'Esterre, described as 'the wily Orangeman' in her biography, made quite a show of his displeasure, marching through the city centre whilst cracking a horse whip that he promised to use on Daniel. She adds that friends of D'Esterre rented a window of a house in Grafton Street, from where they hoped to watch the whipping take place. However, O'Connell wisely kept his distance, which then provoked D'Esterre into challenging him to a duel.

Sister Cusack's date fails to tally with others, as she writes that the duel took place on 26 February, but most sources agree it took place three weeks earlier on Wednesday, 1 February, which must have been an anxious day for Catholic Ireland. One can only imagine Mary at home watching the clock. Not many, including his anxious team who accompanied him, expected Daniel to survive, yet somehow the experienced marksman missed his target. According to the *Dublin Evening Post*, Daniel took his shot and caught D'Esterre in the groin, an inch below the hip, which killed the Limerick man a few days later. Afterwards, Daniel said that he had not wanted to kill the man, only injure him. On hearing of Daniel's victory, future Archbishop of Dublin, Daniel Murray (1768–1852) exclaimed, 'God be praised, Ireland is safe.'

Daniel went into hiding at a friend's house, and Mary was instructed not to tell anyone where he was. He went on to set up a pension for D'Esterre's daughter and made himself available to his widow for legal advice.

Six months later, it was happening again, but this time Mary came into her own. Daniel began to wantonly taunt Sir Robert Peel (1788–1850), the Chief Secretary of Ireland, calling him Orange Peel and claiming that he had been squeezed out of a factory in England. His confidence presumably having been bolstered by winning his first duel, Daniel now challenged Peel to one. Count Daniel O'Connell, Daniel's uncle, who was known as The General, was visiting the family home in Merrion Square at the time and was most impressed with his nephew taking on Peel. Mary, however, was not and neither was she impressed with their guest and her husband excluding her from pertinent conversations in French and Irish, neither of which she could speak. She would have been thinking of their seven children in need of their father, along with the fact that Daniel's income was only just keeping them afloat. His responsibilities to his family should not have allowed him the luxury of challenging men to duels, though Mary probably could not say any of this to him. Instead, she concocted a plan, a dramatic one, but it was the only option open to her. She told the sheriff about the duel and effectively had her husband placed under house arrest. The atmosphere in Merrion Square must have been strained, but she did not falter even when Uncle Daniel expressed his anger, telling him, 'I am sorry to have annoyed you, uncle, but I'd much sooner vex you than let my husband be killed.'

She had won this battle, but as soon as he could, and behind Mary's back, Daniel persisted with his duel, deciding it best to leave Ireland to do it – the chosen location being Ostend in Belgium. Sister Cusack reckons that Robert Peel was frightened for his life and had no desire to exchange fire with O'Connell. Peel's father, also Sir Robert (1750–1830), and also a politician, made use of his contacts in the police and had Daniel arrested soon after he arrived in London, on his way to Dover to board the ship to Belgium; an action for which Mary must have been most grateful and presumably Daniel too as he suddenly had a change of heart. He apologised to Peel for issuing such a challenge and promised all that he would never take part in a duel again.

However, the year was not over yet, and more trouble rained down on Mary's head thanks to Daniel's tendency to say yes to anyone asking him for financial help. This was a habit that various family members, including Hunting Cap, had already severely criticized, but Daniel seemed unable, whether it was from an oversized ego or an oversized heart, to just say no. In 1815, according to Maurice O'Connell, Mary had just managed to get Daniel to promise her that he would stop lending money or standing as security for other people's loans. Nevertheless, we have seen how he would lie to her and simply continue on as he wished. Accordingly, despite having promised Mary otherwise, when a businessman from Killarney, James O'Leary, asked Daniel to be his guarantor, Daniel said yes and guaranteed him a colossal £8,000. Then, when O'Leary's business went under, the O'Connells were in real danger of losing everything. It was Mary's brother-in-law James who told her in March that Daniel was involved, as security, in O'Leary's bankruptcy. She must have sent her husband a rocket of a letter which, unfortunately, Daniel destroyed as he never kept her letters if they upset him. No matter, it is thrilling to read his response to the missing letter, 'I never in my life was so exquisitely miserable as your last letter made me. I wept over it this morning for two hours in bed and I am ready to weep over it again … I blame, indeed I do, my brother James for instilling this poison in your mind … darling believe me, do believe me, you have no cause for your misery. Did I ever deceive you?'

She could have replied yes, you have – what about that episode with Orange Peel – but, instead, she reverted to her usual reassuring and loving self, writing, 'I know it is not in your nature to deceive me. Let me then, darling, entreat of you to forget what is past and do not for one moment think me capable of having no confidence in your protestations.'

It is a marvellous act of love for a husband who had, unintentionally, let her down again and again, whether it was purchasing a house against her express wishes or sailing off in secret to take part in a duel that she thought she had prevented.

Remarkably, Mary does not sound aggrieved when she writes the following year to tell him that a solicitor in Killarney told her that 'there was not a greater buck in … London … than James O'Leary dashing away at his usual rate, most elegantly dressed at the opera and theatres every night and living in one of the most expensive taverns in London. This is the way, darling, he is spending your £8,000.' She made her point despite the loving use of 'darling'. In fact, Daniel's £8,000 had been borrowed from his brother James and a John Hickson from College Green. In addition, it was agreed amongst the family that this latest blunder be kept from Hunting Cap, who had warned Daniel against getting involved with O'Leary. Drastic measures were taken in this regard with Ellen, Daniel's sister, stationing two trustworthy men at two different entrances into Derrynane House, their uncle's home, to urge every single visitor to refrain from mentioning O'Leary's bankruptcy which was being spoken about throughout the land. Meanwhile, Count O'Connell kindly leant Daniel £3,600 to pay back what he had borrowed from John Hickson. In 1821, the count realised that he would never get his money back and made a gift of it.

For the most part, Mary's letters to Daniel were full of comfort and understanding, but it is natural to assume that she often kept her true feelings and worries about money and their future to herself, which must have been a strain. Furthermore, we remember that she was, at this time, continually getting pregnant and losing babies until young Daniel's arrival in 1816. On 16 October, one-year-old Ricarda, their fourth daughter, who was known as 'Ducky' or 'the little red duck' and who clung jealously to her mother after she had 'little Dan', succumbed probably to measles and whooping cough. It is no surprise that after at least twelve pregnancies in thirteen years or so, Mary's spirits and health began to deteriorate over the next two years.

It was decided that she needed a long summer holiday, and so, accompanied by her daughters, son John, niece, the children's governess and some servants, she set out for the spa town of Clifton. She planned to winter in France; however, she proved too unwell for a longer journey.

Five years later, she made it to France, leaving Ireland on 2 May 1822, but it was not for a holiday. Instead, it was a drastic solution to cutting down on the family's living expenses by relocating, potentially for up to a year, to the city of Pau, situated at the northern point of the Pyrenees mountains. This time, all the children bar Maurice went with her, along with her married sister-in-law Alicia Finn and two servants. Daniel and Maurice stayed behind, and the separation was not undertaken gladly, with Daniel repeatedly blaming himself for their precarious finances which were forcing this break-up of family life.

Mary did her best to assuage his guilt, writing, 'You are, heart, much more religious than your Mary and from the moment it was deemed necessary for me to come with my family to France, I put it on the resolution to bear it like a Christian. Do not, my own love, make me unhappy by those reproaches you cast on yourself … You have been the best and most beloved of husbands …'

It took nine days for Mary and her party to reach Bordeaux, where they moved in with Mrs Harrison, an Englishwoman who had been rich until her American husband spent her fortune before abandoning her. One might wonder if Mary drew any parallels between herself and the impoverished woman who was now reduced to taking in lodgers. In any case, here they planned to wait for Alicia's husband, William, to collect them. However, when William still had not arrived by 26 May, Mary ordered two carriages to take her and the family on to Pau, approximately a hundred and sixty miles from Bordeaux. Various particulars of the year in France are known to us thanks to Mary and Daniel's daughter Ellen, a future poet and writer, who kept a journal. The journey to Pau was taken in stages because of Mary's fatigue; the first day, she only managed fourteen miles. After three days of travel, they finally reached Pau, where Mary immediately found herself under pressure to secure temporary lodgings as the woman who was supposedly to take care of them had gone away without organising anywhere for them to stay. This must have been Mary's first time to view properties, a job that Daniel would have done previously, and it proved a tricky business. There were plenty of places for rent, but they were either too small, too rural, too expensive or lacking in furniture and amenities. On 8 June, Mary looked to be settling for a big old house in the rue de Prefecture until, two days later, she got inside the house and found the beds in filthy condition with the agent refusing to change them. Mary refused to move in and, the following week, she found what she was looking for at number 5 cote du Moulin, Basses Ville.

Unfortunately, Pau's hot summer did not suit the family, and Mary did not want to stay where there were no English-speaking priests. She had deliberately been left out of conversations between Daniel and his uncle, The General, because she could not speak French, and it would seem she had not attempted to learn the language before moving to France. She started looking elsewhere and found them a furnished house in the historic town of Tours, approximately six hours by train from Pau, which was available to rent in October. A cooler temperature was a cheerful prospect and, furthermore, Daniel was coming over to help them move and stay on for a month before returning to Dublin in November. They remained in Tours for the following year despite its unpopularity with the family. Ellen wrote in her journal, 'Only that my father has bound us to this horrid house we should have gone to Paris the 1st of June – for Mama is sick of Tours, which does not agree with any of us.'

Having done the year in Tours, Mary brought her family to Paris, in 1823, and found it full of French soldiers who were readying themselves for war with Spain. For her, this must have been a deciding factor and she determined to leave France as soon as possible.

That autumn, Mary and the children moved to Southampton, England, which was to prove no better than France. Mary felt isolated in every way, writing to Daniel that she and the family were being snubbed because they were Irish and Catholic. In one letter, she declared to Daniel that their new home was, 'a most horrid and stupid place for young People. The stiff, starched, proud English will not visit without letters of introduction.' In another letter, she complains that English people are 'the coldest people in the world' and 'not one of those introduced to us … have as yet paid us a visit. We are Irish Catholics. This is against us.'

She wanted to return to Dublin whilst Daniel, in financial turmoil, suggested that Killarney would be cheaper, but this did not suit Mary. In fact, she would rather stay in England than live in Ireland outside of Dublin. Claiming that Dublin was the only place where she felt physically well, she strengthened her argument by pointing out that if the family moved to Kerry, Daniel would be overrun by all manner of relatives wanting something from him, in other words money, which would mean that they would save nothing. On top of that, their shaky finances would become obvious to the entire O'Connell family, which would be embarrassing. For her final argument, she had her daughters' backing. Mary told Daniel that their girls had said that 'they would rather live in the greatest obscurity anywhere than live in any of the country parts of Ireland.'

They stayed in Southampton. One can relate to Mary's reluctance to live permanently near the O'Connell clan. Even after all these years, she remained sensitive to the fact that she had had no dowry and had cost Daniel his inheritance and relationship with his Uncle Maurice.

A week later, Mary agreed to return to Dublin after her brother-in-law James O'Connell advised Daniel that Dublin was the cheapest option since the family already had the house in Merrion Square. Mary made Daniel promise to cut back on expenses; for example, they would go without a carriage and horses and employ no more than four servants. According to Daniel's great-great grandson, Maurice R O'Connell's essay, 'Daniel O'Connell: Income, Expenditure and Despair' in *Irish Historical Studies*, Daniel's uncle Count O'Connell had made Mary promise that she would not return to Ireland until all their debts were paid. This was the uncle that had been obliged to lend Daniel a large sum of money to pay off another creditor and then, six years later, turn it into a gift. It appears that she was made responsible for something that was mostly outside of her control, no matter how hard she tried to rein in Daniel's spending. After two years abroad, it must have seemed that keeping her word to the count might involve her staying away from Ireland forevermore. As she boarded the ship for Ireland, in May 1824, she would only have hoped for the best, for at least she and the children were going home again.

The family's financial problems were far from trivial. Although Daniel was earning good money, he was hopeless at managing their finances. His brothers James and John were obliged to give him loans until they had little left to spare him. James sent letters lecturing his brother about his finances and warning him that he could end up in a debtors' prison. As far as James was concerned, Mary's years in forced exile, which he cooly referred to as a 'tour', had accomplished nothing, 'Their tour to the Continent, which was intended to be of use to your finances, has beyond all doubt contributed to adding largely to your debts.'

Daniel's friend Denys Scully (1773–1830), a writer and emancipation activist, had loaned Daniel £2,000, which he had promised to pay back within six months. It was now eight years later, and, understandably, Denys wanted his money back. James begged his brother to stop becoming involved with other people's expenses. For instance, Daniel received a letter from Father Peter Kenney, rector of Clongowes Wood College, where Daniel showed, according to Maurice R O'Connell, a particular interest in two pupils, Alexander and John Burke of Clonmel. Does this mean that Daniel was paying their school fees? Well, whether it does or not, it was Daniel that Father Kenney contacted about the boys' unpaid fees from the previous year.

Part of the problem was that Daniel and Uncle Maurice, Hunting Cap, had patched over their differences, resulting in Daniel believing that he was back in favour, fortune-wise, when the old man died. In other words, he allowed himself to spend freely because he believed that he would someday be rich and able to pay off his debts. In 1823, he says as much in a letter to Mary: 'I always looked to the resources to come from my Uncle Maurice's succession as the means to paying off and I went into debt on that speculation.'

When Hunting Cap finally died in February 1825, Mary and Daniel decided it would be better for the family to move into Derrynane House. Biographer Erin Bishop thinks that Mary may never have met the Uncle Maurice who, in his absence, had ruled so much over the couple's courtship and married life. Therefore, her first sight of their new home took place only after Daniel inherited it, making her mistress of Derrynane House. She liked it immensely, writing to Daniel that September, 'Every day I get more pleased with Derrynane.' Her new status also stirred ambition. 'I think I should be able to do a great deal of good for the poor people of Derrynane.'

Apart from the house, Hunting Cap's fortune was, as final punishment for his dowry-less marriage, to be divided between Daniel and his brothers John and James.

Typically, Daniel set about having Derrynane almost completely renovated, making the front of the house the new back of the house and adding four reception rooms and more bedrooms and, typically, it cost a lot more than he had expected. In July 1825, their eldest daughter, Ellen, married barrister and politician Christopher Fitzsimon (*d*.1856), and Daniel provided a dowry of £5,000 to be paid over four years.

Whenever Mary and Daniel were living together for long periods, we have less information about her doings as there were fewer letters. For instance, how much say did she have in the Derrynane renovations? Maurice R O'Connell believed that Mary loved spending just as much as Daniel did. For evidence, he referenced Daniel's letters, when she was living abroad, begging her to be careful with every penny in order to hurry on the family's reunion. Furthermore, Daniel's uncle Count O'Connell makes Mary promise to stay away until all debts are cleared. We also note James O'Connell's disparaging comment about her 'Continent tour' and, from that, we might imagine James and other close relatives' disapproval of Mary's frequent house moves in France.

The family still maintained the house in Merrion Square as Daniel needed his Dublin base. He spent approximately six months a year in Derrynane and Mary accompanied him back to the capital. But then London called, after Daniel put himself on the ballot ticket in an 1828 by-election in County Clare, just to see what would happen. When he won by a large majority, the British government wisely pushed through the 1829 Catholic Emancipation Act, which meant that Irish Catholic politicians could now represent their country in Westminster. It was a notable achievement, for which Daniel was hailed as 'The Emancipator' or 'The Great Liberator'.

It also proved financially rewarding when a national testimony, or reward of as much as £20,000, was presented to Daniel for winning Emancipation. Furthermore, Daniel's supporters set up a subscription fund that would pay him a decent income, and so it did after PV Fitzpatrick, Daniel's political manager and financial agent, determined that the tribute should achieve a grand total of £1,000 every month to allow Daniel to concentrate on what was important. Finally, Daniel was able to pay off his debts and quit his law practice in favour of full-time politics. And so, on 4 February 1830, Daniel made history, taking his seat as the first Catholic member of parliament. Mary had accompanied him to London, bringing her two single daughters Catherine (Kate) and Elizabeth (Betsey) to show them off to London society. Initially, Mary was rather enamoured with the city, attending the theatre and the opera, until it began to bore her, and she wanted to come home. She was now fifty-two years old and her youngest child, fourteen-year-old Daniel, was back in Ireland preparing to attend and board at the Jesuit school Clongowes Wood College, in Kildare, just as his older brothers had done before him. We can be thankful for this today as Mary happily began upon a new correspondence with her 'Darling Danny', who had spent his first fourteen years being taught at home by Mary, with daughter Ellen's help. His mother bristled when it was suggested that she coddled or spoiled him. For instance, she writes to her son, 'I am told Mr Duncan [one of Danny's teachers] says to every person that you are a spoiled child by me. I don't really think he should speak of me in those terms ...'

Her forty-eight letters, collected by biographer Erin Bishop, were released as *My Darling Danny: Letters from Mary O'Connell to her son Daniel, 1830–1832*, and they include scenes such as the following when Mary describes her and Daniel going to see a play in London: 'It was so crowded and of course so noisy that we did not hear a single word of the tragedy except part ... of the last two acts. Your Father was received ... with cheers all the way to the box and when he made his appearance there the cheering and waving of handkerchiefs ... was beyond anything you can form an idea. I often wished you were with us.'

In 1832, Mary had what some might describe as a common enough experience for the wife of a famous and popular politician when Ellen Courtenay, a young actress from Cork (*c*.1803–1864) accused Daniel of being the father of her son. To this end, from her Fleet prison cell, London, where she had been jailed for debt, Ms Courtenay wrote a pamphlet entitled: 'A Narrative by Miss Ellen Courtenay, of Most Extraordinary Cruelty, Perfidy & Depravity, Perpetrated Against Her by Daniel O'Connell, Esq (M.P. for Kerry) ...'

She described visiting Daniel O'Connell in Merrion Square, in 1817, when she was just fifteen years old, to ask his advice on a leasehold belonging to her father. She said that because Daniel made her feel uncomfortable, she resolved to deal with him only by letter. However, she was urgently summoned back to Merrion Square a few months later, where she said that he seduced/raped her in his study, and she had their child nine months later. According to the pamphlet, he had refused to publicly recognise the child or to contribute towards his expenses.

It is impossible to be sure today one way or the other. Daniel could be flirtatious, which Mary knew, as she wrote to him in 1809, 'I ought to lecture you well for being such a plague to young girls.' As the couple spent so much time apart, Mary was also prone to feelings of jealousy. For instance, in 1823, after twenty-one years of marriage, she wrote from France to take issue again with his visits to their children's former governess Miss Gahan. Daniel's reply was blunt, ' ... I never in my life showed the slightest tinge of preference to any being above you, and why now, when I would not look at any other woman for a moment, you should persevere in an angry correspondence on a subject so trivial ... I have only to repeat my solemn promise of never again seeing her without your express permission.'

Ellen Courtenay's dates were somewhat unreliable. She said that the child, whom she christened as Henry, was born on 4 November 1818, whilst also claiming that whatever happened in Daniel's study took place in the summer of 1817. She also said she had written the pamphlet out of financial desperation, having tried different avenues to reach him. The pamphlet includes footnotes denouncing Daniel's leadership and political standing, which has suggested to some historians that Ellen's story was not true and was, instead, concocted by political enemies hoping to tarnish the reputation of a popular Irish Catholic leader.

Furthermore, Ellen's pamphlet was published by the notorious journalist and actor Barnard Gregory (1796–1852), who edited the weekly scandal sheet *Satirist* and had plenty of experience in blackmailing celebrities. The arguments continue today as to Daniel's innocence or Ellen's truth and one can interpret letters between Daniel and Mary, throughout the years of 1816–1817, any which way. Meanwhile, the sorry episode is raised here only because it inadvertently proved detrimental to Mary's health and life.

By the summer of 1832, the accusations made by Ellen Courtenay had all been forgotten, having received little or no response from the O'Connell camp. Unfortunately, a dramatic sequel ensued four years later, in 1836, upon Ellen's release from prison. Ellen took to following Daniel when she saw him out walking. The story goes that one day she and nineteen-year-old Henry accosted Daniel as he walked out with his second-youngest son, John, who was now an MP for Youghal. There was an altercation whereby John hit Henry several times with his umbrella and ended up in court charged with assault. Pandora's Box duly erupted, and the highly publicised court case appeared in all the papers with plenty of gossip about the physical similarities between Daniel and Henry Simpson. The timing could not be worse as Daniel was about to conduct a tour of the English midlands and so it was decided that Mary should join him on tour in April, to present a solid and united front to the commentators who were enjoying the scandal surrounding the great Irish Liberator. Mary was far from well but made the necessary journey for Daniel's sake. The following month she went to Tunbridge Wells in Kent to take the waters but returned, with Daniel, to Derrynane, in August, from where Daniel sent a panicked letter to a friend saying that she was getting weaker day by day. Some attempt to revive her health was made by moving her into Daniel's agent John Primose's house, Hillgrove, in Cahersiveen, but it proved to be a temporary break as her condition continued to worsen. She was brought back to Derrynane, where she died on 31 October and was buried in the O'Connell tomb on Derrynane's Abbey Island, separated, as always, from her husband, who lived for another eleven years and was buried in Glasnevin Cemetery in Dublin, in 1847.

At the time of her death, Daniel's best years, it could be argued, were behind him, though he could be proud of their four sons who had followed him into politics. He never recovered from the loss of Mary, and Sister Cusack quotes him as an old man saying that she 'gave him thirty-five years of the purest happiness that man had ever enjoyed'.

In Arthur Ponsonby's collection of Scottish and Irish diaries, he provides this from Daniel, 'I love, from my heart I love, Liberty.' Daniel O'Connell, 'The Liberator', had dedicated his life to freeing Ireland from English rule, along with his campaigning to rid the world of slavery. Ponsonby (1871–1946) notes that Daniel, a rather intermittent diarist, married Mary O'Connell a few weeks after his last entry but never mentioned her in his diary at all. However, before we make too much of that, Ponsonby points out that he also never mentioned the Act of Union. So, his two big passions, the latter born out of hatred, were never recorded in his own writings, outside of his letters. Their letters during their long and frequent separations were perhaps what kept them in step together, particularly when his career expanded so quickly and widely, and Mary was left to bring up their children by herself. She was his greatest and most constant support, the one who always co-operated with him, from keeping their courtship and wedding quiet, and enduring those constant farewells from him as they became parents, to leaving her home behind for two years to improve their finances.

Ultimately, Mary O'Connell enabled her husband to give his all for Ireland, perhaps his first love. As Sister Mary Frances Cusack wrote, 'She was certainly not a woman of any remarkable intellectual calibre, but she had sufficient appreciation of her husband's value to give him the just award of her affectionate approbation in his career.'

Constance Wilde and her first son Cyril.

CHAPTER THREE

CONSTANCE WILDE (1858-1898)

Wife of Oscar Wilde, playwright and poet

Constance (née Lloyd) Wilde's maternal grandfather Captain John Atkinson, Receiver General of the Post Office, lived with his wife Mary in 1 Ely Place, a beautiful Georgian town house, and no doubt mixed in the best of Dublin's society. Mary's brother, politician and barrister Charles Hare Hemphill (1822–1908), the first Baron Hemphill, also lived nearby in Merrion Square, where his neighbours included ophthalmologic surgeon and writer Sir William Wilde (1815–1876) and his wife, writer and poet Lady Jane Wilde, otherwise known as Speranza (1821–1896).

In 1857, Charles Hemphill was a member of a British Science Association expedition to the Aran Islands. William Wilde was the official leader and organiser of the ethnological section of this expedition, which included a big picnic at the prehistoric hillfort of Dún Aengus. William Wilde's son Henry Wilson, Oscar's half-brother, aged nineteen, was a member of the party too. Charles Hemphill was to be a witness at Oscar's wedding when he married Constance Lloyd in May 1884; his signature is on their wedding certificate.

When Constance's nineteen-year-old mother, Adelaide (Ada) (1838–1921), married her twenty-seven-year-old barrister cousin Horace Lloyd (1828–1874), on 28 August 1855, one can only speculate if the Wildes were invited to the wedding, although Lady Wilde might have been too busy tending to her sons, baby Oscar (1854–1900) and his brother William (1852–1899).

Financially speaking, Ada had married well. Her father-in-law was Englishman John Horatio Lloyd (1798–1884), a wealthy barrister and former liberal MP for Stockport. She and Horace set up home in London, at 3 Harewood Square, in Marylebone, where they had two children: Otho in 1856 followed by Constance in 1858. Family life was difficult as Horace and Ada proved disinclined towards parenthood. Horace was much too engrossed in his career and high-society friends to spend his evenings at home. In response, Ada sailed home frequently to Dublin, so much so that the children, Otho and Constance, grew very familiar with their grandparents' neighbourhood as they played with their cousin Stanhope Hemphill (1853–1919) who is likely to have known the Wilde brothers in Merrion Square.

Back in England, Horace moved his family into bigger and fancier houses, finally settling at 42 Sussex Gardens, London, an establishment that required five servants and was just a stone's throw from his father's mansion at 100 Lancaster Gate.

Constance would have been provided with a governess at home, alongside Otho, until she could attend a local girls' school. Highly intelligent, Constance had a love of learning, and excelled in piano, intricate needlework, painting and learning languages. She could read Dante's *Inferno* in its original Italian. On finishing school, she was fortunate in being able to attend a college and she is described as a scholar in the censuses of 1871 and 1881. Although they could not hold a degree, women could choose, if they so wished, a subject to study for an examination. Accordingly, Constance studied the poetry of Percy Bysshe Shelley (1792–1822) and wrote an essay that was so impressive, her tutor, Mr Collins, had little to say about it – something she proudly shared with her brother, in a letter dated 14 January 1882.

On the face of it, Constance was living the dream, growing up in luxury surroundings, with the freedom to pursue an education. However, she lacked confidence in herself, a probable result of her parents' lacklustre parenting skills. Her father's late nights and roving eye may have produced the alleged illegitimate son that turned up at Lancaster Gate with his mother. Constance was a witness to the scene that played out on that occasion.

Extra marital affairs – and children – were something that Horace Lloyd shared with his in-laws' neighbour Doctor William Wilde. By the time the revered doctor married, he was already a father at least three times over. Horace might have thought his sins were little in comparison to his father John Horatio Lloyd's breakdown in the 1830s, which caused him to strip and run naked in a public park. Furthermore, Doctor Wilde's direst hour was still to come and, when it did, it involved a scandalous trial that saw him accused of rape by a young patient of his, who was vindicated by the jury.

Constance and Otho lost their father in 1874 to a pulmonary disease and with that, their newly widowed mother turned against her sixteen-year-old daughter, either ignoring Constance in private or humiliating her in public. One can imagine that treatment stripping a shy, young girl of her confidence. Even worse than that, Ada beat Constance and banged her head against the wall. We know all this thanks to Otho who maintained that this barrage of abuse turned his sister into someone who was fearful, even sulky, in company and prone to explosive rages at home.

Historical biographer Franny Moyle suggests that Ada was jealous of her beautiful daughter. Widowed at just thirty-six years of age, Ada was desperate for another husband with deep pockets in order to maintain the luxury to which she had become accustomed, and perhaps she viewed her daughter as competition. In any case, within two years, Ada had achieved her goal by marrying the affable, wealthy widower, and father of one, George Swinburne-King.

Luckily for Otho, his school was in Bristol, providing him with an escape from a chaotic home. In 1876, he won a 'demy' scholarship to study Classics at Oriel College, Oxford University, whereupon Lady Jane Wilde wrote to her son, Oscar, who had studied Classics in Magdalen College, asking him to look out for Otho. The following year, when Otho was visiting his grandmother in

Dublin, she sent him to call on the Wildes in Dublin and, after that, he and Oscar would bump into one another in Oxford.

Sister and brother, Constance and Otho, kept in touch via frequent letters. In one, Constance raved about a new interest, mesmerism. This was the practice of putting someone into a hypnotic state to influence their thoughts. Constance boasted to George Swinburne-King, their future stepfather, that she could mesmerise her grandfather.

Another subject that became close to her heart was fashion, but not simply for its own sake. When a new shop, Liberty, opened in London, in 1875, selling artisan furniture, oriental goods and 'art fabrics' for bohemian-type dresses that loosely hung from one's figure, with puffed sleeves, Constance became a regular customer. Liberty's clothes promoted spontaneity by allowing the wearer to move freely. This was more than a mere fashion statement; this was kicking against the system that preferred women's limbs and torsos to be corralled into girdles and rigid corsets with no 'give' in them. The Liberty dresses, described as Pre-Raphaelite or Aesthetic, owed their popularity to the likes of model and muse Jane Morris (1939–1914), wife of designer William (1834–1896), and artist and model Elizabeth Siddal (1829–1862), who was married to the painter and poet Dante Gabriel Rossetti (1828–1882). In pursuing her own personal tastes – Otho thought her dresses ugly – Constance proved herself capable of flouting society's rules.

Her mother's upcoming nuptials meant change, not least for Ada who had been receiving an annual stipend of £400 from John Horatio Lloyd, Horace's father, since his son's death. Naturally, her father-in-law saw no need to continue supporting Ada when she was to marry again. However, Ada knew how to force John Horatio's hand in this regard. If he dared to cut her off, she would, in turn, stop supporting his grandchildren and, so, a deal was struck which would ultimately allow Constance and Otho to make a financial break from their mother.

The wedding also raised the matter of location. Where should the newly marrieds live? Twenty-year-old Constance and her mother were living in the home they had shared with Horace and Otho, but now Ada wondered about moving. Constance wrote to Otho to say that she had made the mistake of suggesting that they could look for a house in South Kensington, where a friend of hers lived. Ada baulked at this, typically declaring that a thousand pounds would not induce her to live near any of Constance's friends. This was enough for Otho who took himself off to Lancaster Gate to inform his grandfather and Aunt Emily, who lived with her father, that Constance needed rescuing. John Horatio responded immediately. While George Swinburne-King and his former daughter-in-law moved in together in Constance's childhood home, Constance packed up her dresses, art materials and books and went to live with her grandparents, the Lloyds.

Her new home was very grand but presented its own difficulties thanks to her old-fashioned spinster aunt, Emily, who still lived with her parents and did not understand her niece's desires to be creative. Still, Constance loved her grandfather and was safe from her mother's ridicule and violence. She could flourish at Lancaster Gate, given half the chance. Her social life reflected her interests, and she was a frequent visitor to Grosvenor Gallery, a new contemporary space that opened in 1877, in New Bond Street, which became a hub for fans of the Aesthetic Movement. It was also where an unescorted woman could gaze at art and then eat alone in the restaurant without sticking out by a long mile. There was a library and a club, but perhaps the best thing of all was the gallery's inclination to champion female artists.

Constance met her first serious love interest at the gallery in 1881. Sculptor Richard Claude Belt (1851–1920) was immersed in controversy when he was introduced to Constance. Belt had been commissioned to create an award-winning statue of the poet Lord Byron, but Belt's former employer, sculptor Charles Lawes (1843–1911), claimed that the design was his. This accusation resulted in a six-month trial, with high-profile witnesses and members of the Royal Academy, but Belt won his case. He would not, however, win five years later when he was charged with selling fake diamonds to London's wealthiest. For that, he received twelve months' hard labour. Constance found herself attracted to this successful artist who was unafraid to take risks. Belt's photograph can be viewed online. With his shoulder-length floppy hair, full lips and heavy-lidded stare, he bears an uncanny resemblance to Constance's future husband.

Her next boyfriend was Alec Shand, a friend's brother, to whom she was secretly engaged. Her confidence was growing as was her circle of friends. In the summer of 1880, enroute for the boat to Holland, Constance and her grandfather and Aunt Emily met up with Constance's Irish uncle Charlie Hemphill and his son Stanhope, the cousin she and Otho had played with in childhood. Things took an awkward turn when Stanhope declared his love for her and proposed. In fact, Stanhope's proposal was the sole reason for the family get-together. He met with rejection, accused her of caring for someone else, and was sent on his way. She described her mortification in a letter to Otho and swore that she would never marry. The following year, however, she would sing a different tune.

That summer, Constance's Irish grandmother hoped to marry off her twenty-eight-year-old daughter Ella who was in London, staying with her sister Ada. The old woman suggested that the twenty-seven-year-old unmarried son of her friend Lady Jane Wilde should call at Ada's house during Ella's visit. Oscar's mother thought this a most agreeable idea as she wanted to see Oscar marry well. Money was a problem since her husband's death five years earlier, obliging her to exchange Dublin for London where she shared a rented house with her son Willie.

Ada organised a tea party for Ella, at which both mothers hoped that Oscar Wilde would fall for her. Alas, Ella failed to impress once Oscar caught sight of her niece Constance. In his essay on Oscar Wilde for *Famous Trinity Men*, Thomas George Wilson wrote that it would have been better for both of them had Constance and Oscar never met. In any case, their fates were sealed as attraction was instant on both sides. On 7 June, Oscar visited Lancaster Gate and found Constance struggling with nervousness. Of course, he was as different as could be from her cousin and Alec Shand. Influenced by the Aesthetic

Movement, he wore his hair unfashionably long, and his manner was flamboyant. Constance wrote to Otho acknowledging that though some of their relatives found Oscar comical, she thought that their grandfather liked him. She also confided that when she and Oscar were alone he was free from affectation, which allowed her to relax in his company. There was a public Oscar and a private one that perhaps only she was privy to.

Back in Dublin, Speranza's Saturday salons had been famous for attracting all manner of writers and artists and she had begun anew from her London address, where guests, including Constance and her mother Ada, squeezed into a small drawing room. Oscar and Constance snatched the opportunity to get to know one another better in the middle of a boisterous crowd, with Oscar inviting Constance to see *Othello* at the Lyceum. Determined to go, Constance told her guardians that the invitation had come from Lady Jane instead of her son.

Oscar took Constance and her grandfather to an exhibition at the Pall Mall Gallery. In between these excursions, Constance was discreetly making herself available to Oscar by staying home in case he should visit. The weeks passed by and, in November, Constance received a poem from her stepfather in which he gently teased her about Oscar. That same month she heard that Oscar was heading to America in the New Year for three months, lecturing about English Renaissance Art and 'The House Beautiful'. Constance took pride in his being so in demand and the fact that he would be very well paid for his fifty lectures.

When Oscar's brother Willie got a job on the *Daily Telegraph*, he moved with his mother into a more upmarket house in Mayfair. Constance's relationship must have improved with her mother since they visited Lady Wilde together in her new surroundings, though they did wonder in private at the small rooms. For Constance, it was a chance to hear all about Oscar's first play, *Vera* or *The Nihilists*, about the death of a Russian Tsar, which was being premiered on 17 December at the Adelphi Theatre. Lady Wilde told Constance that Oscar would expect her to see it and Ada agreed to accompany her. The performance was cancelled, however, following the actual murder of a Russian Tsar, leaving Oscar to concentrate on preparing for his lecture tour. He sailed to America on Christmas Eve.

Constance kept herself busy, taking pottery classes as part of a new fascination with ceramics. Ambitious as always, she began to paint plates with a view to selling them at the Amateur Exhibition in Regent Street. She also enrolled in the St John's Wood School of Art which had only admitted its first female students in 1860. Art could provide women with a purpose and even a career as a tutor.

In August 1882, Constance stayed with Grant Duff Ainslie and his wife at their home, the sixteenth-century Delgatie Castle in Aberdeenshire. On seeing the dramatic landscapes surrounding the castle, Constance wrote asking Otho to send her spectacles and a sketchbook and then proceeded to enjoy herself, playing tennis, billiards and going on picnics. She also learned how to shoot, while evening entertainment included demonstrations of guests being mesmerised. Constance was an eligible member of the party and perhaps did not notice the effect she was having on the men. One of the women had been enjoying the attentions of a Mr Huxley before Constance's arrival distracted him dreadfully. When Mr Huxley left, the Ainslies' sixteen-year-old son, Douglas, made his infatuated feelings known to Constance. Unsure what to do, Constance attempted to be a friend that the teenager could confide in. However, this backfired when her hosts heard that she had been in Douglas's bedroom advising him about a problem he was experiencing at school. Constance described all in a letter to Otho. She was told to stay out of Douglas's room, which did nothing for the youngster who now began to show off when she was near. For one thing, he took up betting on horses, while his mother accused Constance of turning Douglas's head. The other guests found the whole matter hilarious and, to top it all off, a fifty-year-old colonel became smitten with Constance and began to flirt openly with her.

Constance told her brother that she would probably ask to return home early. In the end, the decision was made for her when Douglas wrote her a note asking her to visit him in his room when everyone else was asleep. Although he did not send it, he also did not discard it and when the note was found the next day, Constance might as well have taken up Douglas's invitation, for all her protests of innocence, as she found herself packed off home.

Her confidence, which had been so thwarted by her mother's insecurities, must have been boosted by this sort of – albeit embarrassing – attention. Alternatively, biographer Eleanor Fitzsimons suggests that Constance may have become eager to marry to escape such scandalous attention.

Oscar's American tour ended up being a lot longer than three months and he finally returned home in January 1883, only to leave a few weeks later for Paris where he, much bolstered by being treated as a serious artist in America, intended to write. Mary Anderson (1859–1940), a leading American actress, had commissioned him to write a second play – *The Duchess of Padua* – which she would star in. Perhaps hoping to encourage similar feelings in London, Oscar had his hair cut short and determined to work hard at his craft. The trip to America had been a great success, instilling in him purpose and direction. Furthermore, he had returned with money in his pocket, having received an advance on the American performance of his play *Vera* along with his fee from Mary Anderson to work on her play. Surely nothing can make an artist feel more validated than being amply paid for something they have created. It was also brought sharply to his attention that marriage might be the next natural step for a budding successful writer since American and English newspapers had pretty much married him off to future Pulitzer-winning writer Maud Howe (1854–1948), daughter of American writer and poet Julia Ward Howe (1819–1910), after he spent some time with her. The media yearned for a society wedding, as did his mother, and Oscar was obliged to clarify his bachelor status for the time being.

It was Oscar's mother who reunited him with Constance after she invited the Lloyd siblings to Mayfair on 16 May 1883. Constance must have read about the fabled engagement between Oscar and Maud Howe and may have wondered what to expect. However, that first meeting went so well that the following day, Constance and Otho were back for one of Speranza's 'At Homes', which was followed up by a flurry of meetings.

Otho accompanied his sister to Oscar's lecture about his 'Impressions of America' and then helped welcome the Wildes back to Lancaster Gate where he reported to his future wife Nellie Hutchison that Oscar only spoke to Constance. Whatever about Constance's feelings about the attention being paid to her, Otho did not believe that Oscar's behaviour was especially significant and felt that it was just his usual way with women who interested him.

Oscar sailed to New York on 2 August for the *Vera* rehearsals and Constance went to the Continent for a month with her grandfather. On their return to Lancaster Gate, John Horatio's health took a turn for the worse, and Constance was sent to stay at her Irish grandmother's house in November. She had time enough to see Oscar, recently returned, and he gave her a copy of *Vera*, which had failed in America, closing down after just one week. She wrote from Ely Place inviting him to visit her and the Atkinsons in Dublin.

Combining business with pleasure, Oscar sailed for Ireland on 21 November and booked himself into the Shelbourne hotel for four nights, for his two talks at the Gaiety Theatre on the 22 and 23. Constance and her family went to hear him and then he came to tea. Constance wrote to Otho saying that their grandmother was much taken with this new version of Oscar, while their cousin Stanhope would not stop teasing her about him. 'Such stupid nonsense' is how she described the teasing in a letter to Otho.

Then, as biographer Franny Moyle relates, something strange happened. Back in London, Otho heard something unsavoury about Oscar and wrote to his sister confessing misgivings about the romance. One can only wonder at the outcome had his letter arrived on 25 November instead of when it did, two days later, because on 26 November, Constance posted a letter to her brother to tell him that she was engaged to Oscar Wilde. Presumably her brother's letter must have been a shock, yet Constance refused to allow it to intrude on her happiness. She replied that she did not want to know what Otho had heard about Oscar, whether it was true or not. She was committed to her new fiancé, happily in love, and determined not to let anyone or anything interfere with the relationship.

She readied herself for battle, expecting a negative reaction to the engagement from quarters such as the Lloyds. The Atkinsons, however, were delighted, including Constance's mother and stepfather. Not surprisingly, a chastened Otho quickly wrote to assure her that he would welcome Oscar into the family. In fact, it all worked out nicely. Grandfather Lloyd wanted to quiz Oscar about his finances, but apart from that he declared himself happy for the couple.

Oscar's finances were shaky. All the American money was gone, and he still owed money from his college days. He confessed the total debt, £1,500, to John Horatio who, being Constance's guardian, decided to forward £5,000 to a trust fund which would provide his granddaughter with an immediate income from the interest alone. But he stipulated that the wedding was to take place only after Oscar paid off at least £300 of his debts. With a series of lectures booked around Britain, Oscar agreed, promising to make that happen by April 1884. And so, the wedding was set for that April. In mid-December, news of the engagement was released to the press. Constance's life as she knew it was over. Engaged to a celebrity, she found herself the subject of newspaper articles in Ireland and England.

On 23 December, Oscar's friend, the American painter James McNeill Whistler (1834–1903) invited the engaged couple to a special breakfast, presumably so that all their friends could have a good look at her. The engagement was surely a surprise to Oscar's friends since he had arrived back so recently from America.

And what about Constance's friends? She received many letters demanding that the news be verified; was she, her friends asked, really engaged to *the* Oscar Wilde?

Was it the sudden glare of attention that brought about night terrors? When Oscar embarked on his lecture tour, Constance found herself miserable and unable to sleep. At one point, her cousin Lizzy came to stay at Lancaster Gate and slept beside her to lend her courage enough to relax and sleep. Constance and Oscar exchanged love letters, in which she admitted her anxiety, describing how a fierce storm struck one night, with howling winds that made her think of death and separation.

Is it possible that Constance was hearing further rumours concerning whatever her brother had learnt about her fiance? Oscar may even have told her of his previous love affairs – with women, though it is unlikely that he would have mentioned his encounters with female prostitutes as a college student. However, all is speculation, and we can only wonder if Constance had any inkling of anything else.

While Oscar was away, Constance concentrated on wedding preparations. Her dressmaker was designer Adeline (Ada) Nettleship (1856–1932), wife of the painter John, whose clients included famous actresses like Mrs Patrick Campbell (1865–1940), Ellen Terry (1847–1928) and Sarah Bernhardt (1844–1923). Ada specialised in creating 'Aesthetic' dresses with simple lines and gorgeous fabrics. Constance's wedding dress generated a lot of excitement amongst the public who were anxious to see it. In fact, the dress went on show in March, the month before the wedding. However, the wedding was postponed until May, probably due to their lacking enough funds to lease a house that they both loved on Tite Street in Chelsea. The delay might also have spurred on the ailing John Horatio, who released £500, to be redeemed against Constance's future legacy, thus allowing her to take out a six-year lease and have work done on the house.

The wedding finally went ahead at 2.30pm on Thursday, 29 May 1884, at St James's church in Sussex Gardens. The crowd that turned up to see the bride of Oscar Wilde might have been perplexed at her not wearing a wildly colourful dress, though the reporters from ladies' magazines did, for their readers, inject their descriptions with flowery adjectives of her Aesthetic style. There were pleasing puffed sleeves with a low-cut bodice, while the satin dress, creamy with a hint of yellow, was not bustled, meaning that the skirt fell straight down on all sides, with a long train. Oscar's wedding gift to her, a silver girdle (an ornate belt, a throwback from ancient times) hung from Constance's waist whilst her veil, made of Indian silk, was embroidered with pearls.

With John Horatio too ill to attend, Constance was given away by her uncle. After the ceremony, there was a celebratory cake at Lancaster Gate and by 4.30pm the newlyweds were on their way to Paris, for their honeymoon, where Constance's wardrobe – the large hats, long cloaks and floaty dresses decorated with ribbons and embroideries – was a hit. One of Oscar's Paris-based admirers, Henrietta Reubell (*c.*1849–1924), a wealthy and eccentric American woman, who Oscar thought was the image of Queen Elizabeth, wanted Ada Nettleship to make her copies of Constance's dresses.

In her book *Wilde's Women: How Oscar Wilde Was Shaped by the Women He Knew*, Eleanor Fitzsimons writes that Constance's marriage provided her with the independence she had craved. Before marriage, any excursion the twenty-six-year-old wished to take needed permission from Aunt Emily. One might also consider the impact of Constance having her own home. From sharing a house with a bitter and abusive mother, to moving in with Aunt Emily and her rules, both women having restricted her in their own way, we can appreciate the sudden sprouting of Constance's interests during the early years of marriage. This was the first time since her father's death that Constance would experience her home as a sanctuary.

The Wildes arrived back in London on 24 June 1884 and moved into Oscar's old lodgings to await the completion of their house. John Horatio's death on 17 July meant a large increase in Constance's income, with her and Otho inheriting approximately £23,000 between them. This was timely as she took charge of the renovation project and the house's interior, in league with her husband's ideas and their architect, the celebrated Edward William Godwin (1833–1886), while Oscar returned to his lecture circuit. The house would reflect its occupants' passion for art and culture, in every conceivable way, with Otho describing it as the most beautiful house in London.

Constance wrote to her brother about wanting a career, which was something her old-fashioned aunt would never have supported. In this way, marriage gave Constance independence to discover herself. Thanks to her choice of husband, she was free to earn a living and considered going on the stage or becoming a journalist or writing a novel.

Meanwhile, Constance's taste in fashion and décor inspired new devotees to the cult of Aestheticism. As far as her husband was concerned, Constance's quirky look was a welcome addition to his own. They were like a brand couple, each complementing the other. Whenever they attended social gatherings, the press described Constance's full attire. Of course, not everyone was a fan, but Constance went her own way and seemingly influenced her husband's new series of talks about dress, the first of which he delivered on 1 October. Franny Moyle proves Constance's influence by highlighting Oscar's suggestion that a person should aim for rationality in their clothes. For instance, women could dispense with uncomfortable corsets by wearing dresses with high waistbands, just as Constance did. Women could wear flat shoes and be out of danger of tottering forward on high heels, just as Constance did. This was about freeing women from the physical bonds of conventionality, starting with how they were expected to appear in public. Constance was way ahead of her husband in this regard, but she must have welcomed his appreciation for what she was trying to achieve. She was striking out against the current ideal, the hourglass figure that was created by tightened corsets, skintight sleeves and the outsized bustle that should make the wearer's hips and stomach look small in comparison.

However, it was not just about dressing to enable freer movement of one's body. There was also real danger posed by women's clothing. In 1843, Léopoldine Hugo (1824–1843), the nineteen-year-old daughter of French writer Victor Hugo (1802–1885), and Charles, her new husband, drowned after their small boat capsized on the River Seine. Her heavy skirts made it impossible for him to save her and killed him in the process. Another prime example was the shocking fate of Oscar's two half-sisters who had attended a Halloween party, in 1871, wearing the usual crinoline skirts. When the first sister's skirt caught fire, the second went to her aid and despite frantic efforts of their fellow guests, both girls died from their burns. Similarly, women working in factories had to contend with the risk of their overlong skirts getting them caught up in the machinery. In this way, the Aesthetic look was presented as an improvement on women's health and safety.

After Christmas, Constance was preoccupied with last-minute house details. When Oscar headed off to lecture in Ireland in January, she chose to stay home, hiring housemaids and embroidering cushions. Gone were the night terrors and the need to have her husband by her side. There was another reason for her succumbing happily to domesticity. When renovations were finally completed in 1885, it was just months ahead of Constance giving birth to a boy, Cyril, on the morning of 5 June.

There had been another birth of sorts a month earlier when Constance made it into print, having written a response to an article in the *Pall Mall Gazette* about 'Ladies Dress – Esthetic and Artistic', in which a complaint was made about the general untidiness of aesthetes. The female correspondent was all for close-fitting clothes for all women, no matter their situation. Eight months pregnant, Contance took umbrage at this, pointing out how unsuitable tight clothes were for women in her condition and championed Viscountess Harberton's (1843–1911) Rational Dress Society which had been founded in 1881 to campaign for clothing that would make life easier for women. In a list of principles for the perfect dress, the society placed 'freedom of movement' in the number one spot. To this end, Viscountess Harberton possibly designed and certainly wore the 'divided' skirt in place of heavy layers of petticoats. Instead of a woman accepting that her body needed altering with stays and restrictive garments, perhaps she should demand that her clothes be altered to suit her body and lifestyle. This was a revolutionary thinking that not everyone could get on board with. Some, it seemed, worried that loosening a woman's clothes might be loosening her morals.

Following in her mother-in-law's footsteps, Constance turned her Tite Street home into a magnet for famous statesmen, poets, writers, painters and actors. Constance held two 'At Homes' a month and guests marvelled at Oscar's beautiful house and wife. Constance lapped it all up, producing an autograph book to collect signatures from the likes of John Ruskin, Mark Twain and Frances Hodgeson Burnett. A list of the eighty-nine signatories can be found on the Oscar Wilde's Society's website. One guest, the writer and singer Anna, Comtesse de Brémont (1849–1922) wrote of the expression of love and pride on Constance's face as Oscar held forth, the centre of attention.

A month shy of Cyril's first birthday, his mother fulfilled another goal by appearing in Sophocles' *Helen of Troy*, as one of Helen's handmaidens. It played for six nights in May, with Constance's receiving praise for her appearance. Even the Prince of Wales came to see it. This was to be Constance's sole performance onstage, not least because she was three months pregnant again.

Vyvyan Wilde's arrival on 3 November 1886 was a bit of a disappointment for his parents. For one thing, he was not the girl they had been hoping for and for another he lacked Cyril's good health. Oscar wanted a girl in memory of his sister Isola, who had died when she was just nine years old. The newborn was to have been named after her.

The following year, 1887, was a landmark one for the Wildes. Oscar was hired by publishers Cassell & Co to edit their new magazine *The Lady's World: A Magazine of Fashion and Society*. This was indeed good news as the family's outgoings had increased with the babies and their nurses, obliging Constance to borrow from Otho, who now needed repaying as he was supporting two houses after deserting his first wife, Nellie, and their two children to move in with Nellie's friend. At one point, the Wildes considered leasing out the home that they had spent so much time and money on. This must have been a pressure on their three-year marriage, although it was not the only one. By now, Oscar was failing to resist his attraction to men, while Constance, suspecting him only of being unfaithful with actresses whose plays he had reviewed, extended a friendly welcome to the young men that Oscar brought home, referring to them as 'his disciples'. The magazine job was a welcome boost to their relationship as Oscar was reminded about the importance of being Constance's husband. Thanks to her parties, and his mother's too, he had first-rate contacts and access to any number of famous writers, and many guests found themselves approached to write for his renamed *The Women's World*.

Writing-wise, Oscar embarked upon a new medium, that of the short story, while Constance was asked to write a children's story for the Christmas edition of *The Bairn's Annual of Old-Fashioned Fairy Tales*. Her celebrity proved a huge selling point, although this celebrity also had genuine writing skills, and Constance was to go on to produce a children's book, *There Was Once*, a retelling of familiar stories and fairytales. Her book hit the shelves the same year as Oscar's *The Happy Prince and Other Tales* and Constance was now seen as a writer alongside her husband.

A joint review of both books appeared in the *Irish Times* on 2 February 1889:

> 'Mr and Mrs Wilde possess charming children of their own and they have utilised their acquaintance with the infant world in giving to it some delightful fairytales, which even the elders must appreciate. "The Happy Prince and Other Tales", illustrated by Walter Crane and Jacomb Hood, and published by David Nutt is one of the happiest works which Mr. Oscar Wilde has ever produced; whilst Mrs. Wilde's fairytales, also published recently and entitled "There Was Once", are a charming reproduction of the old stories, familiar to our childish days, which Nisbet [sic] has brought out.'

In February 1887, Constance branched out as a public speaker via the Rational Dress Society. Her prominence as a member combined with literary success resulted in Constance being asked to edit the society's new gazette. She agreed to edit the first edition only and ended up running the entire operation for the next two years. In need of capital to enable the society to sell rational clothes and design patterns, the gazette had to make commercial sense fast through subscriptions and advertisements. Constance spent a lot of time targeting potential customers and inviting people, by letter, to subscribe to the gazette. Published by Hatchard's in Piccadilly, the first edition went on sale in April 1888.

Perhaps it was only natural that Constance became involved in politics, an inevitable crossover from her interest in reforming women's lives through their wardrobes. Joining the Chelsea branch of the Women's Liberal Association, she backed Lady Margaret Sandhurst's campaign to represent Brixton in the London County Council. In April 1888, at a conference funded by the Women's Committee of the International Arbitration and Peace Association, Constance gave a speech about the necessity of educating children from a very young age on the importance of peace.

In July 1888, she researched and wrote an article for Oscar's magazine entitled, 'Children's Dress in this Century', highlighting, as always, the superiority of loose clothing and quality fabrics. She had now achieved all three ambitions that she had considered in her 1884 letter to Otho: she had starred in a play, published articles in magazines, written a book and had added a fourth accomplishment, as a political and social activist. She supported future prime minister William Gladstone (1809–1898), and took Oscar to meet him, appreciating the liberal politician's support for female equality and for Home Rule in Ireland, two topics that she herself publicly addressed for the Women's Liberal Association. Oscar showed his support for his wife's activism by inviting her political friends to write articles for *The Woman's World*.

That December, the poet William Butler Yeats (1865–1939) was invited to the house in Tite Street and, afterwards, made the following comment about his hosts, 'I remember thinking that the perfect harmony of his [Oscar's] life, with his beautiful wife and two young children, suggested some deliberate composition.'

Not surprising, given her punishing schedule, Constance's health gave way in May 1889. She went to her mother's house in Brighton for respite, although her timing was unfortunate as Ada's husband had recently left his wife to set up home by himself in Hastings. A letter from Constance to a friend in June 1889 provides an insight into her busy life when she explains that, despite feeling poorly, she spent the afternoon in conversation with thirty guests.

Ever the seeker, Constance decided to work on improving her mental health, assigning herself a book, *Golden Thoughts*, about the philosophy of Spanish mystic Miguel de Molinos (1628–1696) that promoted meditation as a way to understand oneself. Finding somewhere quiet to meditate proved a challenge.

Her interest in spirituality and the occult might have sprung from Speranza, Constance's mother-in-law, who introduced her to her friend, the vegetarian, physician, writer, campaigner for women's rights and theosophist, Anna Kingsford (1846–1888). Founded in New York, in 1875, the non-sectarian, non-political Theosophical Society promoted 'a universal brotherhood of man' and a willingness to embrace Western esoteric tradition, ancient Greek and Egyptian mythology alongside Eastern doctrines from Buddhism, Hinduism and Oriental mythology. Constance attended a meeting in July 1884, and when Kingsford set up her own group, the Hermetic Society, Constance must have followed her because when Kingsford died in February 1888 Constance joined the new Hermetic Order of the Golden Dawn, a secret society requiring new members to undergo a fussy initiation ceremony and choose a Latin motto. Constance chose '*Qui Patitur Vincit*' ('Who Endures Wins'). The Golden Dawn believed in using ancient magical rituals to attain wisdom, and membership required commitment, discipline and secrecy. Over the next year, Constance somehow found the time to study an array of affiliated subjects, including Hebrew, astrology and the Tarot and passed exams to advance her status to a Philosophus within the Outer Order of the Golden Dawn. She refrained from going any further, however, and left the group around the same time that Oscar started writing his novel *The Picture of Dorian Gray*, sparking suspicion that she had only joined to glean information for him, thereby breaking the secrecy rule. However, biographer Franny Moyle cannot quite believe that Constance would have put herself through a year of intense study and examinations just for Oscar's story.

Meanwhile, Constance thoroughly enjoyed going to the theatre with Oscar and his friends and frequented private clubs like the Albemarle that allowed women to be members. Confirmation of her status as a fashion icon was evident when the expanding Albemarle asked her to be their interior decorator.

In September 1889, she brought Oscar to see the striking dockers' mass demonstration for better wages, in Hyde Park, and was struck both by the power they wielded in unison, which impressed her, and the bitter smell of their tobacco and unwashed bodies, which did not. Yet, the dockers inspired her. Concerned that she might be leading a frivolous life, Constance, following some self-prescribed reading, decided to set up a club for like-minded women who wished to dedicate themselves to social improvement, which she launched as The Pioneer Club in March 1891. On hearing about the Utopian Communities being established in America, whereby people lived together to abide by a life based around shared core values, Constance told a friend that she wished she could join them. She opted to settle for doing good closer to home and began visiting impoverished folk within walking distance of her front door.

Was she striving to fill a void left by her husband? Biographer Eleanor Fitzsimons mentions a common belief that the Wildes' sex life had ended with the birth of their second son. Oscar had given up his magazine job to concentrate on writing full-time and his social life frequently kept him out all night. They began to see less and less of one another which caused rows and upset. At one point, Oscar, reading a bedtime story to his sons, warned that bad things happen to naughty boys who upset their mothers, prompting one of them to ask what happened to naughty fathers who stay out late and make their mother cry. Did Constance feel like she was accidentally reliving her mother's first marriage?

In 1891, Oscar introduced Constance to a new friend, Lord Alfred Douglas, or Bosie as his mother called him (1870–1945). In her essay 'Constantly Undervalued, A Centenary Appreciation of Constance Wilde', Anne Clark Amor writes that the Wildes' marriage might have survived Oscar's sexual preference for men had he not fallen in love with Douglas. Constance was an innocent. *The Picture of Dorian Gray*'s release proved controversial, with WH Smiths refusing to sell it, and plenty more criticising it for the debauched pursuits of its central character, while Constance appeared blissfully ignorant regarding whispers about her husband's relationships with young men. Her ignorance, however, would not outlast Oscar's infatuation with Douglas, a relationship that brought Douglas's enraged father, the Marquis of Queensbury (1844–1900), stampeding into their lives in 1894.

That year, Constance, having seen both boys off to boarding schools, came up with an idea to make money: a collection of Oscar Wilde's quotes entitled *Oscariana*, to be released by Hatchards, who had published the *Rational Dress*

Constance with Oscar Wilde and their son Vyvyan, c.1890.

Gazette. Working with Hatchard's general manager Arthur Humphreys on the book, Constance experienced a strong attraction to the married Humphreys, which may have been reciprocated, although biographer Eleanor Fitzsimons feels that it was a chaste affair due to their marital statuses and Constance's growing interest in religion.

'For Oscar Wilde, posing as a sodomite'. This was the card handed into the Albermarle Club by the Marquis of Queensbury, forcing a response from Oscar, following months of hassle. Out of hatred for his father, Douglas encouraged Oscar to sue for libel, thereby exploding Constance's world, and Oscar's too, in 1895. By that stage, the Wildes were mostly living apart, with Constance frequently staying with friends, especially whenever she was unwell. After falling down the stairs in January, damaging her arm and spine, she had to ask Oscar's friend, art critic and journalist Robbie Ross (1869–1918) for her husband's whereabouts and £5 for a month's recuperation in Torquay.

Back in Tite Street, Constance received a note on 1 March from Oscar, who was staying at the Avondale Hotel in London, telling her that he would visit her at 9pm. That evening, he broke the news that he was taking the Marquis of Queensbury to court and presumably pleaded his innocence to her. After that, he took off to Monte Carlo for a holiday with Douglas, without leaving a forwarding address. Constance wrote to Robbie Ross on 12 March, asking him to tell Oscar that she had been forbidden to walk and needed to stay with her aunt for a while. She also wrote that she was going to be operated on the following week, but if Oscar preferred, she would stay home and postpone the operation until after the court case.

On 1 April, in a wonderful show of loyalty and support, she accompanied her husband and Douglas to St James's Theatre to see *The Importance of Being Earnest*. Two days later, Oscar either dispatched Robbie Ross, or Ross went of his own accord, to explain to Constance that the libel trial had collapsed because what the Marquis of Queensbury had alleged was true, that Oscar was in a sexual relationship with Lord Alfred Douglas and now faced charges on multiple counts of indecency involving a string of other men. Up to that moment, Constance had believed, or chosen to believe, that they were all just good friends.

From then on, Constance thought only of her sons, although she did try to help Oscar at least two more times. Her magnanimity and fortitude in the face of such an appalling situation are remarkable. Taking the boys out of school, she quickly hired a French governess to bring them to Europe, where she would join them, in an attempt to spare them the headlines splashed across every newspaper in England and Ireland. When Oscar was released on bail, Constance spent two hours trying to convince him leave the country, but he refused. Similarly, Robbie Ross begged Oscar in vain to flee to Europe with Constance. On 24 April, Oscar's creditors sent the bailiffs to access the house in Tite Street and empty it of its contents, selling off everything, including the boys' toys.

Constance reunited with her sons at Glion by Lake Geneva, writing to a friend about her broken heart and her discomfort at being surrounded by beauty when Oscar was enclosed in the four walls of his cell. She had been advised to sue for divorce to ensure that the boys stayed with her, and she also needed to safeguard the boys' financial future should anything happen to her.

That September, Constance received a letter from writer Robert Sherard (1861–1943), Oscar's friend and William Wordsworth's great-grandson, describing Oscar's awful living conditions and asking her to take him back. Constance's brother, Otho, who was in Glion, witnessed his sister's reaction to Sherard's plea, and he immediately wrote to Oscar, telling him that a letter of apology might just prevent divorce proceedings. Oscar promptly sent a letter to Constance's solicitor, who showed it to her whilst telling her that, whatever happened, she needed to change her second name. In due course, she and the boys changed their name from Wilde to Holland.

Her health was precarious, yet Constance cancelled a health spa to return to England to see her husband and attend to paperwork. On obtaining special permission, she visited Oscar in jail on 21 September and was dismayed that she could neither see him properly nor touch him, that their conversation had to be conducted over two gratings and a passageway. Constance wrote to Robert Sherard that next time she would request a separate room for her visit, and she also thanked him for his ongoing kindness to Oscar.

By now, most of Oscar's friends and acquaintances had deserted him. Anne Clarke Amor, in her essay about Constance, quotes a letter she sent her friend explaining why she had changed her mind about divorce. After seeing him, Constance believed that Oscar cared about her and the boys. In turn, she might be the saving of him if she took him back. She acknowledged the risk involved but knew if Oscar renounced his claim to her life assurance, she would be financially independent and, therefore, if living together proved impossible following his release, she and the boys would survive without him. It certainly seemed that Oscar had renounced Bosie, as he declared to Robbie Ross that Douglas had 'played dice with his father for my life and lost'.

While Constance was in England, the boys stayed with Uncle Otho and his family in Bevaix in Switzerland. Preferring to winter in a warmer climate, Constance took the advice of her friend Lady Margaret Brook, the Ranee of Sarawak, (1849–1936) to join her in Italy. Brook found the family an apartment that was big enough for her, the boys and Otho's family too, in Sori, on the northwest coast.

For Constance, health-wise, the year 1895 ended badly. Struggling to walk, she checked into a private clinic in Genoa, in December, to consult about her lack of mobility, and was operated on by Genoa University's Professor of Gynaecology, Luigi Maria Bossi (1859–1919), who prescribed bedrest before discharging her in January. Eleanor Fitzsimons suggests that this clinic was the real reason Constance exchanged Switzerland for Italy.

On receiving a letter from Willie Wilde's wife in February, telling her that Speranza had died, Constance immediately determined, despite her physical difficulty, to break the news to Oscar in person. This second visit also provided her with an opportunity to clarify matters concerning the life-interest on her private income. Oscar's declaration of bankruptcy meant that his share was being held by the Official Receiver to be sold to the highest bidder. Appreciating Constance's compassion regarding his mother's death, Oscar agreed that she should receive his share of the interest, to be settled on their sons.

Constance was then taken up with the boys' education, placing them in a German boarding school while she stayed nearby with friends until they were expelled after a teacher hit Vyvyan with a rule, provoking him and his brother to hit, and kick, back. She moved them to a small school with just fifteen boys, from which they were also expelled after their fellow pupils, all anti-British, challenged the brothers to a fight and lost. Constance then moved the three of them to Heidelberg, sending the boys to Neuenheim College which was mostly staffed and attended by British ex-pats. Meanwhile, she stayed in the Schloss Park Hotel, where she befriended her landlord and his wife and improved her German. She also renewed an interest in photography and became involved with her local church.

Then something went awry back in England when Oscar's solicitors advised his friend the writer and art critic William More Adey (1858–1942) to make an offer for marriage settlement monies that the bankrupt Oscar had meant for his wife. Adey and Robbie Ross triple-outbid Constance, with their offer of £75. Prior to this, Constance had pledged to pay Oscar £200 annually on his release.

This development prompted Constance to rethink divorcing anew. Oscar blamed his well-meaning friends for antagonising his wife. For once, the confusion was not Oscar's fault, but Constance likely felt that she lacked the luxury of time to investigate matters further. Furthermore, her Irish relatives may have disputed any reconciliation with Oscar. Constance had lots of great friends, but one suspects that this might have been a particularly lonesome time for her.

Christmas was spent with friends in Freiberg. Needing to move her son Vyvyan, who was being bullied in Neuenheim, she brought him to Monaco in the New Year, where he registered in a Jesuit-run college, and she stayed a few days to make sure he was settled.

On 12 February 1897, Constance was given full custody of her sons, and was appointed their legal guardian with her cousin Adrian Hope. Three months later, Oscar, awaiting imminent release, signed a Deed of Separation, thereby giving up his rights to the boys along with income generated from the life interest. Meanwhile, he would have a weekly allowance of £3, which he would lose if he upset Constance in any way, and/or returned to his disreputable ways.

Constance returned to Italy, from where she told a friend that her lack of mobility forced her into buying a typewriter to stay in touch. She could type but not hold a pen steady. Following Oscar's release on 17 May, he sailed to France from where he sent her a sorry letter about everything. If he was hoping his contrition and proximity might result in their meeting, Constance held back from naming a date. Whatever her feelings about the boys seeing their father again, she was very ill owing to an increase in symptoms that included debilitating headaches and numbness in the left side of her face, while her right arm now shook uncontrollably.

Not wanting or able to leave Italy again, she looked for a villa, writing to Oscar that he could visit his family once they were settled, during the boys' summer holidays. Whatever hopes Constance might have entertained for their future were surely doused when Oscar wrote to her from Naples, saying that he would visit in October, too late to spend time with his sons, while the Naples postal mark told her that he was back with Bosie. She exploded and sent him a letter drenched in hurt and exasperation, uselessly forbidding him from seeing Bosie and from living in Naples and rescinded her invitation to come to Italy. That November she discontinued Oscar's £3 weekly allowance, but then sent money through Robbie Ross, who was not to disclose its origin. Bosie and Oscar separated for good in December 1897.

Three months later, in March 1898, Constance performed a final act of kindness towards her husband. She reinstated his allowance, ensuring that he would receive it if she predeceased him. Eleanor Fitzsimons quotes a letter that she sent Vyvyan, in which she tells him not to hate the father who loved him so, explaining how all Oscar's troubles stemmed from a son's (Bosie) hatred for his father (the Marquis of Queensbury), adding that Vyvyan's father had suffered enough.

The following month, April, thirty-nine-year-old Constance returned to the clinic in Genoa, despite family and friends begging her not to have another operation. However, as always, she yearned for the independence and freedom that she had spent her life advocating through her wardrobe and politics. Professor Bossi took a miscalculated risk in removing benign fibroids to allay her paralysis. In a 2015 paper for *The Lancet*, Merlin Holland, Vyvyan's son and Constance's grandson, and Ashley H Robins suggest that Constance was probably suffering from multiple sclerosis, a little-known condition at the time. Four days later, she could not stop vomiting. Dehydrated and exhausted, she lost consciousness and died on 7 April. A devastated Otho had her buried in the Staglieno Cemetery in Genoa. There was no mention of the Wilde name on her headstone, although this was added later.

Charlotte Shaw, painted by Giulio Aristide Sartorio.

CHAPTER FOUR

CHARLOTTE SHAW (1857-1943)

Wife of George Bernard Shaw, playwright

One could argue that George Bernard Shaw's wife, Charlotte Payne-Townshend, had been in love just once in her life and that was with Swedish doctor and psychiatrist Axel Munthe (1857–1949). Before that, there had been seven proposals from four soldiers, the Secretary to the Danish Legation in London a count, an Irish businessman and a barrister.

Munthe did not ask her to marry, and so it was that the eighth proposal, from an eccentric, budding Irish playwright, made her a wife at forty-one years of age. Charlotte had professed that she never meant to marry, though one wonders what her answer would have been had Munthe asked.

She was born in 1857, to a prominent Protestant family that numbered several clergymen amongst their ranks, including Charlotte's great grandfather, the Reverend Horatio (Horace) Townsend (1749–1837), who, following the death of his wife, moved to be near his eldest son, Reverend Chambrè Corker Townsend (1797–1852), and his family in Clonakilty, County Cork.

By 1825, Charlotte's father, Reverend Townsend, was living in Cork, in a spacious, two-storey stone house, about three miles outside Rosscarbery, that he had inherited on his bachelor brother's death; the house and surrounding land had been in the Townsend family since 1686. When the reverend died in

1837, the house, with its extensive library, was left to Chambrè who, in turn, following his death in 1852, left it to his eldest son Horace. Chambrè had hoped his son would enter the church, but Horace preferred to study law in Trinity College. He was a favourite with his younger siblings whose futures he worked to establish after their father's death. Carrying out Chambrè's posthumous instructions, Horace saw his three brothers launched into the profession of their choice, while his six sisters mixed with the best that Cork society had to offer, to find themselves suitable husbands.

If Horace died without issue, his father's will stipulated that the family home, Derry House, was to pass to a stepbrother, but, fortunately, Horace found himself a wife. At least, that is how it appeared at the time.

On 20 October 1855, he married Mary Susanna Kirby (1830–1891) whose family lived nearby in Glandore, County Cork. The Kirbys originated from Yorkshire and were, for the most part, lawyers and small-time country gentlemen. They owned Edstaston Estate near the town of Wem in Shropshire, along with some land in Ireland. The ceremony took place in front of family and friends in Ireland's smallest cathedral, Ross Cathedral, and as Horace watched his bride's approach, he could have had no inkling of how his interests, his home and his very name would be affected by his marriage to Mary Susanna, a woman who had captured his heart with her elegance and confidence.

Perhaps the greatest influence on Charlotte Payne Townshend's life and ambition was her father's unhappiness and her mother's incessant ambition.

In her 1963 biography of Charlotte, owing to the scarcity of any personal information, Janet Dunbar concludes that the Kirbys were overly concerned with money because, instead of stories about various Kirbys' doings and achievements being passed on to younger generations, the descendants inherited only receipts for bills and sales of land.

But, of course, none of this was apparent as the young couple exchanged vows in Ross Cathedral. The groom, known for his shyness, was a kind landlord to his tenants and an easy-going employer to his servants. Meanwhile, his

English bride appeared to have disliked leaving Shropshire for Ireland.

After the wedding, Mary Susanna moved into her husband's house, and nothing was ever the same again. Firstly, she embarked on extensive renovations to Derry's interior, looking to London for inspiration as to what constituted a fashionable home. Secondly, once she had achieved the perfect home, she wanted to leave it, preferring to relocate to London and take her place in English society. According to Dunbar's findings, the new Mrs Townsend did not like the Irish – over-friendly servants and chatty shopkeepers irked her as she preferred people to know their place – and she suggested that Horace either let or sell Derry, both of which he refused to do. The matter was dropped, for the time being, and the first of their two daughters, Charlotte Frances, was born on 20 January 1857, with Mary Stewart, or Sissy, arriving two years later.

It seems like an idyllic childhood. There were nurses, horses, dogs, English governesses and rowing on their very own lake. The girls received a decent education, especially in languages, thanks to travelling tutors who toured the Big Houses, staying for several weeks at a time, to provide intensive lessons in French, German and Italian, before moving on to their next classroom. Charlotte fell in love with books and availed of her father's library, reading French and Italian books as well as the usual fare.

In 1863, Mary Susanna insisted that her reluctant husband add 'Payne', a family name on her side, to Townsend, giving them the hyphenated Payne-Townsend.

Horace's career was flourishing as a popular Commissioner of the Peace, as were his finances thanks to wise investments. His love for the country life was shared by his eldest daughter who accompanied him on his visits to his tenants' homes. Those visits surely provided an education every bit as important as that provided by her governesses as Charlotte would never forget the horror etched on the faces of those who described, for her, surviving the Great Famine of 1845–7.

Indoors, father and daughter could often be found together in his library, where, under Horace's guidance, fifteen-year-old Charlotte began to study

Irish history and familiarised herself with the politics of men like Theobald Wolfe Tone (1763–1798) and Daniel O'Connell (1775–1847) and their dreams for an independent Ireland.

By this stage, Horace's pre–marital contented life was but a distant memory due to his wife's frequent tantrums and screaming bouts, the means she used to force her husband's hand on whatever she had set her mind upon.

In later years, seventy-year-old Charlotte described her mother's rages throughout a 'hellish childhood' in a letter to the writer and archaeologist Thomas Edward Lawrence (1888–1935), also known as Lawrence of Arabia. She wrote, 'My mother was a terribly strong character – managing and domineering. She could not bear opposition: if it was offered, she either became violent or she cried.'

In 1874, Mary Susanna wanted an 'h' added to Townsend (Townshend) which, she felt, would nicely emphasise their gentry pedigree. Horace resisted but his wife was determined. The ensuing showdowns proved a turning point for seventeen-year-old Charlotte, who agreed with her father over the pointlessness of this 'h', as well as detesting the unpleasant scenes that he was having to endure. It is now that Charlotte discovered that she truly hated her mother. In her biography, Janet Dunbar writes how Charlotte was forcibly struck by the rows over this matter, knowing that her father found the idea of adding that extra letter, to his family's name, as being stupid and even 'distasteful'. Attempting to make a stand, Charlotte told a surprised Mary Susanna that she had no right to speak to her husband like that. Inwardly, as Janet Dunbar writes, Charlotte left the room wishing for her mother to fall down dead.

Mary Susanna's shedding of Derry began innocuously enough with renting a house in Cork for a few weeks, to shop and introduce her daughters to the best of that city's society. Sissy revelled in the balls and the dinner parties, while Charlotte yearned for conversation that generated more substance than flirty compliments and small talk. That is not to say that she was not liked, but she would try to introduce books, history and religion as topics which generally found few takers.

If Horace thought that Cork city had soothed his wife's restlessness, it must have been a jolt when she rented 25 Merrion Square in Dublin, using his daughters as her excuse. In Dublin the social net could be cast more widely than in Cork; why the girls might even be invited to Dublin Castle.

Dublin was a hit. The company of the wealthy Mrs Payne-Townshend and her daughters was sought by the best type of people. Charlotte made use of Dublin's grand libraries by day but still struggled to stimulate interesting discussions at parties. However, Dublin was merely a side-step for Mary Susanna, who announced, in 1877, that she had found the perfect house for them: 21 Queen's Gate, London. She told her husband that Derry would be their country house, but that she was done with living in Ireland or, as she preferred to call it, 'that accursed country'. She had it all planned out. Derry House would be maintained by Horace's relative Willie Townsend, who looked after a number of estates in Cork.

Should Horace have refused to budge? He would be moving away from his job, friends, tenants and staff, along with his dream of establishing a railway for Clonakilty. In short, he was losing the only place he called home. Mary Susanna got her way, but at what price? In London, Horace spoke little and showed no interest in playing host at the lavish dinners thrown by his wife, who continually scolded him for his reticence. Then, Mary Susanna made a serious error with Charlotte when she made a comment that her daughter never forgot. One day, after Horace failed again to be properly sociable to their visitors, Mary Susanna railed at her girls, 'Who could get into Society dragging such an incubus as that?'

Charlotte exploded at her mother. The scene is described in Janet Dunbar's biography. There was huge upset and Charlotte forced herself to face a daunting truth. She yearned for freedom but had no options unless she married. For a girl of her upbringing, staying single meant being her mother's companion day after day, until one of them died. Yet, how could she risk marrying and ending up miserable like her father, or her mother, for that matter? As far as Charlotte could see, marriage was a form of 'bondage' and, therefore, she chose to wait for a funeral rather than go in search of a husband. Refusing to marry was also a way of thwarting her mother's obsession to see both daughters wed.

Charlotte rebelled further by taking a course in first aid, pointing out that this was the lesser of two evils as her actual preference was to be a doctor, an impossible dream for her sex and class. In June 1880, she received her St John's Ambulance Certificate of First Aid Qualification.

Meanwhile, visits home to Derry proved upsetting for Horace who struggled to renew his former position of familiarity amongst his tenants who seemed not to miss him at all.

The year 1881 was a busy one for the Payne-Townshends. Succeeding in her ambition for a London home seemed to have galvanised Mary Susanna. The family visited Ireland, driving through Bantry and Killarney and visiting Drishane, the home of Charlotte's cousin Edith Somerville (1858–1949), the future half of bestselling duo Somerville and Ross, who wrote, amongst other titles, *Some Experiences of an Irish R.M.* (1899).

That October, the family sailed to Paris to see the first International Expedition of Electrical Apparatus and surely half of the family relished the decision to split up for more exploring. Mary Susanna took Sissy off to Nice, whilst Horace and Charlotte headed off on their own tour of France and Spain, although their trip was marred by his rheumatism and her ear infection. The foursome met up at Cannes for Christmas and saw in the New Year from Nice.

The continental trips did not improve the marriage as Mary Susanna continued to nit-pick at her husband over every little thing. The girls escaped the tension at home by accepting any invitations that came their way. Charlotte was dead against marriage, and Sissy, determined to marry only for love, had fallen for an officer, Hugh Cecil Cholmondeley (1852-1941). Meanwhile, her sister was busy being just good friends with several men who appreciated her intelligence and the fact she was not looking to be walked down the aisle.

In 1884, Charlotte took off for Paris with her father and cousin Edith Somerville. There, the girls had their palms read and Charlotte was told that she would marry a distinguished person and live a long life with him.

Sissy's engagement was announced that autumn, with the wedding set for the following year. Unfortunately, Horace took to his bed in the New Year, confounding his doctors as to a diagnosis. He died a few weeks later, in February, and Mary Susanna buried him at Edstaston, a final blow for Horace who might have preferred to have been buried at his beloved Derry. Sissy married Hugh Cecil Cholmondeley a few weeks later as Horace's dying wish was for the wedding to go ahead. Afterwards, Sissy and Hugh moved to Hampshire, leaving Charlotte alone with the mother she hated and, perhaps, even blamed for her father's death.

In 1890, Charlotte brought her mother back to Derry to recover from a recent illness. Once there, she determined to carry out her father's dream of a Clonakilty Railway. It took almost a year and required her to travel all over, rallying support from her father's old friends, businessmen, small farmers, villagers and anyone else who might benefit from a new railway line, and, in March 1891, the application for a Clonakilty and Rosscarbery Railway was approved. Wanting only to see Charlotte successfully married, Mary Susanna was exasperated by her eldest daughter's railway pursuits and accused Charlotte of not loving her the way she should, especially after all the sacrifices that she had made on her behalf. This was a constant refrain.

Writing about Horace's passing thirty-seven years later, in a letter to TE Lawrence, Charlotte seethed about her domineering mother who, she thought, with hindsight, should have been beaten by her husband. Charlotte believed that her father's premature death was a result of Mary Susanna taking him away from Derry and having to endure her constant criticism.

As for herself, Charlotte believed that she had been damaged by an innate sense of duty that sought to rein in her instincts and emotions. She fought her mother, in defence of Horace, which clashed with a genuine belief, and guilt, that she should be only respectful to her mother. From an early age, she determined never to have children who might suffer as she did.

Charlotte confessed to Lawrence that when her mother died she was glad and often wondered if her longing for her mother's demise somehow brought it about.

Her wealth was her salvation. Charlotte had yearned for freedom which she finally obtained on her mother's death, on 9 September 1891. Renting out 21 Queen's Gate, she moved to a house in Hamilton Place. Derry House was now hers, but she left it with Willie Townsend, its long-term caretaker. London would remain as her base, although she made regular visits to Derry and kept up with Irish politics.

Alongside money, Charlotte had also inherited her mother's need to travel. The following September she made a typical journey involving eight destinations between Lucerne and Gibraltar. Travelling provided an escape when any of her male friends became too familiar. Following a letter from General Clery, urging her to open up her heart more, Charlotte sailed to India on 25 November 1892, where she met up with friends and attended a state ball and a panther shoot.

Her dread of the institution of marriage was as strong as ever. She returned home and continued to see General Clery and even allowed him to kiss her more than once, but when he proposed, she could not say yes. Oh, she liked him an awful lot, but she wanted something more for her life. She had hoped that her visit to India would trigger something within, but she had found herself merely mixing with her wealthy English friends, who dissuaded her from engaging with the natives, whose adherence to their own religions had fascinated her.

She was searching for something unfathomable. Two years later, she travelled to Egypt, staying on Lord and Lady Waterford's yacht and lunching with the likes of Field Marshal Kitchener (1850–1916). Travel usually broadens the mind but what is to be gained when one is only surrounded by nobility and luxury?

From Egypt, she sailed on to Italy, joining friends in Rome who introduced her to Doctor Axel Munthe, the Physician-in-Ordinary to the Crown Princess of Sweden. Charlotte had never met anyone like him. His consulting rooms were patronised by the rich, but he also had a room in a slum district where he treated the impoverished and even animals.

Feeling unwell, Charlotte went to his surgery, where Doctor Munthe declared that she needed to relax more, suggesting that she try Venice since he was heading there with the Crown Princess. The independent Charlotte did exactly that, and they regularly met up. In Munthe, she found what she had always wanted, decent conversation with an intelligent and vivacious companion.

Two weeks later, she was back in Rome and found herself bewildered. Her feelings for Munthe were love; at least that was the case for her. In her book *Forgotten Wives*, Ann Oakley describes Alex Munthe as a complicated person who took advantage of rich, idle women who succumbed to his charm. He and Charlotte continued to invite one another out for dinners and lunches but little else. Charlotte began declining invitations from her friends in case she missed a summons from Munthe. Here was a man who was friends with royalty but also worked hard to help the destitute. It is little wonder that she felt so stimulated in his company. For his part, her independence and yearning to do something worthy may have appealed to him. He had her meet the Little Sisters of the Poor, where she made a sizeable donation to their convent.

The summer temperatures were rising, signalling the exodus of the rich from Rome. When Munthe told her he was leaving too, she confessed that she would miss him. He replied in kind, asking for her photograph to join his collection of mementoes of his friends.

Having no photographs to hand, Charlotte went one better, commissioning a pastel portrait of herself from well-known painter Giulio Aristide Sartorio (1860–1932), which required several sittings. Seated behind a table, she wore a cream blouse that flared out at the shoulders into long sleeves, emphasised by her pose, elbows on table with hands raised and clasped together as if she was about to pray or ask the viewer for something. With head slightly tilted, her gaze is steady and confident; truly, she looks radiant in pastel, radiant in love. Her expression suggests an intimacy with the viewer, that is, the portrait's recipient.

But the painting was too much for Munthe, who wrote months later, 'I cannot and will not accept it. If you do not want it, I shall make Sartorio take it back.' Such a presumably expensive gift may have embarrassed him, along with possibly the content, although he professed to have thoroughly enjoyed the Kipling novel that accompanied the painting.

By now, Charlotte was back in England and losing hope in Munthe ever wanting more than friendship. Seeking to distract herself from her unhappiness, she asked a friend should she donate her fortune to the poor as she was experiencing terrific guilt since returning from Rome. Munthe had shown her how one person could make a difference to so many.

So, she still wanted to do something with her life but what? In fact, she was on the cusp of great change, and it was largely thanks to that fortune that she had briefly thought of giving away.

She began attending meetings on improving rights for women, and made new friends, including Sidney Webb (1859–1947) and his wife, the writer Beatrice Potter (1858–1943), who would usher in many new interests into Charlotte's life, not least of all an unlikely husband.

Beatrice Potter and Sidney Webb had met in 1890, through the Fabian Society, which sought to promote socialist ideas and evoke a sort of peaceful revolution in British politics, in the belief that society's ills could be remedied through study and scientific research. Sidney was immediately attracted to Beatrice, whilst she needed some encouragement and time, during which she told Sidney that she thought marriage was suicide, before finally marrying him on 23 July 1892. Typically, their honeymoon was spent researching Irish trade union manuals in Dublin.

They introduced Charlotte to Fabianism and told her about their London School of Economics and Political Science, founded the previous year, with two others, where Beatrice lectured on trade unionism. Charlotte was intrigued and wanted to know more.

Beatrice describes Charlotte in an oft-quoted diary entry for 16 September 1896 that ends, 'It was on account of her generosity to our projects' and 'for the good of the cause that I first made friends with her'. Charlotte donated £1,000 to the school library and rented rooms overhead in Adelphi Terrace for £300 a year. She proved herself a very good friend indeed.

Charlotte also responded positively to Beatrice's idea of taking a house in the country, to which they could invite fellow Fabians. Beatrice rented the rectory of Stratford St Andrew in Suffolk, where Charlotte went that August, 1896, for six weeks. A few Fabians were already in situ, including future Labour MP Charles Trevelyan (1870–1958), Graham Wallas (1858–1932), who had been best man at the Webbs' wedding, and aspiring playwright George Bernard Shaw (1856–1950).

It was a working holiday with scheduled meetings every morning about the Webbs' school and the new library. The afternoon was given over to long walks or bicycle rides, while after-dinner entertainment was usually provided by Shaw reading from his latest work.

The party shrank when Trevelyan left, followed by Wallas, and then Beatrice came down with flu, and Sidney stayed by her side, throwing Charlotte and Shaw together for those walks and bicycle rides, resulting in kisses being exchanged beneath the evening sky.

Beatrice captured those weeks in her diary. Her critical tone might stem from the fact that she had wanted Charlotte to fall for the quiet and steady Graham Wallas. Beatrice wrote that Charlotte had fallen in love with 'the brilliant Philanderer and he is taken in his cold sort of way with her'. Beatrice had known Shaw several years by now and, as Michael Holroyd tells us in his Shaw biography, Beatrice was initially Shaw's love interest, though he would not risk losing Sidney's friendship and, so, kept it to himself. But Beatrice had seen him with other women and there could be no marrying for Shaw, she was sure of that.

Meanwhile, that 'brilliant Philanderer' wrote to actress Ellen Terry (1847–1928): 'We have been joined by an Irish millionairess who has had cleverness and character enough to decline the station of life – "great catch for somebody" – to which it pleased God to call her, and whom we have incorporated into our Fabian family with great success. I am going to refresh my heart by falling in love with her. I love falling in love – but, mind, only with her, not with the million; so someone else must marry her if she can stand him after me.'

In truth, there is a George Bernard Shaw quote for every mood, but he did seem to genuinely like Charlotte. On 17 September, the Webbs, Shaw and Charlotte cycled back to London, staying overnight in various spots, taking five days to reach the Webbs' house in Grosvenor Road, whereupon Beatrice invited Charlotte to stay for a few weeks. She accepted, and this is where Shaw visited her in between work commitments.

George Bernard Shaw kept up a barrage of letters all the way. In one letter, he demands to know how much longer she intends to stay away. In the next, he demands to know why she chose this particular time to desert him, 'just when you are most wanted'. Then, he boasts about the bevy of females keeping him company. He also regales her with a story about one of those females, the painter Bertha Newcombe (1857–1947), and how she ended up being his most recent ex when he told her that Charlotte and himself were engaged. When Bertha wrote to ask him about this, he cruelly embellished the falsehood, providing a wedding date, details about their new house and the money that would be bestowed on him by his new rich wife; this treatment of Bertha was cruel as she had been devoted to Shaw for five years. Apparently, Bertha never got over Shaw, as she never married.

Perhaps trying to keep their relationship professional, Charlotte confided, as one Fabian to another, her torment over the fact that land reforms for the Irish peasants were being hindered by their rich landlords, her friends, and described the poverty that she saw everywhere, but Shaw refused to engage seriously, and replied flippantly, '… As long as Ireland produces men who have the sense to leave her, she does not exist in vain. The address of my Ireland is 10, Adelphi Terrace [Charlotte's address]…'

His letters were deliberately playful. He writes about wanting to see her but then exclaims, 'Imagine! Past forty and still going on like this. I hope when I am past sixty I shall be going on like it, and for you, even you shall have been a thousand times faithless and have forgotten me with a nice husband ... but ... you will find him very stupid after me.'

Charlotte wrote that she missed him and then wished she hadn't when he replied, 'Don't fall in love: be your own, not mine or anyone else's. From that moment that you can't do without me, you're lost, like Bertha.'

Her absence was sparking something, though exactly what was unclear. Charlotte surely remembered Axel Munthe's coincidentally exiting her life after she told him that she would miss him. Perhaps wisely, she replied to Shaw's mixed message with the date of her return. He wrote that he 'must' see her as soon as she was home: 'I must: and that "must" ... TERRIFIES me. If it were possible to run away – if it would do any good – I'd do it ...'

Charlotte duly arrived home, and Shaw went to see her that very evening. They began spending more time together. On 4 November, Shaw wrote to Ellen Terry in typical, jokey fashion, asking her if he should marry his Irish millionairess. 'She ... believes in freedom, and not in marriage: but I think I could prevail on her; and then I shall have ever so many hundreds a month for nothing.' He was bewildered when Terry took him seriously and chided him for chasing Charlotte for her money. Later, he is indignant when one of his female friends asked Charlotte for a loan. He refers to her wealth in several letters to friends, perhaps worried about anyone thinking he was fortune hunting. Most men in his position might find themselves similarly unnerved by such financial disparity.

Charlotte began to inch her way into Shaw's working life by learning how to read his shorthand, take dictation and type. It was inevitable since she wanted employment, and he needed help. When a second summer house was rented by the Webbs, in Dorking, for their Fabian circle, Beatrice was as critical as ever, seeing no genuine feelings for Charlotte on Shaw's part and annoyed that Charlotte was holed away typing Shaw's notes and looking miserable.

Meanwhile, horticulturalist Augustine Henry (1857–1930), a friend who had advised Charlotte against giving away her fortune, wrote asking her about her life plans. Charlotte explained that she was attending lectures at the London School of Medicine for Women out of interest and a desire to get to know the school with a view to providing financial assistance. Medicine, she declared, was the most noble profession of all and she wished to help women study it, perhaps by setting up a scholarship enabling one girl every year to attend the school for free. She also described the School of Economics and Political Science, explaining why such a thing was needed in the first place, ultimately to consider the age-old question of why the poor are so poor and the rich so rich.

Augustine replied immediately, anxious that his friend – and her money – were being led astray. Charlotte answers, 'I am in the rather unusual position of being perfectly free … I am independent financially. I am unconventional by nature.'

In the very next sentence, she described her life as 'a wreck' because she had rejected what normal people usually want: love and marriage. Her declaration of independence reads bittersweet: 'Under these circumstances there is nothing to prevent my doing exactly as I choose.'

And what is it that she chooses to do? She lists out her loves for Augustine: brightness, sunshine, art. She could simply go somewhere which would supply all that, but what about those who could never do what she is free to. Is it worthy, she asks, to use her money to further only her own happiness? And supposing a wealthy woman is determined to help reduce that gap between the rich and the poor, well, then, she will need help working out how to do that or if it can be done at all. Thus, she defends her involvement with the Fabians.

In May 1898, Shaw is crippled with gout, and Charlotte, newly returned from months abroad, her safe space, visits him at 29 Fitzroy Square, London, where he was living with his mother and sister. It was her first time to visit his home, and she was appalled at the mess and the state of Shaw, who could barely walk. Charlotte instantly hated Lucinda Elizabeth (Bessie) Shaw (1830–1913) for neglecting her son. It is hard to know how much Shaw had told her of his own troubled background. He had left Dublin and his genial but alcoholic father to follow his mother and sister to London, both women aiming to sing professionally. Charlotte's discovery of his chaotic home was the turning point. Perhaps her need to save Shaw from his mother stemmed from guilt over her inability to save her father from Mary Susanna. Charlotte fetched Shaw back to Adelphi Terrace on 5 May for a long talk that culminated with their engagement.

The wedding took place on a wet Wednesday at 11.30am, on 1 June 1898 in the Registry Office in London's Strand district. The groom was forty-two, a year older than his bride, and on crutches. One suspects that Charlotte's mother, Mary Susanna, would have hated Shaw's Irish accent, lack of title and shaky finances.

Shaw provided several amusing versions of how he acquired a wife. However, years later, Blanche Patch (1879–1966), Shaw's last secretary, claimed to have the true story in her memoir, *Thirty Years with GBS* (1951). Her boss told her that on Charlotte's return from her Roman holiday she found Shaw in a wretched state and determined to rent a house for them in the country and to employ two nurses to care for him. Shaw had objected, pointing out that she could not have a single man living under her roof, telling her that they had to get a marriage licence.

And so began the next forty-five years of Charlotte's life.

For the first eighteen months of their marriage, Shaw was an invalid but a hardworking one, writing three plays including *Caesar and Cleopatra*.

It could be said that Charlotte's wedding present to him was freedom to live the writer's life. She took charge in every way. They may not have married for love and who knows how thoroughly they consummated their relationship, but it does appear that this partnership with his wife saw Shaw transformed from a mildly successful playwright into an international literary figure.

Of course, Charlotte eradicated any money worries, that is obvious enough, but more specifically she took care of his biggest worry. For instance, she settled an annuity on Bessie Shaw, the playwright's sixty-nine-year-old mother, for life. The annuity was set up and paid for by her son, but if he could not meet the payments then Charlotte would do so anonymously. Charlotte disliked her mother-in-law, who wanted to call her daughter-in-law Carlotta because she looked like one! It is no surprise to learn that they rarely met in person.

Unlike his mother, Charlotte took great care of Shaw, ensuring that he would always have a comfortable roof over his head, whilst his vegetarian needs would be met at every meal. On a practical level, she sorted his accounts and took on, as much as she could, his correspondence commitments. In time, she would answer Shaw's letters, only bothering him with essentials.

Careerwise for Shaw, Charlotte made at least one enormous contribution when she welcomed Siegfried Trebitsch (1868–1956) into their Adelphi Terrace home in 1902. Trebitsch, an Austrian playwright, poet and novelist, had a dream; having read Shaw's plays, he wished to translate them and see them performed on stages throughout Europe.

Armed with a letter of introduction from Henrik Ibsen's translator William Archer (1856–1924), Trebitsch knocked on the front door and was shown into the sitting room, where he met Charlotte Shaw, who nicely asked him his business, all the while checking, Trebitsch felt, to see if he and his intentions were a worthy intrusion on Shaw's time. He must have passed muster since, at Shaw's sudden appearance, Charlotte slipped out while Trebitsch introduced himself.

Within seconds of Trebitsch offering himself as a translator, Shaw exited the room, summoning Charlotte to calm down the 'lunatic' sent by William Archer. Charlotte returned, apologised for Shaw's attitude, and called after her retreating husband that their visitor should be heard. In Trebitsch, she recognised a fellow fan of her husband's writing along with the potential of the translator's vision for the plays.

Within a year of Charlotte's calling him back to the sitting room, Shaw's play, *The Devil's Disciple* (1897) went into production at the Raimund

Theater in Vienna, while the plays were published by German publishing house S. Fischer, all thanks to Trebitsch who felt he owed his position as Shaw's translator to Charlotte.

Shaw had heeded Charlotte then and probably should have heeded her in 1904 when he embarked on a commission for poet and co-founder of the Abbey Theatre, William Butler Yeats (1865–1939), who requested a play for the December launch of Dublin's new theatre. Shaw's usual tactic was to discuss his characters with his wife, and, in this case, she begged him against over-egging or using exaggerated characteristics to denote 'Irishness'. He scorned her romanticism for the Irish and went his own way, and Yeats refused the play, *John Bull's Other Island*, although it proved a huge success in London, where it premiered at the Royal Court Theatre on 1 November 1904.

Charlotte found her own way into the theatre business, appreciating its possibility to strike a match for a progressive society. She read many French writers and on finishing the play *Maternité*, by realist dramatist Eugène Brieux (1858–1932), Charlotte determined to translate it for an English audience. Didactic in tone, Brieux's plays confronted social problems and, in 1901, he caused uproar when his *Les Avariés* (Damaged Goods) mentioned venereal disease. *Maternité* criticises those refusing to recognise motherhood as a concrete issue in need of legislative protection and due care for the good of the human race. This surely appealed to the wealthy daughter, whose aristocratic status had prevented her from becoming a doctor, and the feminist who always championed women's rights.

Charlotte began working on it immediately, confident of seeing it played on an English stage thanks to her position on the executive committee of the Incorporated Stage Society, which put on showings, for members only, of new and experimental plays, including those that had been banned. Charlotte submitted her finished manuscript to the censor for its performance licence, only to be told that 'this play ... will never be licensed in England'. Accordingly, the Stage Society embraced it, for its own audience, for a performance on 8 April 1906 that was described by its proud translator as 'a dignified and competent one'.

Charlotte was far from done with Brieux's plays. When not even the Stage Society dared to stage *Damaged Goods*, Charlotte was adamant to see it in print and proposed its inclusion in a trilogy alongside *Maternity* and *The Three Daughters of M. DuPont*, with a preface by Shaw. She contacted a delighted Brieux and bought the rights to publish English translations. The only problem was finding a publisher brave enough for *Damaged Goods*. When none materialised, Charlotte refused to give up, believing that it was only a matter of time; meanwhile she went on to translate the rest of Brieux's plays.

As an executive, Charlotte also oversaw several of Shaw's plays performed by the Society that might not have otherwise been seen on stage. Furthermore, on at least two occasions, she helped Shaw with ideas for plays, although he may not have realised it. *The Doctor's Dilemma* (1906) exists thanks to her reminding Shaw of a conversation that they had witnessed between physician Sir Almroth Wright (1861–1947) and his assistant about squeezing in another patient to their treatment schedule. Wright's query 'Is he worth it?' resulted in a play that is as relevant today as it ever was.

In his book *G.B.S. and the Lunatic*, Lawrence Langner (1890–1962) describes visiting the Shaws in 1922 and asking after new plays. When Charlotte told him that 'they' had been unable to find a good subject, he was visibly confused, obliging her to confess that she sometimes found ideas for 'the Genius' – her words. For example, she had always admired Saint Joan of Arc as did her husband and they had visited the saint's birthplace, Domrémy, in north-eastern France. Knowing that Shaw was stuck for a subject, she bought books about Joan and sprinkled them around the house. According to Langner, Charlotte's eyes twinkled as she remembered Shaw's excitement over his wonderful idea for a new play, 'It's to be about Saint Joan!'

In 1910, Charlotte's dream of seeing her Brieux trilogy in print was realised, though she disliked the reason behind it. Brieux had recently been made a member of the French Academy, which made everything alright because, in

Charlotte's words: 'Mud that may be thrown with impunity at a struggling social reformer and propagandist, must not smirch the robe of one of the Immortals.'

Alongside preparing the Brieux plays for publication, Charlotte decided to select her favourite passages from her husband's plays and have them published too. She never missed an opportunity to promote Shaw's works and used her dinner table to both further her husband's fame and indulge his enjoyment at meeting famous people.

Charlotte was practised in the art of hosting luncheon parties, where the guest list included the likes of American writer Mark Twain (1835–1910) and French sculptor Auguste Rodin (1840–1917) who, thanks to Charlotte's persistence and the £1,000 she lodged in his bank towards 'expenses', was persuaded to make his famous bust of Shaw.

While hosting these luncheons, Charlotte had to cope with Shaw's flamboyance in public. Leonora Ervine (*d.*1965), wife of dramatist St John Green Ervine (1883–1971), tells of arriving for lunch with other guests, only to be greeted by Charlotte who whispered, 'I do wish G.B.S. wouldn't wait to make an entrance but would receive with me.'

In direct contrast to her mother, Charlotte afforded her husband whatever she thought would help him in his ambitions and career. Mary Susanna had stripped her husband of all his passions, while Charlotte provided Shaw with a life of ease, apart, that is, from when she insisted on him accompanying her on her travels. Initially, Shaw reluctantly packed his bag for her, but then, as his fame grew, he needed to escape its demands by travelling elsewhere to write in peace.

Time and time again, Charlotte proved herself a mentor to writers, published or not. One of these was Erica Cotterill, a besotted fan of Shaw's, who began sending him long letters in 1906 that, more often than not, he ignored. The following year, she insisted on coming to see him and brought a play she had written. Typically, it was Charlotte who made the time to read the play and offer suggestions on how to improve it, telling Cotterill that if she reworked the play, she would bring it to the attention of the Stage Society.

However, Cotterill only wanted Shaw's attention, and nothing came of it.

It could be said that Charlotte is the sole reason why TE Lawrence's international bestselling debut memoir exists today. The British officer spent three years writing about his experience of the Arab campaign during WWI. Having met Shaw through a mutual friend, he screwed up the courage to ask the playwright if he would read the manuscript entitled *The Seven Pillars of Wisdom*, declaring that if it could not be improved, he would burn it. Shaw agreed to read it but did not say when. When the three hundred-thousand-word manuscript arrived in the post, Shaw passed it on to Charlotte, who loved it.

Once more this was an unpublished writer who desired George Bernard Shaw's response but had to make do with Charlotte's. But what writer of any calibre would not be touched by Charlotte's enthusiastic letter? 'I devoured it from cover to cover … it is one of the most amazingly individual documents that has ever been written …' Thus began a correspondence that lasted from 1922 until Lawrence's death. She was his first and perhaps truest champion, convincing him of the brilliance of his work and the need for it to be published. Previously, Lawrence had told Shaw that he had written it just for himself and maybe six others.

On 26 February 2004, Charlotte's first edition of *The Seven Pillars of Wisdom*, a copy made 'special' by Lawrence, by way of acknowledging her as one of the book's architects, sold at a Christie's auction for $95,000.

She had many friends, including the Countess of Fingall, Elizabeth (née Burke), who described Charlotte as being 'kind and calm and full of humour, a delightful companion, and I preferred her companionship to that of her more brilliant husband'.

Charlotte never lost her love for travel despite failing health in her seventies. In 1931, she and Shaw went to South Africa, where she was lucky to survive her husband's accidental plunging of their car at full speed into a ditch. In her seventh-fifth year, she enjoyed her first plane trip and, the following year, she and Shaw flew over the Great Wall of China.

CHARLOTTE SHAW (1857-1943)

Charlotte Shaw with George Bernard and friends Sidney and Beatrice Webb, on their way to Russia, 1932.

Charlotte, the granddaughter and great-granddaughter of clergymen, never stopped searching for that 'other'. She told TE Lawrence about Doctor James Porter Mills who advocated meditation and self-awareness. In fact, she had written her own accessible version of Mills's teachings, which Mills insisted on publishing as a textbook for his students. Charlotte supplied the title *Knowledge is the Door*, and a thousand copies were sold.

In later years, she moved onto the Russian philosopher Pyotr Demianovich Ouspensky (1878–1947) and his approach to developing the consciousness, exchanging opinions on spiritual matters with like-minded friends like historian and philosopher Gerald Heard (1889–1971).

A couple of years before her death, Charlotte wrote to Heard, describing how an unidentified book – possibly prescribed by Heard – 'put the final pinnacle on the edifice built up by Ouspensky and all the others'. She agreed that this subject made demands on the willing student, adding that if she had been free to, she would have given up everything to pursue it, 'But I was not free …'

The note of regret for paths not chosen is palpable.

Her last years were painful, with her frail body almost bent in two with Paget's disease of the bone (*osteitis deformans*). It was Shaw's turn to take care of her. When she died at 2am on 12 September 1943, the home-nurse decided to let the eighty-seven-year-old Shaw sleep on. He was already a widower six hours by the time he woke.

Shaw wrote to friends describing Charlotte's final days when she hallucinated that their flat was full of people and demanded he call the manager about the intrusion. Shaw told Kathleen Scott (1878–1947), sculptor and widow of doomed polar explorer Captain Robert Falcon Scott (1868–1912) that he calmed her by explaining how the intruders existed elsewhere and only she could see them because she was clairvoyant and, therefore, it was pointless to call in the manager since he would not see what she did.

Charlotte's will proved controversial. She wanted, upon Shaw's death, the National City Bank to use her fortune – minus several annuities and legacies to servants and friends and immense death duties – to bring 'masterpieces of fine art within the reach of the Irish people'.

Of course, she meant well, but her explanation ruffled several feathers, as she referred to the 'awkward manners' and 'defects' of the Irish people who were in dire need of 'teaching and training', an unfortunate throwback to her mother's attitude, though biographer Holroyd tells us the will was partly written by Sidney Webb.

Charlotte had been a woman of action, defying her mother's and society's expectation as to how a wealthy Victorian lady should behave. She believed in placing herself and her money at the service of others; she was a rich socialist who championed women's rights and who also believed that education should be available for anyone who wanted it, including aristocratic heiresses. She made things happen, from railway lines in Cork to advancing the careers of writers she admired. And she also knew how to enjoy her money, buying the best of clothes and taking frequent trips abroad.

Even in death, Charlotte ensured her money would be instrumental in the education of others as well as promoting artists and their work. Her recognition of the importance of art in everyday life and her generosity were inspirational. Remembering the young woman in Sartorio's portrait, whose expression signalled hope for a different sort of future and the patience to wait it out, we might agree that Charlotte provided for herself admirably, in every way.

Emily Shackleton

CHAPTER FIVE

EMILY SHACKLETON (1868-1936)

Wife of Ernest Shackleton, Arctic explorer

Emily Dorman was born in Sydenham, in Kent, in 1868, one of six children to wealthy solicitor Charles Dorman (*c.*1829–1901) and his wife Jane or Janie, née Swinford (1836–1875). When she was two years old, the family and two servants moved to Lewisham, Kent. Over the next few years, the success of her father's career was reflected in the increase of servants from two to six, along with the acquisition of a country house in Tidebrook, Sussex. Unfortunately, not much else is known about Emily's early life other than she could sing and had a passion for poetry, particular anything by English poet Robert Browning (1812–1889). Her father is credited with instilling an appreciation for literature and nature in his children. In her book *Polar Wives: The Remarkable Women Behind the World's Most Daring Explorers*, Kari Herbert writes that Emily's father was well liked and loved orchids. In fact, Charles Dorman was chairman of the Royal Horticultural Hall and was one of the first to grow orchids privately in England. We can assume that Emily was close to her father, especially following her mother's death in 1892, and that might explain why she was still single in 1897 when her friend Ethel Shackleton (1879–1935), who lived nearby in Aberdeen House, Sydenham, introduced her to her seafaring brother. Of course, there had been other admirers and even proposals of marriage, Emily was an attractive woman, but she had rejected them all. Thanks to her father's wealth, she did not need to settle for anyone who did not meet her or her family's expectations. At twenty-nine years of age, she might have wondered if she would ever marry or maybe she worried about her father missing her. In any case, her introduction to Ernest Shackleton gave her no warning of how her life was about to change.

The Shackletons were a big family, with eight girls and two boys, and for Emily, their home may have felt similar to her own. Head of the house, Doctor Henry Shackleton (c.1847–1920), hailed from County Kildare in Ireland. After obtaining an Arts degree in 1868, from Dublin's Trinity College, he leased a farm in Kilkea, County Kildare, and, four years later, married a local girl, Henrietta Gavan. As devoted as he was to his garden and farm, he decided in the late 1870s that farming could not sustain his growing family. Apart from gardening and reading, he was also passionate about homeopathic medicine, which was practised by an uncle of his, and so, in 1880, Henry decided to start over by moving his family to 35 Marlborough Road in Dublin, in order to return to Trinity College to study medicine. After graduating in 1884, Doctor Shackleton moved his family across the Irish Sea and set up practice in South Croydon in Surrey.

Today, writer and Ernest Shackleton biographer Michael Smith believes that Henry, whose father was of Quaker English stock, took his family to England to escape growing unrest in Ireland, particularly around land ownership.

A final move, six months later, due to Croydon's lack of interest in homeopathy, brought the family to Aberdeen House, 12 West Hill, Sydenham, where Henry built up a practice and a gorgeous garden. He specialised in roses and was sought after as a judge for flower shows and, like Charles Dorman, he instilled in his children a love for literature and the outdoors.

So, Henry Shackleton and Charles Dorman, one a rose and the other an orchid expert, had common interests, but would they ever have spoken to one another if Emily had never met Ernest?

Henry encouraged his children to dream big and two of his daughters proved themselves independent in every way. Eleanor (1879–1960), a trained nurse, emigrated to Canada in 1909 and was followed three years later by Kathleen (1884–1961) who became a journalist and illustrator for the *Montreal Star* newspaper. One wonders if Emily detected such ambitions in her friend's family, which might have stirred ambitions of her own. Generally, young middle-class women did not go out to work. The Shackletons were not wealthy, but neither were they poor, and Eleanor and Kathleen were obviously inspired by their father's passion for life and, presumably, their brother's too since, when he was home, Ernest was their window into other worlds.

On Saturday, 3 July 1897, Ernest arrived back from Japan, on leave from the Merchant Navy. It was the height of rose season so one can imagine the sight and scent of his father's garden providing a balm for his troubled soul. According to his friend and biographer, the British geographer and meteorologist Hugh Robert Mill (1861–1950), Ernest spent his journey reflecting on his life to date and longing for change. During the catch-up conversations with his family, his sister Ethel told him that she had recently become friends with Miss Emily Dorman, whom he knew to see. He finally met her in the drawing room of Aberdeen House before sailing away once more on 17 July for seven months.

After that first meeting, Mill writes that though Ernest and Emily may not have immediately fallen in love, a life-changing friendship was born. When Emily next saw him in February 1898, he had two weeks' leave before his next voyage. She told him of her love for the poetry of Robert Browning, which instantly converted him to being a fan of a poet he had previously dismissed.

The writer and critic Churton Collins (1848–1908) presented lectures on Robert Browning in the early 1890s, and it is possible Emily attended these. In 1922, she referred to papers and her notes on two of Browning's lengthy poems, 'Paracelsus' and *The Ring and the Book*, and reproached herself for not dating them, only signing her name alongside what might be the location, Anesley Centre, which may be missing a second 'n'.

Her meetings with Ernest were cultural, with visits to the British Museum and the National Gallery. Writing to Mill in 1922, Emily noted that she saw a good deal of Ernest in 1898, 1899 and 1900, in between his trips, which would set the pattern for their marriage. She also described requesting Ernest to recite their favourite poems and admitted that, ultimately, all they had in common was their love of literature. However, her father liked Ernest, though some friends thought she was foolish to waste her time in this way.

She was six years older than him and, influenced by those friends, she tried to use the age gap as an excuse not to become involved with him, but Ernest was smitten. Back in 1898, before a spark of yearning was ignited for the Antarctic, Ernest decided that she was the change he had been seeking. When his ship *Flintshire* ran aground that December, he asked for twenty-fours hours' leave, to wish his father an early happy birthday. He also used the opportunity to visit Emily and declare his feelings. At some point, he stubbed out his cigarette against the wooden chimney, which dented and charred it. They both tried rubbing it clean, but it proved impossible. However, no one was ever to notice it. Emily confessed to Hugh Robert Mill that she had always dreamed of owning that chimney piece, but knew, in 1922, she would never own a house large enough to warrant it. On that visit, Ernest stayed until 10.30pm, and Emily later recalled how he kissed her hand before leaving.

He became a regular visitor, in between his voyages, to both of the Dorman houses. Biographer Michael Smith, in an article for *Sussex Life*, describes this time as Ernest's probation period for Charles Dorman, who would likely have preferred that any suitor of Emily's should be more financially secure than a middle-ranking officer in the Merchant Navy.

It would also appear that Emily was keeping her options open as biographer Kari Herbert quotes from a letter that Ernest sent Emily in the spring of 1901, where he alluded to another man who knew her longer than he did. In Roland Huntford's biography of Ernest, this man is identified as Sidney Boulton (1856–1932). Was Emily doubting Ernest's potential as a husband or, was her father perhaps encouraging her towards the wealthy Boulton?

Ernest acknowledged his relative poverty and wished that he had met her first. We get a sense of Emily's reticence when he refers to how he used to, in the early days, beg her to love him, just a little bit.

On the other hand, Emily told Hugh Robert Mill that when Ernest attended dinner parties at their holiday house she always made sure that he sat beside her. Also, when Ernest took five months' leave in 1900, to concentrate on writing his first book – about sailing 1,200 volunteers to South Africa, to fight in the Boer War – Emily admitted to seeing a lot of him then. One can understand her reticence; he was twenty-six to her thirty-two, and he did keep going away for months on end. But she must have been impressed that he had co-authored a book. One specially bounded copy had even been presented to Queen Victoria (1819–1901). As it happened, royal connections would prove very beneficial to Ernest, both personally and professionally.

Ernest decided that he needed to do something big in order to convince Emily and her father that he was worthy of her. He tried joining the Royal Navy Reserve but discovered that he would have to wait a year to enrol. Then he heard about the pioneering National Antarctic Expedition, whose ship, *Discovery*, was being built in Dundee for its commander, Lieutenant Robert Falcon Scott (1868–1912), for the first-ever exploratory trip to the Antarctic. Ernest successfully applied to join Scott's team, as a junior officer. This was it; he had his foot on the first rung of the ladder to glory. According to Hugh Robert Mill, Ernest viewed the project as a short cut to fame and big money. And it worked, in that Emily finally agreed to marry him. One longs to know if her doubting friends now changed their minds as the country was caught up in excitement for this great adventure. They might have been finally persuaded when the new King Edward VII (1841–1910), whose mother Victoria had died eight months earlier, and Queen Alexandra (1844–1925) stepped onboard *Discovery* and looked to be genuinely fascinated by the ship's interior and equipment. The king, who was hugely interested in naval matters, delivered a passionate farewell to Scott and his crew, whilst his wife complimented the carnations in Ernest's cabin that Henry Shackleton had sent his son.

Discovery set sail on Tuesday, 6 August 1901. Having secured Emily's agreement to marry him, Ernest wrote to her father, asking him for his daughter's hand in marriage and ensured that his letter not be delivered until *Discovery* was well on her way to the Antarctic, just in case his proposal was rejected. Frank Nugent, in his book *Seek the Frozen Land: Irish Polar Explorers, 1740–1922*, congratulates Ernest on his shrewdness in writing to Charles instead of meeting with him. Also, Ernest's timing was excellent, as that royal visit and the ensuing publicity made him much more attractive as a son-in-law. However, by the time that Ernest received Charles's reply, dated 8 August, affirming his blessings for Emily and himself, Emily's seventy-two-year-old father was already dead.

Her father's blessing may have sealed the deal for Emily, but one wonders if she retained any doubts about her engagement given that she had two long years without seeing her fiancé as she grieved for her father. Who did she fall back upon in the absence of the two men who were most important to her? In fact, Emily liked to keep herself busy and co-wrote a book, *The Corona of Royalty*, about the coronation ceremony. It was published in time to celebrate King Edward's coronation in 1902.

Ernest returned to England in June 1903, in time for the annual gathering of the Royal Geographical Society, where his peers knew that he had been sent home by Scott from the Antarctic following an inconclusive medical examination. Ernest had been severely weakened by scurvy but had felt he was on the mend. Some polar historians suspect that Scott might have been jealous of Ernest's popularity and used his health as an excuse to remove him from the limelight. However, biographer Michael Smith believes that Scott was right to send the ailing Ernest home as, apart from scurvy, he was also affected by poor circulation and heart problems. In any case, following two months' respite in New Zealand, Ernest arrived home in fine fettle. Because Scott and *Discovery* would not return until 10 September 1904, Ernest found himself as the sole voice of the famous expedition and was much in demand as a speaker.

On 11 January 1904, Ernest started his new job as secretary for the Royal

Scottish Geographical Society, in Edinburgh, located in today's National Portrait Gallery in Queen Street, a short walk from number 14 South Learmonth Gardens, which was to become the first home for Ernest and Emily. Emily describes visiting Ernest's office while they were overseeing the decorating of their home. They walked in to see one of Ernest's staff cheekily hitting a golf-ball around the room. Instead of issuing a reprimand, Ernest asked for the man's golf stick for what might have been his first attempt at the game. Unfortunately, the novice whacked the ball so hard, it shot through the closed window, right across the street and into gardens some distance away.

Did Emily expect that this was going to be their life together, Ernest working office hours and home for dinner every evening? Initially, he did embrace his job. His lecture on 'Farthest South' attracted twenty-five new members and over a hundred pounds' worth of advertising for the Scottish Geographical Society's magazine. He also had a telephone installed along with a labelling machine called an addressograph that could address a week's worth of envelopes in a matter of hours. In fact, Ernest loved his job so much that he did not want to bother with a proper honeymoon.

The wedding of Emily and Ernest took place on 9 April at Christchurch, Westminster and was officiated by Emily's brother, Reverend Arthur Dorman. We might assume that had Robert Falcon Scott returned from Antarctica, he might have been there too as, aside from family, the guests included devotees to polar exploration, while Cyril Longhurst (1879–1948), secretary of the *Discovery* Expedition, was Ernest's best man. Ernest's family probably hoped that marriage would happily ground him in England forevermore.

The *Greenwich and Deptford Observer* described the ceremony in its Friday edition, 5 April 1904. Emily wore a dress of white oriental satin and old Brussels lace, and her tulle veil fell from a tiara of orange blossoms. Her jewellery included Ernest's gift of a diamond and sapphire ring, along with a pearl and diamond pendant from her sisters. After the ceremony, the newlyweds and their two hundred guests adjourned to nearby Queen Anne's Mansions for refreshments.

The brief honeymoon was a less than forty-eight-hour visit to the ancient town of Peterborough, about seventy-five miles from London. It might have been there that Emily wrote a moving letter to her sisters, the paper dampened by her tears. One can understand her emotional state with the absence of her parents heightened on her big day, but she assured her sisters that she was truly happy and loved being married.

The couple were back in Edinburgh by Monday evening and enjoying a picnic dinner in their new home despite the fact that they had no electricity, and their new servants had not yet arrived.

They spent their first married summer learning to play golf nearly two hundred miles away in Dornoch, which had a fine reputation regarding golf, with the earliest record of the game being played there in 1616. It is just possible that the Shackeltons might have encountered the professional English golfer John Henry Taylor (1871–1963), who also spent the summer of 1904 practising his swing in Dornoch.

Emily would have discovered that she was pregnant sometime in June or July, and the rest of the year must have been dominated by Ernest's newfound passion for exploring, something that likely increased with Scott's return, that September.

In February 1905, Emily gave birth to a boy who they named Raymond (*d*.1960). Impatient to make proper money, Ernest was becoming bored of his office job. Emily told their friend Hugh Robert Mill that her husband was always trying new schemes that he believed would make his fortune, from his share in an American tobacco concern to a Hungarian gold mine, but that these schemes would never make them rich. Five months after their son's birth, Shackleton resigned from the Scottish Geographical Society, having been promised a better paid position as personal assistant to the wealthy industrialist William Beardmore (1856–1936).

No longer tied to an office, Emily and Ernest spent the summer at St Andrews, playing golf twice a day, starting early to avoid the crowds. Emily proved the better golfer, while Ernest was a man obsessed with discussing the sport. Julia Dorman, Emily's older sister, joined the couple and complained that Ernest only ever talked about golf.

By May or June 1906, Emily was pregnant again and delivered a baby girl, Cecily (*d*.1957), on 23 December. While she was readying herself for her baby's arrival, her husband was quietly working on his own project which he kept to himself as, according to Mill, he did not want to add to his wife's anxieties. This hardly makes sense since what he was planning was bound to have enormous repercussions for himself and his family. Three days after his daughter was born, England was covered in snow which may have inspired Ernest, in a letter to a friend, to wish to be back in Antarctica.

Within a week or so of writing that letter, he confessed to William Beardmore that he wanted to organise his very own expedition to the South Pole. Beardmore agreed to guarantee a loan of £7,000 and, with his dream becoming a reality, it was time for Ernest to break the news to his wife.

Obviously, Emily put on a brave face for her husband's biographer in 1922, only admitting that she was heartbroken at the thought of a long separation. She may also have been hurt or offended at being told about the expedition only after its possibility was confirmed. Using her pregnancy as an excuse, Ernest had excluded her from months of his dreaming about attempting to be the first person to reach the South Pole. Furthermore, he chose to make his announcement in a comical manner, or, at least, what he thought was comical. Hugh Robert Mill described Ernest's approach, his telling Emily how wonderful it would be, for him, if he could tell Cecily stories about his climbing mountains in Victoria Land (eastern Antarctic) and learning about its quaint inhabitants who led a magical existence far away from her mundane world. His actions remind us of that six-year age gap between husband and wife; Ernest was still a boy at heart.

In any case, Emily offered no resistance and supported her husband's decision. Kari Herbert quotes a letter from him to Emily telling her that when he received her wire, encouraging him to go on his voyage, he cried. He is so full of gratitude that he promises to be home in a year's time with honour and money and tells her that releasing him to the Antarctic means that she gets to make history too. He also promises that, once home, he will never leave her again.

In fairness, what choice did Emily have? Over the last couple of years, she had watched Ernest try to lead a 'normal' life, embracing steady jobs, and a variety of money-making schemes, only for his restlessness to surface time and time again. How could she attempt to dissuade him from this next adventure that just might make all his wishes come through and, therefore, bring him peace? As Emily told Hugh Robert Mill, it was futile to keep an eagle chained to a back garden.

After he announced to the Royal Geographical Society on 11 February 1907 the particulars of his expedition, an awkward moment ensued when Captain Robert Falcon Scott, who planned to return to Antarctica, wrote to Ernest asking him not to use *Discovery*'s base at McMurdo Sound, a bay off Antarctica, on the Ross Sea, exactly where Ernest had planned to station his ship. Scott's request, described today by Irish explorer and writer Frank Nugent as 'unreasonable', had the potential to derail Ernest's ambitions, and he found himself outnumbered as mutual friends and colleagues urged him to heed Scott's wishes, even if it meant not reaching the South Pole. With a heavy heart, Ernest signed an agreement to avoid the old base.

With less than ten months to prepare for the voyage, the couple left Edinburgh in 1906 and moved into a rented house at Palace Court, Bayswater Road, in London, for a month or two, and Ernest took an office about twenty minutes away, at 9 Regent Street, Waterloo Place.

Emily would have been forgiven for feeling that she was already practising for their parting as she would hardly have had any time alone with Ernest in the run-up to his departure. For instance, he sailed to Norway to buy things like sleeping bags, ski equipment, sledges and furs that would be used for boots and mittens. Back in England, he traversed the island in his quest for appropriate food for the months ahead and managed, from his office, a team of agents who were, on his orders, buying ponies in Manchuria, Asia, to be shipped to New Zealand, where dogs were being bought for the trip. An agent in Australia was sourcing scientific equipment and an agent in Norway was sending him whatever else he needed. Emily might have felt that, in a way, he had already left her behind, mentally and emotionally.

On Sunday, 4 August 1907, six years after their inspection of *Discovery*, King Edward and Queen Alexandra visited the *Nimrod*, Ernest's ship for the expedition. They were accompanied by Princess Victoria (1868–1935), Prince Edward (1894–1972) and Prince Arthur, the Duke of Connaught (1850–1942). The King made Ernest a member of the Royal Victorian Order, 4th Class, while his wife presented Ernest with a flag to be raised at the South Pole.

The following day, Emily boarded the *Nimrod* as her husband's guest of honour for a farewell dinner and then attended another farewell dinner the following day, for *Nimrod*'s officers and crew, at the Torbay Hotel, in Torquay, where the Shackletons were spending the summer. When the *Nimrod* set sail the following day, on Wednesday, 7 August, for the first stage of the trip, to New Zealand, to pick up supplies, Ernest remained behind to continue trying to raise more sponsorship, including securing media contracts for his return, including newspapers that would print his articles and photographs and agents who would get him speaking engagements. He was determined to squeeze in every opportunity to capitalise on the expedition's success as a writer and lecturer. Perhaps Emily experienced some relief that *Nimrod*, at least, was on its way, expecting that Ernest might have some time for herself and the children. Two months later, she bade him farewell from Dover Pier on Thursday, 31 October. He wrote to her telling her that leaving her was the worst moment of his entire life and he felt unable to describe his gratitude for her allowing him to fulfil his destiny.

Emily returned to their house in Edinburgh, where one of her sisters moved in with her. How quiet the place must have seemed after the frenetic excitement of the last seven months or so. It was quite an achievement to have organised an expedition so quickly. Although Ernest was heading off to being fêted by 30,000 strong crowds in New Zealand, Emily's accomplishment in parenting two young children and managing her household alone would go unmarked. A year must have felt like a long time, and she could only hope that he would make good on his promises to be home within twelve months and never to leave her again.

In her biography about her grandmother, *A Great Task of Happiness: The Life of Kathleen Scott*, Louisa Young writes about the wife of 'an absentee Antarcticist'. In 1910, Kathleen waved off her husband Captain Robert Falcon Scott on his *Terra Nova* expedition to the South Pole. Leaving their one-year-old son, Peter (*d*.1989), at home, the couple had enjoyed two last weeks together. As the voyage got underway, emotions were running high amongst the wives and their husbands. The climax was a fantastic row that erupted between Kathleen, Hilda, the wife of Edward (Terry) Evans (1880–1957), Scott's second-in-command, and Oriana (Ory) (*c*.1874–1945), who was married to Edward Adrian Wilson (1872–1912), Scott's head of science for the expedition. Young quotes Captain Lawrence (Titus) Oates's (*b*.1880) humorous response, 'Mrs Scott and Mrs Evans had a magnificent battle; they tell me it was a draw after fifteen rounds. Mrs Wilson flung herself into the fight after the tenth round and there was more blood and hair flying about the hotel than you see in a Chicago slaughterhouse …' These long separations took their toll on the explorers' wives who assumed full responsibility for house and family and could not ignore the possibility of never seeing their husbands again.

The *Nimrod* voyage was fraught with difficulties, with the weather proving far worse than expected. Ernest realised the safety of his crew and ship could only be guaranteed by his breaking his word to Scott and setting up base in *Discovery*'s McMurdo Sound. It was not an easy decision to make, and Ernest poured out his tumultuous feelings about the matter in a letter to Emily, dated 26 January 1908. He told her that the decision had aged him, he wanted to do the right thing but had to consider the forty men onboard and their families back home. To attempt to winter anywhere else would be suicidal.

A year later, Ernest made another enormous decision when, in January 1909, he and three exhausted, hungry companions got within 97 miles of the South Pole, which was the nearest that anyone had ever come to the end of the world, and there they raised Queen Alexandra's flag before readying themselves for the 700-mile trek back to the *Nimrod*. Ernest was big and bold enough to recognise that had he continued another hour he would be risking all their lives.

In 1922, Emily remembered how her anxiety steadily increased as the days passed without a word about him. On 23 March, her sister suggested that she head off to the baths for a swim, which was her favourite way to relax. As she swam, she was oblivious to the fact that Ernest and his crew had sent word of their safe return to New Zealand. Once home, she found herself inundated with telegrams of congratulations along with a four-word cable from Ernest, the two most important ones being 'Home' and 'June'. Twenty months after their farewell in Dover, Emily was reunited with her husband in Dover, at 3pm on Saturday, 12 June 1909.

The following day, they slipped away, driving to her father's old house in Tidebrook where they walked in the woods as Ernest described what he had been through. Emily told Hugh Robert Mill that Ernest had no regrets about missing out on the South Pole, although it seems like he wanted her to believe that he had sacrificed reaching it for her sake, telling her that he knew she would prefer a living donkey over a dead lion. They had just forty-eight hours together before the public made its claim on the now-famous explorer.

Emily may have felt like she had just been catapulted into another world. On Monday, 14 June, the gates to Charing Cross Station had to be closed when a crowd of ten thousand well-wishers turned up to welcome Ernest back to London. Friends and family were allowed onto the station's forecourt, including Doctor Henry Shackleton, his daughters and grandchildren Ray and Cecily. Ernest's son was dressed in a sailor-suit and wearing a cap which had *Nimrod* on it. From there, Ernest, Emily and the two children took an open horse-drawn carriage through the streets, which struggled to get through the cheering crowds. Over the next couple of months, there was a succession of formal dinners, lunches, garden parties, official receptions, an invitation from Buckingham Palace and lots of speeches and medals.

That October, Emily accompanied her husband on a tour of Europe for a busy round of meetings and lectures. In Copenhagen, Ernest's lecture to the Geographical Society was attended by the King and Queen of Denmark along with 2,000 others. Once the royal and wealthy had been entertained, the following day, Ernest repeated his speech for Copenhagen's poor, something that might have, years later, prompted Emily's wish to bring out a cheap version of Hugh Robert Mill's biography of Ernest following the first luxury edition.

At a banquet in Norway, Emily noted how the Norwegian explorer Roald Amundsen (1872–1928) gazed at Ernest as he spoke about Antarctica, and she believed that this was the exact moment that Amundsen, who had been planning an expedition to the north, changed his mind and decided to go to the South Pole.

We can probably assume that Emily supported Ernest's refusal of the Congo Medal in Brussels. The elderly King Leopold II (1835–1909) had established the Congo Free State in 1855 and, thanks to Irish diplomat Roger Casement (1864–1916), who exposed the evil committed in Leopold's name against the local population, British newspapers were loud in their criticism of anything to do with the Congo.

In December, Shackleton's name made the list for knighthood by King Edward VII and, on 19 March 1910, Sir Ernest and Lady Shackleton boarded the RMS *Lusitania* for Ernest's lecture tour in the United States and Canada. Roland Huntford, in his book *Shackleton*, quotes from an interview that Emily gave for the magazine *Woman at Home*, before they set sail, in which she declares that she only wanted to be known as the wife of Ernest Shackleton. Huntford writes that at least one American journalist found her to be different from the wives of famous men. Describing Emily as 'statuesque', the journalist complimented her high intelligence, which they described as being 'unusual', and appreciated her distinctive personality which enabled her

EMILY SHACKLETON (1868-1956)

Emily and Ernest Shackleton

to stand with, but also apart from, her husband. This unexpected interest in Emily may have prompted her to be more vocal than usual. For instance, she considered how she differed from her husband, declaring that while he always saw the bigger picture, she homed in on the 'small things', giving the example that what impressed her most about America was the wide availability of iced water. But she might have been joking since she went on to sincerely praise America for allowing its middle-class girls to study and embark on a career without being judged negatively. Back in England, it was not socially acceptable for women like Emily to go to college or get a job. Had she had dreams of pursuing a college education, at least before becoming a wife and mother? Those classes she attended, about Browning's poetry, might have given her a taste for further study. Also, she rejected several marriage proposals and remained unattached until her thirties so just maybe she was hoping, even waiting, for a change in the rules of social etiquette for middle-class women.

One wonders about her satisfaction with the life she was leading when, in the same interview, she denounced fairy stories, preventing her children from reading them because of their typical ending with a girl achieving eternal happiness only after marrying the hero. Emily felt that they were morally reprehensible and responsible for half the misery in the world. It was just wrong, she said, for girls to have such notions 'dinned' into them, thus ensuring that they grew up with the ingrained belief that marriage was the pinnacle for the female race. It might be worth noting that her daughter Cecily never married.

Or perhaps the interviewer just caught Emily after she had heard her husband's latest plans. It was probably in the United States that Ernest mentioned another expedition he had been thinking about for a while. Roland Huntford writes about Ernest's new decision to earmark his lecture fees for another adventure south, and not, as Emily believed, for clearing his debts back home. Not surprisingly, her response was less than effusive. Apparently, five-year-old Raymond was clamouring to be an explorer when he grew up, but his mother refused to start worrying just yet, her philosophy being that difficulties could only be faced when they actually happened. For the wife of a polar explorer, this was a sensible approach.

There were frustrations in the United States following hugely successful lectures in Washington and Boston. Less effort, it seems, had been applied to promoting his talks in smaller towns, which meant that the crowds were woefully reduced in size while, in some cases, according to Mill, Ernest spoke to empty benches. On their way to one town, the Shackletons discovered that they were sharing the train with the posters that should have been advertising his talk *before* their arrival. Ernest's mood dipped and they decided to skip off early to Canada for lectures there. Returning to the United States for two weeks, they solicited advice from an agent who advised cutting their trip short as the lecturing season was coming to an end. Mill references Ernest's disgruntlement after attending a luncheon with a bunch of New York millionaires who showed no interest in him. We must remember that Emily is Mill's source and might have sugar-coated how bad things were. At one point, Ernest considered giving up on America and going home and we can only guess what Emily went through as his travelling companion. At the very least, she would have missed her children.

Back in Canada, they met with Ernest's sister Eleanor, who was a nurse in the Children's Hospital in the city of Winnipeg, where three thousand turned up to see him. Typically, Ernest donated his lecture fee to the hospital. He and Emily set sail for home on 10 June. No doubt both were looking forward to a long holiday in Sheringham, Norfolk, with Ray and Cecily, where they were to play lots of golf. Emily told Mill that Ernest had himself made up as an elderly man and passed himself off as an obscure uncle of his, fooling the children and their other relatives who were with them.

Sheringham must have been a success as they moved down from Edinburgh the following month, renting Mainsail Haul, a furnished house. Ernest left for another big lecture tour of Europe and only returned in early December. Five months later, in April 1911, the family was on the move again, this time to 7 Heathview Gardens in London's Putney Heath. Emily was about five months pregnant, and Ernest was off on his trips again, only hearing about the birth of their son, Edward, on 15 July, when he arrived in Boulogne.

Emily might have felt that she had been existing to a deadline since the summer of 1910, when Captain Robert Falcon Scott left England, and Roald Amundsen left Norway, for their respective expeditions to the South Pole. She must have known how Ernest envied them. Since returning from the United States and Canada, Emily witnessed her husband's continued unsuitability for business and, despite the hundreds of paid lectures he had given, he was still struggling to turn a profit. As she wrote, in a letter to Mill, in 1922, she never heard anyone compliment Ernest on his business sense.

It was an astute Emily who won Ernest a government grant of £20,000 in 1910. On being introduced to the famous journalist Sir Henry Lucy (1842–1924) and his wife, Emily Anne White (1847–1937), Emily seized the opportunity to confide in Emily Lucy about the dire impact the expedition had placed upon Ernest's finances. The outcome of this conversation could not have been planned better. Mrs Lucy repeated all to her husband, who described his astonishment in the *Daily Express* that Ernest was out of pocket for an expedition that had benefited his country, prompting Prime Minister Asquith's government to award Ernest £20,000 for his troubles.

Throughout the rest of 1910 and 1911, Ernest kept an ear to the south, eager for any Antarctic news. Mill quotes a letter Ernest wrote to a friend in New Zealand, on 12 January, in which he confessed his wish to put together another expedition and escape all his business worries. He mentioned that his family was well, but that he did not see them much. We can imagine Emily being bound up in domesticity with three young children while he chased that elusive pot of gold. In 1922, she admitted to Mill that Ernest was thoroughly unhappy in 1912 and 1913, adding that these were her worst years too.

When Scott and his team finally reached the South Pole on 16 January 1912, they found the Norwegian flag blowing in the wind, having been placed there by Amundsen on 15 December 1911, informing the British crew that they had failed in their mission to be first. The world would hear of Amundsen's success that March. With the public's appetite whetted anew for polar stories, Ernest found himself and his lectures, once more, in demand.

April brought the astonishing news that the new White Star liner RMS *Titanic* had sunk after hitting an iceberg on her maiden voyage to America, with the loss of 1,500 souls. Ernest was involved in the official inquiries into the cause of the collision.

The summer of 1912 was a happier time with the Shackletons renting a holiday home for two months at Seaford, in Sussex, where Emily and Ernest spent many hours on the golf course. In 1922, Emily remembered Ernest entertaining the children by reciting his favourite lines from the poem 'The Triumph of Time' by Algernon Charles Swinburne (1837–1909), in which a man, who is unlucky in love, yearns for the sea, a metaphor for oblivion. This may have been the Shackletons' last significant time together as a family.

Less than a year after the *Titanic* tragedy, in February 1913, came the wretched news that Robert Falcon Scott and his four companions never made it back to their ship. When Scott's diary was found in his tent, alongside his frozen body, and that of Doctor Edward Wilson (*b*.1872) and Lieutenant Henry Bowers (*b*.1883), it provided details of their final days, describing the great sacrifice made in vain by Lieutenant Lawrence (Titus) Oates who had begged his friends to leave him behind as his strength was gone. When they refused to, he left the tent, to disappear forever, to release them so they could continue on without him, camouflaging his intention with those famous words, 'I am just going outside, and may be some time.'

Of course, Emily would have thought of Kathleen Scott and the other widows, knowing that her own husband, having previously declared that he was happier being home, was planning another trip to the Antarctic, despite his lack of money. She might also have thought of the men's mothers, and, in later years, she became close friends with Oates's mother, Caroline.

She would, however, never be friends with Kathleen Scott, whose husband probably never forgave Ernest for breaking his promise to avoid McMurdo Sound and it was inevitable that his widow took his side. In 1923, Emily remembers how Lady Scott prevented Ernest from speaking at the R.G.S. memorial for Scott. She also relays her distress to Mill about an unfair judgement of Ernest in Scott's published diary. Ernest had asked Lady Scott to remove it back in 1913, but the offending paragraph remains in the later editions of 1924. She considers writing to Kathleen, who had married again, this time to writer and politician Edward Hilton Young (1879–1960), but decides against it as Mrs Young was always 'so hard' on Ernest. However, she writes to Kathleen later that year after a portrait of Ernest is refused by the National Portrait Gallery because he has not been dead the requisite ten years. This spurred Emily to first telephone the Young household to check if Mrs Young was at home and, hearing that she was, Emily wrote to ask if she might visit Kathleen to discuss something that was weighing heavily on her. Emily never received a reply.

In 1922, Emily credited a lack of money as the source of Ernest's stress and unhappiness in 1912 and 1913, and it was an issue for her too. She must have been so grateful to her father for that annual £700 that kept her and the children afloat and, possibly, even more grateful that her father was no longer around to see that his initial doubts about Ernest had been well founded. No one is perfect, but it would have been only natural if Emily regretted that her husband was not a better provider and did not prize exploring the Antarctic over living with her and their children. Scott's death propelled Ernest forward with his plans to return to that treacherous place. For Emily, Scott's demise would have been a perfectly sensible reason for Ernest to stay home.

When the *Endurance* left England for Buenos Aires on 8 August 1914, for the first leg of Ernest's Imperial Trans-Antarctic Expedition, he was not on it. In his book *The Ship Beneath the Ice*, Mensun Bound writes that Ernest's refraining from mentioning his absence on the *Endurance*, as she departed, suggests that he preferred for people to think he was onboard. So, why did he stay behind, only leaving Liverpool on 25 September to reconnect with his crew and ship in South America? Some point to his ongoing struggle to raise necessary funds, while others sense a more personal explanation in the letter he sent Emily, once he was safely out to sea, about their quarrelling.

The letter, dated 26 October 1914, is partially quoted by Kim Heacox in his book *Shackleton: The Antarctic Challenge*, with Ernest writing that he did not like leaving her on bad terms and that he knew she would have been happier with a more domesticated man. Emily was struggling openly with this second trip, unable to produce the unequivocal support she had given to the *Nimrod* expedition. Ernest tells her that exploring is the only thing he is good at, and, in this regard, he will not yield to anyone.

The same letter is referenced by Roland Huntford, who goes further than Heacox's assessment. Ernest tells Emily that he refuses to be upset by what she said about her old beau Sir Sidney Boulton, because he knows that she is not the type of woman to be carried away, especially when she has a wonderful asset in the children who 'anchored' her. Such double standards would have been normal then. The father was free to sail the world, while his children anchored their mother beneath one roof. Huntford's interpretation is that Emily's feelings for Boulton had been reignited, but it is also possible that, in the middle of an over-heated quarrel, a frustrated Emily had merely quipped that she should have married the man who would have stayed by her side.

As a couple, the Shackletons were under a lot of stress, but Emily did her part. In 1922, she told Hugh Robert Mill that she disliked fame yet, in July 1914, she boarded the *Endurance* for the very public hour-long visit made by Queen Alexandra, whose husband King Edward VII had died four years earlier, and her sister, the Dowager Empress of Russia Maria Feodorovna (1847–1928). Perhaps Emily was touched by a widow's determination to continue her husband's work. She brought the children with her, and a moment of hilarity ensued when three-year-old Edward refused the queen's invitation to walk with her, preferring to stick with his nurse.

A photograph taken of the occasion, which appears in Roland Huntford's biography, shows Queen Alexandra concentrating on little Edward who stands in front of his mother. It is a black-and-white photograph, slightly blurred, but Emily, wearing a bright-coloured blouse and skirt, stands out from the royal sisters who are both dressed head to toe in dark, fur-lined coats and hats. Emily and her son cast the only smiles at the photographer.

Thanks to several brilliant biographies about Ernest, one can piece together the multiple stresses affecting him and Emily in 1914. Presumably, first and foremost, for Emily, the prospect of another prolonged absence for an undetermined amount of time was stressful enough. Their children were aged between nine and three and, as the sole parent for the foreseeable future, any problems that cropped up with their schooling or health were hers to solve alone. However, one also needs to consider the timing of Ernest's departure. To be left at that particular time of world uncertainty, as a string of treaties rapidly pulled countries into an all-out conflict, would have brought further concerns for Emily. Of course, if he had stayed, Ernest would have joined the fight in Europe but that might well have felt different in that he would be going off to defend her and the children. And while a soldier could receive and send letters home, a Polar explorer ultimately disappeared across the horizon, completely out of reach.

Today, many biographers believe that Ernest was having affairs. In fact, it is alleged that William Beardmore, who had sponsored Ernest's 1907 expedition, was motivated not so much by science or generosity but by the opportunity to enable Ernest to sail miles away from his much younger wife, Elspeth (1874–1955). Not surprisingly, there is no mention of such things in Hugh Robert Mill's biography. However, in a letter to Emily, he does allude to another unpleasantness concerning Ernest's brother Frank who had been jailed for fifteen months for fraud in 1913. There had been a trial and naturally the name of Frank's famous brother had cropped up more than once, which must have been mortifying for his sister-in-law to find her family associated with such a person as Frank. And while Ernest was leaving all that embarrassment behind, there was no such escape for Emily.

In 1916, she moved herself and the children into 14 Milnthorpe Road in Eastbourne. News reached her in May that Ernest was safe, but it would be another year before she saw him again, in May 1917. By then, he was forty-two to her forty-eight years and had been through a journey like no other. To distract her, while he was gone, Emily had become involved with the Girl Guides, as Eastbourne Divisional Commissioner.

Her husband's return threw her usual routine into disarray but thanks to decent servants and good children, she gladly neglected her domestic duties as she acclimatised to having a husband in residence once more. And, as she told Mill, she also relaxed her usual vigilance regarding their expenditure. In 1922, she blames herself for their financial predicament but also defends herself with the admission that she did not know that much of what they were spending had been borrowed from the bank.

Ernest told her that this would be his last trip, but, by now, she probably knew better than to believe him. Several biographers paint a sad portrait of Ernest at this time, with accounts about his drinking, his relationship with his actress lover and the fact that he spent little time in Eastbourne with his family. As always, there were money problems, and he longed to get involved in the war that was still raging all these years later.

There were one or two blissful weeks in 1917 when the couple rented a flat to be alone together, but that was expensive and had to be curtailed. Yet Emily chooses to disclose this information to Ernest's biographer in 1922, which seems a most private thing to mention, including her use of the word 'bliss' about those weeks. Is this Emily's way of letting other women know that she and Ernest were still enjoying a physical relationship?

When he had been home for a while, Emily wrote to a friend about Ernest's restlessness, and her hope that, for his sake, he would soon receive a posting from the War Office, which he did in 1918.

Then came the final expedition in 1921, with Emily providing the name for the ship, *Quest*, that set sail on 21 September. Just after *Quest* reached the sub-Antarctic island of South Georgia, Ernest had a fatal heart attack on the morning of 5 January 1922. His body was embalmed for its return to England, but Emily sent an urgent message instructing Ernest's crew to bury him on South Georgia. She did right by him until the very end, knowing that he would prefer to stay in his beloved Antarctic, where he had been his most brilliant in every way.

Emily's generous nature is one of the things that stands out in her letters to Hugh Robert Mill. When she wrote to him on 18 April, asking if he would consider writing a biography about Ernest, Mill's agreement was immediate. With her widowhood barely begun, Emily was happy to launch herself into a project that allowed her to nurture her husband's legacy. On a practical level, however, she needed money and fast. It is estimated that Ernest had left her about £40,000 in debt (over a million pounds in today's currency), obliging her to accept such kindnesses as Mill's decision to award her his share of the book's profits, while family and friends helped with the children's school fees.

When a Shackleton Memorial Fund was established to support Ernest's mother and his children's education, Emily requested that the bulk of it be made over to her mother-in-law who Ernest had been financially responsible for, along with two of his sisters, following his father's death in August 1920. One can understand his need to strike it rich, with so many relying on him.

Within three months of Ernest's death, a journalist, Harold Begbie (1871–1929), published a hastily written biography of Ernest, thus inspiring Lady Shackleton to approach Ernest's publishers about an official biography. Ernest had already written about his Antarctic trips, but Begbie proved that people were eager to know more about him.

Emily's letters to Mill, as she gathers information for him, provide an insight into her life, her busyness as a single mother and her work with the Girl Guides. On two occasions, she even mentions the pounds she is shedding. This weight loss, she explained, was a result of her physical labour when she decided to do without servants, in an effort to live frugally.

As a distraction from her grief, the book was double-edged in that assisting Mill required her to reread Ernest's love letters to her and his diaries, and she confessed to experiencing agony more than once.

She remained close to Ernest's mother but struggled with his sister Aimee who, when the Memorial Fund was delayed, sent Emily a 'nasty' letter telling her to pay their rent. Emily cannot stop herself from sharing this sort of extra curricular information with Mill, explaining that because she is writing after midnight, she is 'getting garrulous' and cannot remember how many 'r's are in garrulous.

On 16 August 1922, Emily writes to Mill about sending letters from 1913, the problem year, telling him that he will now understand the pain she had hinted at. She plans to burn the letters when he returns them and offers to discuss that year in more detail with Mill in person. One can read anything into this, but she adds her belief that she failed Ernest because she was 'too sure'. Is she referring to his need for other women? She finishes by confessing her need to remember that Ernest used to call her his 'blessing', every year.

As for 1914, her unhappiness then can be attributed to the fact that their three children had whooping cough and then Emily also succumbed to it. Meanwhile, Ernest went abroad because, of course, he did not want to catch the cough too. There was a long, worrisome period of six weeks for her.

Overall, Emily's love for her husband blazes through her letters to Mill.

He dutifully sends her each chapter on its completion, and she professes her delight with his work. But she is not afraid to voice her disagreement. In a letter dating 29 April 1924, she tells Mill that Ernest would not want any doubt attached to what he had described as 'the 4th Presence'. The biographer had attempted to play down Ernest's belief that an invisible fourth person had accompanied himself, Tom Crean and Frank Worsley on their mammoth trek across South Georgia in May 1916. Mill made the necessary changes. It is tempting to conjure up an image of Scott's spirit silently egging on the team, wanting to get them back to safety, something he had been unable to do for himself and his four companions in 1912.

According to Emily and Ernest's granddaughter, the Honourable Alexandra Shackleton, whose father was Edward, Emily doted on her two sons who both called her Honey. She, in turn, called them Honey I (Raymond) and Honey II (Edward). Her relationship with Cecily was a difficult one, a natural occurrence, perhaps, from living together after the two boys left to pursue their careers and marriages. Cecily became a talented cook, according to her mother, and they did very well without servants.

Emily's finances improved in later years, thanks to an increase in the income from her father's estate. In 1929, King George V (1865–1936) granted Emily a 'grace-and-favour' apartment at Hampton Court Palace, usually reserved for retired soldiers and diplomats, where she died on the morning of 9 June, in 1936, after a long illness. She is buried in St Giles's church in West Sussex.

Annette Carson

CHAPTER SIX

ANNETTE CARSON (c.1855-1913)

Wife of Edward Carson, lawyer and politican

There is a piece of online footage, from a 1960s interview, in which the longtime widowed, and elderly Lady Ruby Carson (1881–1966) recalls her first visit to Belfast following her marriage to lawyer and politician Lord Edward Carson (1854–1935) in 1914. The video begins with Ruby climbing the uneven porch steps of her home, with the aid of a walking stick and interviewer Ivor Mills's arm. Her voice is strong as she declares that while she knew that people were coming to meet her husband that day in 1914, she was unprepared for the size of the crowd waiting to greet them. As they sailed into Belfast Harbour, their ship sounded out three times on, what she described as, the 'hooter'. She saw workers from Harland & Wolff down tools and race to clamber onto the roofs of buildings to get a look at the newlyweds. Finding herself suddenly overwhelmed, Lady Carson feared that the boisterous crowds would not approve of her and confessed as much to her husband, just before they headed down the gangway, 'This is quite dreadful, they may not like me.' However, he merely replied, 'I don't see why not, because I do!' Years later in her interview, her entire face lights up and she giggles as she proudly repeats to Mills her husband's response.

On disembarking, the newly married couple drove through the streets of Belfast and went to stay with their friends, the Craigavons. Two days later, they elected to make their way down the Shankill Road in an open car, solely for the community who wanted to see her. In their excitement, people threw everything into the car, including a horseshoe. Two old women climbed up on the car to thump Ruby on her back and instruct her, 'Be good to him, Mrs Carson, be good to him!'

Women, it seemed, really liked Edward Carson.

Ruby was not the first Mrs Edward Carson, but perhaps she was entirely more suited to the role of the wife of a public figure. For one thing, her health was strong, and for another, at twenty-seven years younger than her husband, her energy knew no bounds.

Her predecessor was Sarah Annette Kirwan, initially believed to be from Clontuskart in County Galway. In the summer of 1879, twenty-five-year-old Edward Carson, a law student, was boating with his best friend James Shannon, somewhere near Dublin, likely Kingstown (today's Dún Laoghaire), and spied a slim blonde on the shore. James, who knew her to see, said that the girl lived with her father, widower and Galway man Henry Persse Kirwan (*c*.1818–*c*.1884), a retired County Inspector of the Royal Irish Constabulary. Her mother, Ann Foster, also from Galway, had died when she was a child. Instantly smitten, Edward badgered his friend for an introduction. Since there is no mention of a chaperone, perhaps Edward was struck at the sight of an attractive young woman out walking alone. Carson biographer H Montgomery Hyde writes that Edward appreciated the woman's smart appearance and dress. Hyde also writes that Shannon was reluctant to play Cupid until Edward threatened to approach Annette without him. And, so, Edward got his introduction to Annette who, it appears, was equally enamoured with the young law student as they were engaged before summer's end.

Apart from £50 in his bank account, neither Carson nor his fiancée had any money, a fact that appalled Carson's father, the architect Edward Henry Carson Senior, who refused to attend the wedding at Monkstown parish church on 19 December 1879. The ceremony was officiated by the Reverend Frank Hall, Carson's old schoolmaster, and the marriage certificate was signed by Annette's father and best man James Shannon. Perhaps the only show from Edward's side was his younger sister, Bella.

The newlyweds honeymooned in London, where they enjoyed spending Christmas and probably all of Edward's £50.

On their return to Dublin, in January 1880, they were obliged to move into a house in Herbert Place belonging to Annette's 'uncle', barrister and Kilkenny magistrate John Joseph Kirwan. This was her father's cousin who had raised Annette after her mother died. In his book *Judging Redmond and Craig*, Alvin Jackson writes that it was believed that Annette was her father's illegitimate daughter; in other words, her mother was not Henry Persse Kirwan's deceased wife. If this is true, it goes some way to explaining Annette's extreme discomfort, later on, in high society. This belief may have occurred owing to a mix-up regarding the scant details available about Annette's early years.

In the meantime, Annette had married an ambitious man and a born rebel at that. Marrying against his father's wishes – and he had been his father's favourite son – was merely the beginning of a pattern that Edward would follow for the rest of his life. For instance, when he was advised to stay away from his stricken best friend James Shannon, who was dying from contagious diphtheria, Edward went ahead and visited him anyway.

Annette would have had to hold the fort while Edward poured all his energy into his career. H Montgomery Hyde wrote that, in these early days, briefs were few and far between, but on receiving one, Edward would stay up half the night working on it, with Annette's encouragement and support. Their first child, William Henry Lambert, known as Harry, arrived the next year in 1880, his birth providing the catalyst that allowed his paternal grandparents to finally accept his parents' marriage. The reunion was short lived, however, as Edward's father died suddenly in early 1881, the same year that Annette gave birth to her second baby, Aileen. By now, they were renting a small house at 9 Herbert Place. Since his father had never been a wealthy man, Edward now had to provide for his widowed mother as well as for Annette and their two children. These financial commitments might explain the four-year gap between Aileen and her younger sister, Gladys Isobel, born in 1885, followed by her brother Walter Seymour in 1890.

The marriage was, for the most part, a happy one or, at least, it was initially. Annette was a devoted wife, and several of Carson's biographers, including Geoffrey Lewis, praise her for nursing Edward through the diphtheria that killed both James Shannon and his wife. Furthermore, following a risky operation to remove gallstones, a couple of years later, Annette's constant care ensured Edward's return to health.

In her essay, 'Edward Carson, A Family Man', Theresa Envers writes that Edward and Annette were very much in love and enjoyed frequent visits to the theatre as well as breaks away to celebrate whenever he won a case.

Annette lost her father just before Christmas, in 1884, on 3 December. According to his obituary, she was with him when he died at home, at 68 Frankfurt Place, Dublin, a short walk from her house at 9 Herbert Place.

The following year, Edward's success as a junior barrister allowed them to give up renting and buy a large house at 80 Merrion Square which was but a few minutes away from his childhood home at 4 Harcourt Street. They also bought a small holiday home in Dalkey, where Annette and the children spent their summers, with Edward joining them on the weekends.

On 5 December 1885, the newspaper *Berrow's Worcester Journal* printed a very brief paragraph, under the heading 'Violence and Rowdyism', describing Edward and Annette being attacked by a gang in Castle Street, High Wycombe, during which he was smeared with mud and left with cuts and bruises. Meanwhile, Annette, mother-of-three, proved her hardiness as she escaped by sprinting off and climbing not one, but two fences, into a builder's yard, from where she descended several feet to the railway track. The paragraph's brevity leaves the modern reader with more questions than answers, but one guesses that they must have attended a meeting or rally as the reporter writes that several other prominent local Conservatives were similarly targeted. The episode reveals an Annette that might otherwise have remained hidden from us. One wonders if her ability to look after herself was the result of being raised in the care of male relatives.

In 1886, the Carsons met the Londonderrys and, in particular, Lady Theresa, Marchioness of Londonderry (1856–1919). The British socialite, with a passion for politics, became a lifelong friend and supporter of Edward and his career. Geoffrey Lewis, in his biography *Carson: The Man Who Divided Ireland*, described their intense relationship as that of patron and protégé. They were near enough in age, but Lady Theresa positioned herself as Edward's mentor while he would go on to confide in her about a wide range of issues, both professional and domestic. Lewis also believes that Annette's ensuing feelings of jealousy and insecurity over this rapidly deepening friendship were wilfully ignored by her husband for the good of his career.

In 1893, Carson decided to quit Dublin to practise law in London and made his successful debut in Westminster on 2 February. For the moment, Annette and the children remained in Merrion Square until Edward could relocate them to London, which he did, after finding a flat in Cromwell Road, where the family lived briefly until Edward bought a house in Rutland Gate, Knightsbridge. At some point, Edward also bought a large holiday house in Rottingdean, a small village in Brighton. Annette may have been familiar with the village as her cousin, Reverend Frederick Tower, had been the vicar there. Biographers believe that Annette's unhappiness may have resulted partly from her loneliness and having too much time on her hands. Her husband worked long hours, and the three younger children were away at school. Meanwhile, her eldest, seventeen-year-old Harry, emigrated to Rhodesia, today's South Africa.

Furthermore, it is known that Annette felt out of her depth with their elevated social life. In fact, Lewis, in his Carson biography, describes her as being frightened of the powerful hostesses she encountered. Thanks to Lady Londonderry, the Carsons were beginning to mix with the best of London's society. If Annette was born illegitimately, as biographer Alvin Jackson claims, this would have been a source of anxiety to her, making her feel unworthy in esteemed company.

Edward's sister Bella stayed with the couple from time to time and witnessed Annette's exasperation at the deluge of correspondence that arrived from her husband's female friends, especially from Lady Londonderry, for Edward's eyes only. Geoffrey Lewis writes that, for Annette, Lady Londonderry was the most irritating of all Edward's friends as she frequently went to the House of Commons to watch him in action, nicknamed him 'the Solicitor' and constantly invited him to dinners at her house.

Annette was to prove her mettle once more, in August 1901, as she walked alone near her house in Rutland Gate, when five teenage boys surrounded her, blocking her passage, and one of them made a grab for the wrist purse attached to her left arm. Rather bravely, forty-six-year-old Annette tried to stop him with her open umbrella. Her refusal to hand over her purse obliged one of her attackers to seize her left hand, forcing her fingers back, severely injuring one of them, until the purse snapped from its chain and the gang ran away with its contents: five pounds, over thirty shillings and a first-class train ticket to Brighton.

The altercation caused her neighbour to look out his window and send his valet, Alexander Duret, in pursuit of the thieves. In fact, Duret managed to nab one of them, eighteen-year-old George Glangeld, described by the *Bristol Times* as a news vendor, although the *Dover Express* said he was a barber. At the police station, Glangeld caved immediately, saying that he didn't have the purse on him because the others had taken it. He supplied the names of his friends, which led to the initial arrest of seventeen year old Peter Platt. Officers on the scene were confident that they would catch the rest of the gang before too long. Indeed, the *Liverpool Echo*, reporting from the Old Bailey, on Thursday 15 August, named two other prisoners, John Pines and Thomas Snell. All confessed to being present at the time of the robbery but disagreed that any violence had taken place. One newspaper reported that the boys pleaded that hunger had driven them to such drastic action – the sight of the purse proving impossible to resist. In other reports, they said that they saw a woman approaching and instantly decided that if she had a purse they would take it. Consequently, they were charged with robbery without violence and sentenced to imprisonment with hard labour, with Glangeld's the longest stretch at twenty months.

Annette was in court too, accompanied by Edward, with her arm in a sling, and she identified Glangeld as one of her attackers. It is such a shame that her voice is almost lost, with few direct quotes from her in the articles that appeared in numerous newspapers. Instead, we hear from Detective Sergeant Morgan who arrested eighteen-year-old John Pines and sixteen-year-old Thomas Snell at Victoria Station on Saturday night. He described how the two boys gave themselves up, 'It is quite right. We were both in it with Glanny (Glangeld).' They also told him that Peter Platt was innocent of the crime. We hear from a second arresting officer, John Pickering, who quoted Thomas Snell, 'Platt was not in it. There were four of us. I took the purse and gave it to Pines.' Then we hear John Pines agreeing with Snell, 'Yes, that's right. There was £2 7s. 6d in it. We only had 14s. each. Some of the money fell out as we were running away.' Pines also admitted to throwing Annette's purse into the Thames.

One article, however, printed in *The Times* on Saturday, 24 August, contains Annette's words and a little more detail about that day in court. Before the prisoners were brought in front of the judge, they were paraded out back with other men in the courtyard and it is here that Annette, with Edward at her side, had to encounter them again. It must have taken courage to gaze at each man before finally identifying Glangeld. She also picked out Thomas Snell from the five or six men in front of her. When asked by the chief clerk about Snell's part in the attack, Annette replied, 'He was the youth who took the purse and forced my fingers back. I have no doubt about that.'

Annette did not write any letters that survive today, or keep a diary and, therefore, we end up judging her or, that is, her life with Edward, through his eyes and we must allow that he is not always fair about that life and appeared in want of sympathy from his female correspondents. For example, when the Carsons went on holiday to Maderia in 1909, Geoffrey Lewis quotes Edward's letters back to Lady Londonderry describing how boredom forced him to play roulette in order to make time go faster, 'I am sorry I came away … the loneliness of isolation …. I play roulette all the afternoon to pass the time, not very intellectual, is it?'

There is a family photograph taken outside the Carson home in Rottingdean that shows Edward looking detached from his family. The four Carson children are now adults. The women are seated, Annette in between Gladys and Aileen who must be visiting as she is wearing a jacket and a hat. Each has a small terrier-dog in her lap. Both Aileen's eyes and her mother's eyes are closed possibly due to the sun's glare. The black-and-white photograph is grainy, but it is probably summertime as the two large windows behind the family appear to be open. Also, both Annette and Gladys are wearing blouses and long skirts. The back row is more interesting. Edward stands in between Walter on his left and Harry to his right, all clad in full suits with starched collars and dicky bows. His sons appear to be talking to the photographer; Harry, with his left hand raised, might be issuing instructions on how to work the camera. Perhaps his wife is the photographer or Aileen's husband. The odd thing is that whoever is taking the photograph is standing off to the side of the family. The other odd thing is a very gloomy-looking Edward, wearing sunglasses and staring over Annette's shoulder, is not engaging with anyone in his circle.

By this stage, Edward preferred to visit the Londonderrys at their home in Mount Stewart in County Down, unaccompanied by Annette. In another letter to Lady Londonderry, written sometime around 1912, he describes the 'rot' he experiences following the arrival of his family who unknowingly inflict upon him 'the usual routine' that murders his zest for life.

Annette's health began to fail in 1910, and Edward's selfish response was to tell Lady Londonderry that 'I find it hard to realise and get accustomed to her being an invalid.' This from the man Annette had nursed through

The Carson family. Back row, left to right: Walter, Edward (wearing sunglasses and staring over Annette's shoulder), Harry (with raised arm). Front row, left to right: Gladys, Annette and Aileen.

serious illnesses earlier in their marriage. However, she cannot have seen much of Edward that year as he was engaged in one of his most demanding and famous cases, defending young George Archer-Shee, a thirteen-year-old naval cadet who had been accused of stealing from a fellow student at the Royal Naval College, Osborne, a training college for Royal Navy officer cadets on the Osborne House estate on the Isle of Wight. Edward was familiar with this school as his son Walter was a past pupil.

Three of Annette and Edward's four children may well have inadvertently proved a source of anxiety for their parents. For instance, if, as some biographers believe, Edward had hoped for his two sons to be inspired by his achievements and follow him into law, he was to be sorely disappointed as it transpired that both boys had their own ideas. Their eldest boy, Harry, had little interest in excelling at his expensive school and was, according to Geoffrey Lewis, 'wildly extravagant', his gambling debts needing to be covered by his father. When he decided to take off to Rhodesia, in Southern Africa, to be a farmer, Edward duly acquired a farm for him, thanks to his connection to English mining magnate, politician and Prime Minister of the Cape Colony, Cecil Rhodes (1853–1902).

However, farming did not work out for Harry as, amongst other things, his addiction to gambling took its toll. When the second Boer war broke out in 1899, Harry joined the Rhodes Cavalry but never distinguished himself as a soldier. Instead, according to Geoffrey Lewis, who refers to Harry as a 'taboo subject' within the Carson family, Harry arrived home with a South African wife, Harriet May, originally from Scotland, who was nicknamed 'the Boer' by her in-laws, which hardly seems complimentary. According to the 1911 census, thirty-year-old Harry and his wife, of six years, twenty-seven-year-old Harriet May, had two sons, four-year-old Edward, who had been born in Africa, and three-year-old Ian, born in Sussex. The household, at the time of the census, also included three servants. A few short years later, all would be woefully different for Harry.

As soon as he was old enough, Harry's brother Walter defied their father's expectations by joining the navy. Lewis writes that Edward and Walter's relationship only improved during wartime when Walter showed himself to be adept at manning the new submarines. Of course, it is easy to make something out of the boys' choices; Harry whisks himself off to Southern Africa while Walter literally sails away, both ultimately straining beyond their father's jurisdiction. Although it must be noted that both boys were funded by Edward to go their own way.

Meanwhile, Gladys, their youngest child, was frequently ill. She and her sister Aileen, described by Geoffrey Lewis as being 'beautiful' and 'high spirited', were devoted to their father, though Gladys would assert her own independence when, at the age of twenty-five, in 1910, she contracted tuberculosis and was sent off to a sanitorium in Switzerland, where she met and fell in love with an American.

As usual, her father poured out his feelings in a letter to Lady Londonderry, telling her he did not 'relish' foreigners, in particular foreigners like Gladys's boyfriend who he described as a 'terror'. By this stage, Aileen had married Gerald William Chesterman (1872–c.1974) and, as far as we know, did not cause her parents any undue concern.

In yet another letter to Lady Londonderry, Edward referred to his children as a 'rum lot', meaning strange or odd. It is frustrating not to know if his wife shared this assessment or if it caused problems between them. As time would tell, Annette had the stronger relationship with their sons.

Annette spent more time in Northgate House, in Rottingdean, where she was often alone. Perhaps being robbed and roughed up by those teenage boys back in 1901, had left its mark on her. One can only guess at how she passed her time. It would have been usual at the time for the lady of the house to pursue gardening, and she may have availed of the large glass conservatory at the back of the house and may also have enjoyed reading. Mike Laslett, honorary archivist and curator of Rottingdean Heritage, credits the Carsons with lending money to the villagers in 1909, to buy the Reading Room in High Street, which still stands there today.

Two years later, the residents of Northgate House were listed out for the 1911 Census form for England and Wales. Fifty-seven-year-old Edward Henry Carson is a barrister-at-law, his birthplace is Dublin and he describes himself as 'British' in the box for nationality. Sarah Annette Carson is fifty-six years old and, rather surprisingly, her birthplace is given as Raphoe, in County Donegal. Twenty-five-year-old 'single' Gladys is the only offspring present, with no American beau in sight (she never married). Meanwhile, the family is outnumbered by their staff of six, including five servants and a thirty-five-year-old professional nurse, Helen Mary Ferguson, testament to Annette's poor health.

Where, or what, is the Donegal connection to Annette? According to *The Constabulary in Ballymoney*, her father, Henry Kirwan, was based for a time in Donegal, specifically Raphoe. On joining the Irish Constabulary on 26 August 1840, he was sent to serve in County Antrim where he remained until January 1846. After that, he was stationed in Longford, Donegal, Monaghan, Cork,

Leitrim, Meath and Tipperary, and by 1 October 1867, had been promoted to County Inspector. Annette was born about 1855 and, unfortunately, since births were not registered in the state until 1864, it is impossible today to pinpoint the location of her birthplace. The census form was filled out by one hand, the handwriting is the same throughout, and the writer made a mistake by filling out the ages of the females beneath Edward's age, instead of using the separate column provided for women and, so, their ages have been struck through and rewritten beneath the right heading. Would Edward have made a mistake like this? Well, yes, he did. In 2015, Whyte's Auction House sold a slip of paper signed by Edward in black ink and there is no denying the fact that he filled out the 1911 form. However, his handwriting appears a little different from the handwriting that appears on the 1901 census form, though we can assume that this is also Edward's penmanship, albeit with a few more flourishes.

Researcher and writer Eleanor Fitzsimons offers an explanation for the Raphoe entry as Annette's birthplace. Between 1901 and 1911, the rules changed regarding the census form. The former merely required one to write 'where born' which, for both Edward and Annette, was Ireland. The latter asked for specifics, wanting the name of the parish where someone was born. Edward provided the answer and, so, Annette's birthplace must have been Raphoe, as opposed to the more usually supplied location, by Carson biographers, Clontuskart.

Annette died three years later, on 6 April 1913. Her death was reported in several British newspapers and, collectively, today's reader can only hope that they provide pertinent details about her life. It is peculiar to have to rely on newspapers since she was not a celebrity in her own right. Or was she? For instance, a tiny mention of her being robbed appears in *The Cornishman*, on 22 August 1901, and includes the provocative phrase, 'Lady Carson ... was well known in Dublin even before her marriage with the Solicitor General of England.' No explanation is provided for that 'well known', while the snippet, which appears in a column, headed 'Rank and Fashion', is only to inform the public that Lady Carson's daughter, who is not named, will be presented the following year.

According to the obituary that appeared in the *Evening Irish Times* on 7 April 1913, Annette had been grievously ill for some time. Before any mention is made of her husband, her father is named as Mr H Persse Kirwan, formerly of County Galway. Her marriage to her 'distinguished husband' in 1879, just two years after he was called to the bar, meant that she shared with him his early trials as well as the later successes. She was described as a 'dame' of the Primrose League, although there is little mention of her in the league's records aside from her presence at various meetings.

Inspired by Prime Minister Benjamin Disraeli's (1804–1881) concept that Britain should come together as one nation, the Primrose League was founded in 1883 by a small group that included Winston Churchill's father Lord Randolph (1849–1895) to spread Conservative principles throughout Britain. Neither political nor religious, it believed in Disraeli's ambition that the life of all citizens should be cared for equally by the country's institutions and government policies.

London's Weekly Dispatch also mentions the Primrose League and that Lady Carson had a 'practical' interest in politics and the League. Annette also loved animals, especially dogs. She was tall and very goodlooking, a charming and popular hostess and an inspiring influence in her husband's brilliant career.

The *Lincolnshire Echo* complimented Annette on standing by her husband's side for a 'strenuous' thirty-four years of law courts and politics. Anyone who knew her appreciated her 'sympathetic and earnest character' and can imagine the help she provided her husband in difficult times as he would have availed of the same judgement and counsel that Annette applied to the Primrose League. The *Liverpool Daily Post* notes that Lady Carson had been very popular in Irish society and also enjoyed her husband's popularity in Conservative circles.

And so on. Yet, Annette still feels like a shadow in her husband's story.

Rottingdean photographer George Bowles took a photograph of Annette's funeral cortège and Northgate House can be seen in the background. A wonderful description of her funeral appears on 12 April 1913 in the *Brighton Gazette* by someone who may have known her. They write that Lady Carson made her home in the hearts of the villagers who appreciated her kindness, humility and sympathetic ear. The tone is unapologetically sentimental; she had been like a mother to Rottingdean who mourned her now as a bereaved child. They describe the coffin being placed in the hearse and surrounded by flowers. One lone bunch of purple flowers is placed on the lid of the coffin and this is from Edward, with the words: 'Grateful for 34 years of love and devotion, her loving and afflicted husband.'

The cortège is made up of the family group leading the way to the church, followed by various politicians and members of Parliament, then the Northgate household and, lastly, 'a few friends'. Yet, the floral tributes provide evidence of her warmth and many friendships. Large clusters of red and white flowers were supplied by the family.

Cards and flowers were sent from as far away as Melbourne, Australia.

The funeral cortège of Annette Carson, passing by the family home.

Some of the messages are, one might feel, written out of respect for Edward, while others are more heartfelt, including this from Emma Tenterden, 'In loving memory of my dear friend and in ... hope that we shall meet again.'

Edward's younger sister, who watched Annette marry him all those years ago, also supplies flowers with the simplest of messages, 'From Bella'. Yet, perhaps the most telling of the tributes is that of Harry, her eldest child, who wrote, 'To my darling mother, and dearest pal, from Harry.' That 'pal' and, yes, 'darling' too, drums up the image of a woman with a sense of humour who was fun to be around, at least for those who knew her best.

She was buried in the graveyard of St Margaret's church, a short walk from Northgate House. An actual pyramid of flowers formed out of the large number of wreaths that were heaped onto her grave, including a Union Jack, sent by one lady, made up of red, blue and white flowers. Two other women laid an array of colourful spring flowers around the grave, and, on an otherwise dull day, the sun came out just as Annette's coffin was placed into the ground.

She is in good company, surrounded by artists. To her immediate left is the Glaswegian journalist and novelist William Black (1841–1898), while a few steps away, on the south-west buttress of the church, two plaques mark the resting place for the ashes belonging to painter and designer Sir Edward Burne-Jones (1833–1898) and his painter and engraver wife Georgiana, née MacDonald (1840–1920). According to the church's website, Burne-Jones chose this exact spot because it could be seen from the window of his home at North End House, thus allowing the surviving spouse to bid their dearly departed a cheery good morning from their breakfast table. Georgiana's sister Alice was the mother of writer Rudyard Kipling (1865–1936), who lived in Rottingdean from 1897 to1902.

Annette's last years were far from happy. Lewis writes that she had become something of a spendthrift and addicted to betting on the horses, a pastime that she shared with her eldest son. She had also put on a lot of weight and, following a possible series of strokes, was unable to get out of bed for weeks on end, unable even to brush a fly from her face. Once again, we must return to Edward's letters to Lady Londonderry in which he described Annette's final hours. At one point, she asked to see 'my old man' and when Edward bent over her, she reached up to embrace him and be kissed in turn. So, she surely loved him until the very end. Edward declared to Lady Londonderry that Annette 'was with me all my career' and that he had done his best to make her happy.

The summer before Annette died, Carson went to the spa at Bad Homburg, in Germany, a favourite destination of his, although he complained to Lady Londonderry that it was becoming more German and less English with every passing year. It is unclear as to whether Annette was with him. He was outside watching a tennis match, the seat beside him vacant, until, that is, an attractive young woman, sat down and engaged him in conversation.

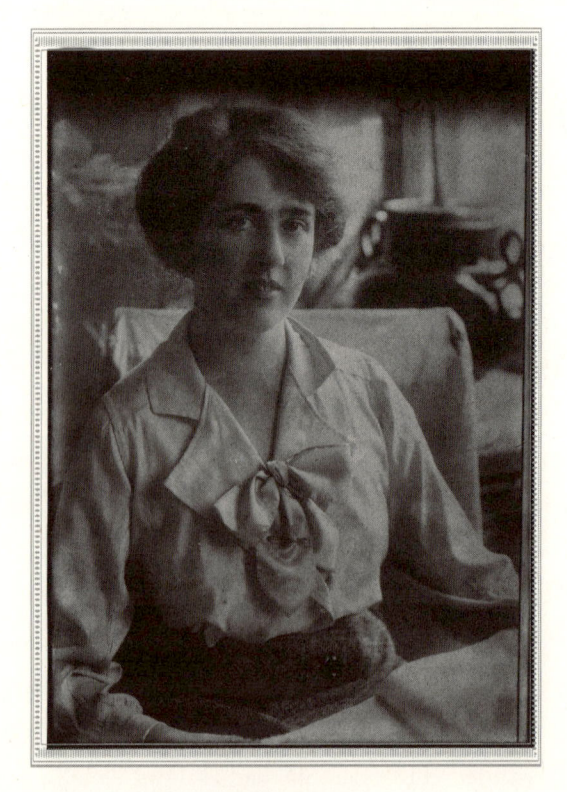

Ruby Carson

Her name was Ruby, and she was from Somerset, where her father was an officer in the army. She was also thirty-three to his fifty-eight years. However, just like Annette, it seems that on meeting Edward she found him instantly attractive in every way. She likely knew who he was as, apart from his politics, he was the celebrity barrister who had helped put Oscar Wilde behind bars, in addition to clearing the name of thirteen-year-old George Archer-Shee when he was accused of stealing a five-shilling postal order from a classmate. This is the case that would end up on stage in 1946, as *The Winslow Boy*, thanks to playwright Terence Rattigan, and made it to the screen, under the same name, in 1948.

We may never know how much they saw of one another in Germany, but that Christmas, in 1912, Ruby sent Edward a tie that she had knitted for him. On Boxing Day, he sat down and wrote to thank 'Dear Miss Frewen', referring to her as 'a very nice friend'. His letter was in German as, according to Geoffrey Lewis, a nod to their first meeting. However, if one assumes that Annette could not speak German, one would be forgiven for suspecting that Edward preferred to keep this correspondence with Ruby a secret. After all, he had instructed that Lady Londonderry's letters should be rerouted to his club as the frequency of her messages upset Annette.

Ruby and Edward's friendship developed in letters, although, unfortunately, only his letters to her survive. However, it does appear that she had set her sights on him. It is impossible to know how much the ailing Annette figured in her mind, but knitting a tie for a man she had met the previous summer seems like an indication of intimacy.

According to the *Newry Reporter*, Edward and Ruby married quietly on 16 September 1914 at Charlton Musgrave church, in Somerset. The wedding party consisted of Ruby's parents and siblings, the Marquess of Londonderry, Bonar Law (1858-1923) the future Prime Minister of the United Kingdom and Ruby's friend Mrs Hall Walker, matron and commandment of the Hall Walker Hospital for Officers, newly opened since August. The only one of Annette's children to attend was Aileen. She championed Ruby's jolliness and youth, writing to her father, 'I don't think I could have borne to let any of

Lady Londonderry's "choosings" steal you from me.' Aileen had looked after her mother during her last weeks and, afterwards, made herself available to her father as his housekeeper and companion. It was surely a relief that he was to be cared for once more.

Lady Londonderry had determined that Edward should marry again and appears to have had her own ideas about a prospective second wife. In her memoir, *Seventy Years Young*, Elizabeth Burke Plunkett, Countess of Fingall, describes her friend Lady Theresa Londonderry as a fine woman who was in love with love and always interested in her friends' love lives. Furthermore, she was apt to be upset if they did not take her advice in this matter.

Earlier that year, in May, the *Western Times* printed Edward's annoyance at being asked about a possible wedding, 'All statements are entirely unauthorised, and I resent the interference with my private affairs.' Perhaps smarting from Edward's robust refusal to discuss his private affairs, the *Western Times*, on 19 September 1914, scores a hit, telling its readers that considering the most 'emphatic' denials made about being engaged, the recent marriage of Edward and Ruby must surely have come as a big surprise for everyone.

The couple's honeymoon was impacted by sombre news from Belgium. The world was at war and the two Carson boys were to play their part.

In 1918, Harry was discharged from the army, having been seriously wounded in Ypres. Two years later, he took a position with the Royal Army Ordnance Corps (RAOC). It would seem that Harry's best days were already behind him. In 1922, the *Edinburgh Evening Newspaper* printed a story about his being destitute, his one possession being the suit he was wearing, and there is no mention of his wife. Perhaps he was paid for telling his story. He admits to being estranged from his father for the previous ten to twelve years and upon being asked further about the estrangement, Harry replies that 'matrimonial differences' were to blame though he pointed out that his father was educating his two sons. It is unclear what he meant, but it is surely possible that Harry might have struggled with his father's second marriage coming so soon after his mother's death. Furthermore, his stepmother was just one year younger than him, born in the same year as his sister Aileen. Did Harry suspect that his father's new relationship might have begun before Annette died? Or did Harry simply mean that his own marriage had fallen apart.

Three years later, on 23 April 1925, Annette and Edward's youngest daughter, Gladys Isobel Carson, died of chronic heart disease, having spent the previous two years, in a London nursing home. During the war, she had captained the Brighton branch of the Women's Auxiliary Force. According to her brief obituary in *St Pancras Gazette*, her father was her most constant visitor and did everything he could to improve her health. Gladys was buried in St Margaret's graveyard with her mother. She was just forty-one years old.

That same year, Harry ended up in the London bankruptcy court. An article about him, titled, 'A Chequered Career', appeared in the *Daily Mail* and one feels the absence of his mother. We learn that after Harry left the army, in 1918, following his injury, he received a pension of £1 a week. He rejoined the army in 1920, serving until September 1921.

After that, he had a series of jobs and was, at the time of his court case, making £4 a week as a billiard marker. The court found that Harry had no assets and debts totalling £904, which he attributed to living beyond his means before 1914 and, also, guaranteeing another person's loan. The *Gloucestershire Echo* adds the information, in October 1923, that the furniture at Harry's wife's address had been claimed by Lord Carson. It seems that Harry had lost everything he possibly had to lose.

Harry was interviewed by the *Manchester Evening News* on 19 October 1923. He had just turned forty-three and talked about his happy childhood, when the family lived in Dublin, where his father worked. He spoke of being born with a silver spoon in his mouth and how he and his siblings were devoted to Annette. He attended St Columbus College, Dublin, and then was sent by his father to Malvern College in England because, Harry said, his father had always wanted one son in the navy and one in the army. This conflicts with biographers who have surmised that Edward Carson was disappointed by his sons' refusal to study law.

Harry said he was seventeen when he sailed to South Africa, finding himself instantly thrust into a completely different life needlessly complicated by the fact that he spent all his money on the voyage. This left him unable to pay tax on his belongings, on arrival at Beira, and so everything was confiscated, including his revolver. Still two hundred miles from his destination, Harry had to sneak onboard a goods train for the three-day onward journey and confessed to crying with relief when he disembarked.

When the farm did not work out, Harry became a trooper in the British South African police and took a while to adapt to the rough-and-tumble life, remembering how he would drink a bottle of brandy before breakfast. He spoke of marrying a South African girl and about his chaotic relationship with money. On turning twenty-one, he inherited £500 from an uncle, which he promptly spent on 'all matter of riotous pleasures'. Wanting a change, he sailed home in 1906, whereupon his father sent him to Ottawa to take up a commission in the Canadian militia, but Harry arrived in Canada to find no such commission waiting for him. Determined to return home, he had spent all his money and was forced to take a lowly position on a cattle boat heading to Glasgow, a twelve-day journey he described as 'dreadful'. The only food available was curry, three times day, and his duties included feeding and cleaning up after the cattle onboard. Once home, he took a job as an inspector of the military canteens in Dublin. Two years later, bored with the quiet life, he returned to the army, obtaining a commission in the 3rd County of London Sharpshooters Yeomanry.

By this time, he had fallen out with his father, but Edward never banned him from the family home, pointing out that their son was welcome to visit his ailing mother. Harry said his mother always forgave him, no matter what he did, and helped him out until her death. When Annette died, Harry promised to mend his ways and, so, Edward paid him £2 a week but neither promise nor payment lasted.

Harry died in 1930, following a long illness, in King's College Hospital, London. A rather moving interview with him appears in *Reynold's Illustrated*

News, in May 1930, with the shocking heading 'Peer's Son Who Threw Away Chances and Sold Matches in the Street, Dies a Social Outcast in a London Hospital'. One might be tempted to imagine that Harry's greatest traits, his honesty and steadfast good nature even in the face of calamity, might have owed something to his 'best pal', his mother. Harry blamed himself for the mess he had made of his life. He spoke of Annette with devotion and completely understood his father's final refusal to help him, 'It isn't surprising that my father tired of my mode of living. I was hopeless, not a master of myself. As soon as I touched money, I seemed to lose my reason.'

His younger brother, Walter, married Violet Taswell Richardson in 1916, two years after Edward married Ruby. The following year, Violet gave birth to stillborn twins, a fact which was cruelly printed in the *Leamington Spa Courier* in the Births section. In 1928, Walter took up his new command of *Cyclamen*, one of several sloops (single-masted boats) whose patrolling of the coastline in the Persian Gulf had seen an end to piracy, murder and gunrunning. He was the Local Fishery Naval Officer from 1931 to 1933 and requested retirement from the navy in 1939. Perhaps having been through one world war left him with no appetite for a second one. But what did he do in the intervening years?

In March 1946, he was found dead in a flat in Jermyn Street, Piccadilly, a suspected case of gas poisoning. He was just fifty-five years old and was survived by Violet and their son and daughter. The *Leicester Evening Mail* runs with the tragic header 'Peer's Son Gassed Himself' after the West London coroner recorded a verdict of suicide. Walter had been living in the flat for the previous eight to ten weeks. His married daughter professed to finding Walter in good spirits when she saw him the night before he died and, aside from some health issues, could not explain why he would take his own life. Her name was Annette, although she would never have met her namesake. Walter was methodical in his actions. He locked his door, wrote several letters, including one to the coroner, explaining his death, turned on the gas heater, taped a rubber tube he must have purchased, that stretched from the heater to his bed, got under the blankets and ensured the bottom half of his face was covered, the tube at his neck.

Aileen, perhaps the happiest of Annette's children, died at her home in Worcester in August 1964. She was eighty-three years of age.

In September 1936, twenty-three years after Annette's death, the *Belfast News Letter* printed something peculiar. Edward had died the previous October, survived by Ruby and their son, Edward (1920–1987) and Walter and Aileen. Apparently, back in 1913, Annette died intestate, without a will, leaving '£5001 5s with net personality of £1001 5s.' It is curious that her barrister husband did not ensure that she made a will; she was ill for such a long time before she died. And then he died without taking any letters of administration of Annette's property. All that money was just sitting there when Harry was barely existing on a series of dead-end jobs. Incredibly, in 1936, Annette's money is granted to her successor, Ruby, a 'stranger in blood' who is not related to Annette. How did this come about? Surely, Annette's son and daughter had prior claims? Yet, there it is, in the *News Letter*, in black and white: after Edward's death the letters of administration of Annette's property 'have now been granted to his second wife, the Right Honourable Ruby Baroness Carson … the sole executrix.'

CHAPTER SEVEN

SINÉAD DE VALERA (1878-1975)

Wife of Éamon de Valera, politican

Historian Diarmaid Ferriter, in his *Judging Dev: A Reassessment on the Life and Legacy of Eamon de Valera*, writes that Sinéad de Valera deserved her own biography. Fortunately, when her youngest son, Terry (1922–2007), published his own memoir in 2004, he included within it his elderly mother's writings, as prompted by his questions, about herself and her life. For this reader, it is far too short but one might surmise that this was typical of the award-winning teacher, writer and poet who shunned the limelight of celebrity yet was beloved by all who met her.

Sinéad de Valera was born Jane Flanagan at ten o'clock on the morning of Saturday, 1 June 1878, in a small house in Skerries Street, Balbriggan, County Dublin. Her father, Laurence Flanagan (*b*.1836), a Kildare man who could remember the Great Famine, was a carpenter with a passion for books. He taught himself French and acquired a deep knowledge of English literature. He also loved his country and supported Charles Stewart Parnell (1846–1891) in his mission for Home Rule in Ireland.

When Queen Victoria (1819–1901) visited Ireland in 1900, Flanagan was in charge of a building crew at St Peter's church in Glasnevin, Dublin, and as

Sinéad de Valera

the royal procession passed by the church, he instructed his workers to keep their hats on and turn their backs on her.

Jane's mother, Margaret Byrne (*b*.1838) was from Balbriggan and met her husband when he was working on a house there. The couple emigrated to America where they befriended nationalist writer and journalist John Mitchel (1815–1875), whose quiet demeanour Laurence much preferred to the flamboyant political figure of Daniel O'Connell. The Flanagans returned to Ireland a few years later and then left once more to try their luck in Glasgow, where they realised that it was easier to make a living in Ireland.

On seeing his infant daughter's headful of auburn hair, Laurence nicknamed Jane (also known as Jennie) 'Doll'. When Jane was seven, the family were living in Dublin, where she went to St Francis Xavier School. A bright child, she was a huge favourite of Miss McVeigh who, despite being a poor teacher, inspired Jane to follow in her footsteps, which Jane did by becoming a student teacher, a monitoress, at the age of twelve. Apparently, she looked so young and fragile that she was called Tiny by her friends. She began teaching infants and five years later entered teacher-training college where the principal, a Jesuit priest, Father Waters, was most impressed by her. She became known for her ability to recite and give meaning to all manner of poetry, which was an offshoot of her love for the theatre and the stage. Her father brought her to see her first play when she was twelve and she was instantly smitten. Father Waters offered to pay for Jane to attend university, which she was most grateful for, but he died suddenly before anything was organised.

Jane spent most of her school holidays with her unmarried Aunt Kate, who ran a shop in Balbriggan. These were happy days, and she recalled the customers who frequented the shop, including the beggars who made a precarious living by singing or playing music on the street outside. Other types of beggars were the intimidating toughies, who dressed like sailors and were usually minus a limb, and hassled people for coins. An experience in later years with one of them, where he addressed Jane with words that she could never repeat, upset her so much that she confessed to still having nightmares about it fifty years later.

Jane described herself as having a nervous disposition. She could not listen to ghost stories and hated thunder and lightning. When Terry was six years old, and the de Valera family were living in Elm Villa, Sandymount, he saw a ghost, a woman, but could not make his mother believe him. He saw the woman again and then, a third time, he watched the family dog get agitated and bark at thin air.

In adulthood, Terry became interested in the occult and discovered who the woman may have been, a previous occupant of their house who was believed to have taken her own life there. Terry went so far as to interview elderly residents around Sandymount who remembered the woman and described to him the figure he had seen as a boy. His mother forbade him to speak about the ghost and he obeyed until they moved house, a few years later, when he then informed the whole family of what he had seen. Sinéad told him, in later life, that had she believed him at the time, she would have had to move immediately.

Jane saw Charles Stewart Parnell towards the end of his career when he came to Balbriggan to give a speech. A huge crowd welcomed him at the train station. Her brother Larry, who was lame, could not march with the crowd but drew up a placard which he proudly held aloft. On one side, he wrote Charles Stewart Parnell, while the other side advertised Cooney's Paste Blackening boot polish. On seeing the makeshift placard, Parnell went and shook Larry's hand, something the young boy and his sister would never forget. She was struck by how tired Parnell looked and remembered only the conclusion of his speech with the words, 'God save Ireland'.

When she was thirteen, Jane attended Parnell's funeral in Glasnevin, bringing Brigid, her six-year-old sister, for company, and cried her eyes out as the cortege passed by.

In September 1896, she enrolled at the teacher-training college in Baggot Street, where she came into her own as a gifted student, excelling in all her subjects, aside from needlework. Her first teaching job was in a school in Edenderry, County Offaly, where she struggled under a harsh disciplinarian, the principal, Mrs Moran, who would make contact in later years to apologise for how she had treated her young teacher.

Edenderry was where Jane embarked upon an extensive reading programme for her own pleasure, falling in love with the works of William Shakespeare, Charles Dickens, John Keats, Lord Byron and George Eliot, to name but a few. No doubt she was influenced by her father's passion for literature.

Whatever form Mrs Moran's questionable behaviour took – no details are provided – surely compensation was found in her brother, William Kennedy, who befriended the young teacher. Jane called him Uncle Bill and he introduced her to Irish current affairs. He was involved in the Nationalist Movement, having taken over writer and politician Arthur Griffith's newspaper, *The United Irishman*.

The Edenderry branch of the Gaelic League was founded in 1899, sparking Jane's interest in learning Irish. The league came into being in 1893 to provide Irish language classes for all in an effort to return Irish to its rightful place as Ireland's primary language.

Jane returned to Dublin in September to teach at her old primary school, St Francis Xavier's, where she spent the next three years, although, once again, it was not a happy time as she had little in common with her three other older colleagues who were 'West British' in attitude and manner. That November, she joined the Central Branch of the Gaelic League, and, in her memoir, she credits the league with providing the inspiration for the Easter Rising, quoting republican leader Patrick (Pádraig) Pearse (1879–1916), 'The Irish Revolution really began when the seven Proto Gaelic Leaguers met in O'Connell Street.' She was paraphrasing. Pearse's actual words were, 'For if there is one thing that has become plainer than another it is that when the seven men met in O'Connell Street to found the Gaelic League, they were commencing … not a revolt, but a revolution.' Note that Pearse uses the name O'Connell Street long before it was thus renamed in May 1924.

She describes that first evening in November, shyly knocking on the door of 24 O'Connell Street, to ask about joining the Irish class which had begun in

September. Jane soon found herself top of the class in examinations, winning prizes in competitions, and being asked to teach Irish to other students. It was around this time that she preferred to be known as Sinéad, the Irish version of her birth name Jane.

She quickly found herself in demand and in 1900 she was teaching Irish to women in the Colmcille branch on Arran Quay which was funded by Capuchin priests, and she also taught at the Connacht branch of Craobh Mhic Éil. In 1906, she was nominated as a delegate to the 1906 Ard Fheis Cúchalainn Branch, General Post Office, Cork.

Journalist and politician Ernest Blythe (1889–1975) attended Sinead's Irish class as an eighteen-year-old and describes how her classes were so popular that latecomers would have to stand, there not being enough seats for everyone. He also claimed that all the boys were in love with her, including, it would seem, himself.

Sinéad also joined republican activist Maud Gonne's (1866–1953) society *Inghínidhe na hÉireann* (Daughters of Erin), founded in 1900, where members took the name of an Irish saint or heroine and read papers about great Irish women to one another. Sinéad chose Fidelma, a female prophet in Irish mythology, before deciding to concentrate all her spare time on the Gaelic League which was making a difference with its focus on educating as many as possible about their heritage and language. *Inghínidhe na hÉireann* was dissolved in 1914 and merged into *Cumann na mBan* (The Women's League).

Sinéad remembers a trip to the Hill of Tara with friends from the Gaelic League. As they supped from a well, someone wished that Ireland would soon have her own king. 'Oh, no,' said Sinéad, 'a Republic', whereupon one of the older members, a woman, added, 'And may you be the president's wife.' Today, we might prefer that Sinéad was instead told that she should be president, but she accepted the compliment all the same.

Another highlight is when she took the lead role in the play *The Tinker and the Fairy*, written by Doctor Douglas Hyde (1860–1949), Ireland's first president. The stage was writer George Moore's (1852–1933) back garden in Ely Place. Moore also directed, though he encouraged the actors to do their own thing. The writer was much impressed by Sinéad's presence on the stage and presented her with an umbrella. Sometime later, she met the poet William Butler Yeats (1865–1939), who thrilled her by saying, 'I believe you and the wind were the success of the day.' Meanwhile, Irish playwright Edward Martyn (1859–1923) told her that she had what it took to be a professional actress.

In later years, writing about her love for acting, Sinéad confessed that she harboured some regret and longing, presumably for what might have been. Moore told her he could get her more stage work, and she received an invitation to join the Abbey Theatre. She acted in a few more plays with Douglas Hyde and was praised by the likes of republican activist Michael Davitt (1846–1906).

Meanwhile, as a teacher, she made a great impression on Arthur Griffith, founder of Sinn Féin and later president of Ireland, who wrote in December 1907: 'On Sunday week at 4 o'clock, Sinéad Ní Fhlannagáin [Sinéad's full Irish name] of the Ard-Craobh of the Gaelic League delivered a very sympathetic lecture to the children of Clann na hÉireann branch and their friends.'

So, it could be said that she was well on her own way to success both in terms of acting and of being a nationalist before one of her students derailed her unexpectedly.

Éamon de Valera (1882–1975), a twenty-eight-year-old mathematics teacher, started attending her Irish class in 1908. He was four years younger than her but that did not deter him from pursuing her. That Christmas, she was sent a plant and card which was merely signed '*Ó chara*' (from a friend) and suspected it was from 'Dev'. Sinéad was obviously the type of woman who made an instant and positive impression. Men, in particular, seemed very drawn to her. Her early photos show her to be a striking woman with dark hair and a gentle, open expression. Furthermore, 'Dev' was seeing her at her very best and surrounded by admirers. An outstanding teacher, Sinéad won a gold medal for her teaching methods in the 1907 Oireachtas competition.

Meanwhile, she described him as an 'exacting student'. After meeting outside class at a few céilís, they decided to get engaged the following June, with Dev wanting them to marry that very August. However, he had to wait until 8 January 1910 when they got married at nine o'clock on Sunday morning in Arran Quay church, St Paul's, in Dublin. Both had wanted the ceremony performed in Irish, obliging the priest to learn the language as fast as he could. Even so, Father Martin was so nervous on the day that, according to Sinéad, he married them several times over before he got all his words right. The guests were made up of family and close friends and the wedding breakfast was held in Four Courts Hotel on Inns Quay.

Their first house was 33 Morehampton Road, in Donnybrook, where their first child, Vivion, was born later that year, on 13 December. Sinéad loved to tell a story about sending her new husband out for supplies for their new home. He went to an auction and returned with an enormous chandelier, a battered cello and two copper plates painted over with rural scenes. Two years later, Sinéad gave birth to their eldest daughter, Máirín, on 12 April 1912. Sinéad quickly emerged as the sensible one, the one who dealt with the bills and kept the household running smoothly. And this became essential for the couple in 1913 when the Irish Volunteers – the republican response to the Ulster Volunteer Force – were founded, and Dev began spending less time at home. Sinéad gave birth to a second son, Éamon on 11 October 1913 and a third, Brian, on 26 July 1915.

Early in 1916, Sinéad sensed that something was up though her husband told her nothing and she would never have imagined that an actual armed rising against the British was being planned. She described the night of Holy Thursday, 20 April, when Dev went to bed in his clothes with his gun by his side. The following day, Good Friday, they knelt in their kitchen at 3pm and prayed as a family. Dev slept elsewhere that night and the following too, in Lieutenant Michael Malone's (1888–1916) house, who assured Sinéad that their victory would be 'bloodless'.

On Easter Sunday, Sinéad, who may not have known that she was pregnant, had a headache and was in bed when Dev called in to say goodbye. It would be the next day before she realised that that might have been the last time she would see him alive. The Sunday papers were full of Eoin MacNeill (1867–1945) calling off the Rising, something which she barely registered. When Easter Monday morning rolled in, The (Michael Joseph) O'Rahilly (1875–1916) arrived at the house, followed by a messenger sent by Dev asking her to send him his kit. Sinéad says that even then she did not fully grasp what was happening, not until Bridget, the maid, returned early from her evening off and told her that the Volunteers were digging trenches in St Stephen's Green.

Unfortunately, Sinéad told us nothing more about her doings throughout that week when Pearse, trade union leader and republican James Connolly (1868–1916) and their soldiers took over the General Post Office (GPO) in Dublin. Dev, leader of the 3rd Battalion, was stationed at Boland's Mills in Ringsend, which allowed surveillance of anyone approaching from Kingstown (Dún Laoghaire). With four children under the age of seven, no doubt Sinéad was kept busy with her usual routine, while what would become the most famous Rising in Irish history was over by Sunday. Pearse surrendered and the participants were rounded up and placed under arrest.

The next phase of this episode was shocking but succeeded in swiftly replacing the general population's annoyance at the rebels, who had brought chaos to Dublin, with heartfelt pity and solidarity. Surely the decision to execute the leaders of the rising, thereby making them martyrs, was one of Britain's most significant mistakes in all her dealings with Ireland.

Sinéad found out about the planned executions on 4 May when Bridget, the maid, asked her what 'extreme penalty' meant, having heard that the rebel leaders would be receiving it. Presumably reacting to her mother's expression, almost four-year-old Máirín told Bridget not to bring any more bad news.

Sinéad was grateful that her sister Bee was staying with her. Over the next few days, the sisters had to cope with hearing about daily executions and having the house invaded by the G-men, or Dublin Metropolitan Police, who would not let family or friends come near them. Sinéad was able to release the children, during the raids, to her neighbour, an Englishwoman who loved Prime Minister Lloyd George (1863–1945) but proved a steady friend at a difficult time. During one raid, when officers were searching through Dev's papers, one of them asked Sinéad what his nationality was, reminding her that she had left Dev's American birth cert in her parents' house. Bee and Sinéad held their nerve as the house was ransacked, but after the officers left, they broke down and cried. Bee retrieved the birth certificate, and two female friends brought it to the American Embassy. Sinéad visited the Ambassador and vice Ambassador several times and – typically – apologised for her intrusions, to which she was told that she was 'as welcome as the flowers in May'.

Sinéad believed that most people felt that Dev would be killed. Stepping onto a tram one day, a woman shouted at her that the world was praying for her husband. However, a reprieve in the executions was announced and Dev was, instead, sentenced to penal servitude for life. He wrote to her, telling her she could visit him and bring two others. She brought six-year-old Vivion and Máirín. They were forbidden to converse in Irish and it was a sober conversation, with Sinéad promising to be both mother and father to their children.

She had to leave Donnybrook in May and relocate to her parents' house in Phibsborough as all the money she had was £30 from selling Dev's motorcycle. The house was already crowded with her two sisters and brother still living at home. Later on, there would be donations from America and Australia, but for now, she relied on family and good friends. The three older children were sent to Balbriggan to stay with Sinéad's aunt Kate and there they would stay for the next year.

Years later, Máirín, in an interview for her father's biography by the Earl of Longford and Thomas P O'Neill, was at a loss to explain how her mother managed to get by at this time.

Sinéad's parents were elderly and frail, while her beloved older sister, Mary, was seriously ill with cancer. Because there was no money to hire a nurse, Sinéad had to take care of them all, including her baby Brian, and do all the housework and cooking while heavily pregnant. Her brother and sister had jobs and so could offer little help. Mary died in August and then Sinead's father had a stroke which was not fatal, but it was clear that his mind was deteriorating. She gave birth to a son in her parents' house on 3 November 1916, calling him Rúaidhrí in memory of nationalist Sir Roger Casement (*b*.1864) who had been executed on 3 August. By this stage, Dev was imprisoned in England. The baby was delivered by Doctor Tuohy, father of artist Patrick (1894–1930), who refused payment in response to the sacrifice made on his behalf by men like Dev.

Four months after burying her sister, Sinéad lost her mother on 11 January 1917. Unbeknownst to her, one of their friends, who was imprisoned in England for his part in the rising, had asked a prison officer about Dev's whereabouts. On being refused information, he was convinced, along with many others, that Dev was dead. Meanwhile, Sinéad struggled with two infants and a father who appeared to be slowly losing his mind. Good news, however, finally arrived in June with the release of all 1916 prisoners. Crowds gathered on the streets of Dublin to welcome the men back from England. Sinéad stayed home, in Phibsborough, with her babies and confused father. A neighbour knocked to tell her that Mr de Valera was on his way. She remembers thinking how strange he looked in his prison garb and noticed bug bites on his hands. Her husband was home at last, but not for long.

An election was held in County Clare, that July, to fill the seat left vacant by the recent death of MP Willie Redmond (1861–1917). Dev won by a huge majority. In September, their search for a new home brought them to Kinlen Road in Greystones. The older children were fetched from Balbriggan and the family were reunited.

The following year brought fresh troubles when the British government had Dev arrested in May, along with other prominent members of Sinn Féin, including Countess Markievicz (1868–1927) and William T Cosgrave (1880–1965). Dev was charged with plotting to import arms from Germany, and returned to prison in England. Sinéad, expecting him home on the last

GREAT IRISH WIVES

The De Valera family, Bellevue, Cross Avenue, Blackrock, July 1935, (back, left to right) Sons Rúaidhrí, Vivion, Éamon and Brian; (middle, left to right) Máirín, Sinéad, Éamon and Emer; (front) Terry.

train, had answered the door to a policeman who warned her that the house was about to be raided as it was believed that she was sheltering Countess Markievicz. In fact, it was a cousin from England who was staying with her. In June, her beloved Aunt Kate died and in August, Sinéad gave birth to a second daughter, Emer. Dev wrote to say he was glad that Máirín had a sister.

Autumn proved terrifying due to the Spanish Flu, a deadly flu that would, over the next two years, kill approximately fifty million people worldwide.

Following a day out with Bee in Greystones, Sinéad and the children waved her off at the station, whereupon she noticed Vivion looking pale. One by one, all the children succumbed to flu, including two-month-old Emer and Molly, the maid. Miraculously Sinéad did not catch the virus, which was, she believed, the only reason why none of the children died. She took care of everyone as the hospitals and doctor surgeries were completely overrun.

Aided by fellow republicans Michael Collins (1890–1922) and Harry Boland (1887–1922), Dev escaped Lincoln Prison on 3 February 1919 and quietly slipped back into Ireland, where he went into hiding. The great escape proved a real boost to Dev's popularity as people marvelled over the story and wondered where he was. Sinéad did her best to stay out of the spotlight as false reports circulated that she had received a letter from Dev. When a photographer knocked to ask if he could take a photo of her and the children reading the non-existent letter, she refused.

Her eighty-three-year-old father died on 12 March 1919, and although her husband was in Ireland, it was too dangerous for him to attend the funeral. Furthermore, he had yet to meet his daughter Emer. One night, Collins and Boland brought Dev to Greystones. The children were not told that their father was home, although Brian and Rúaidhrí did ask Sinéad if she was bringing coffee to the gentleman in the dining room.

The next few weeks must have felt precious. Sinéad had her first night out in years, attending a reception in the Manson House and meeting old friends. As 3 June was Sinéad's forty-first birthday, Dev kept the day free to spend with the family. This was the first time in four years that he was not behind bars for his wife's birthday.

However, the family gathering was not to be. A messenger turned up before lunch to inform Dev that he was going to America. Collins had finalised the details enabling him to sail incognito – Dev hoped to raise support, and money, in America both for an independent Ireland and for himself as Ireland's unofficial president – but he had to leave immediately. In truth, Sinéad hardly saw her husband during the five years that she spent in Greystones. One day, she overheard Rúaidhrí ask Brian who this Dev was. 'I think he is Mummy's father' was the reply.

Dev's American tour, from June 1919 to November 1920, was both wildly successful and also wildly problematic and he did miss his family. In Dev's absence, Michael Collins made himself available to Sinéad, bringing her news from America and money, and even playing with the children, bringing them jigsaws and books. And, perhaps, he was learning Irish from Sinéad who referred to him in a letter as 'my Irish pupil'. Meanwhile, feeling that he had to do something to help his beleaguered president, Harry Boland arrived at Sinéad's door, in May 1920, to coax her into sailing to America. She hated the idea of leaving the children; her eldest, Vivion, was only ten years old. However, it was impressed upon her that her husband, Ireland's president, needed her and perhaps a patriotic slant was also applied.

Collins organised a false passport for her, under the name of Margaret Williams, and a female friend agreed to accompany her. Her son Terry writes that his mother was not a good traveller, a fact which was compounded by her constant fear that at any moment it would be discovered that she was not Miss Williams; Collins had got her height wrong, putting down 5ft 10 inches instead of 5ft 4 inches. Furthermore, she was very seasick and arrived at New York in the middle of a thunderstorm. Nothing about the trip suggested it was going to be an enjoyable one, and, indeed, it was not.

In their biography of Dev's secretary, *The Life and Times of Kathleen O'Connell*, Patrick and Paul Murray quote a letter, dated 18 November 1920, Sinéad sent Kathleen on her return from America. Sinéad writes that she regrets making the visit, describing it as a 'big mistake' to go so far for just six weeks. Decades later, Sinéad also referred to the trip as one of the biggest mistakes she had ever made. Dev was more shocked than joyful on finding her in his hotel room in the Waldorf Astoria. He had no time to spend with her and was sorely stressed from being thwarted at every turn by Irish American nationalists, journalist John Devoy (1842–1928) and politician Judge Daniel Coholan (1867–1946), who both had taken a strong dislike to him.

The six weeks dragged by for Sinéad; she spent a lot of time alone in the hotel, and it would only be natural if she felt rejected by her husband even though it was not his fault. She missed the children who were being minded in Greystones by her sister Bee and brother-in-law Dick Cotter. Meanwhile, times were fraught in Ireland as a war of Independence was finally being fought against the British, and one can imagine Sinéad's fear and upset on hearing about the sacking of her hometown, Balbriggan, on the night of 20 September 1920. Her siblings Larry, Kitty and brother-in-law Andy were caught up in the chaos unleashed by British soldiers who went on the rampage after one of their number had been shot dead by unseen forces. Since the real culprit(s) had escaped, the soldiers attacked the civilian population, and beat two young men to death, leaving their broken bodies in the street. After that, they torched twenty-five houses along with a hosiery factory.

With Sinéad's departure date approaching, there was concern as to how she and her friend could safely travel back to Ireland. Finally, it was agreed that the two women should go home via Canada and so they travelled north to Montreal, but all the hotels were booked out. Eventually they were put up in a house where the occupants spoke only French. For Sinéad, it was an unsettling night and when she slept, she had horrible nightmares. They set sail for Ireland in early October.

Dev arrived in Ireland just before Christmas, but it was too dangerous for him to return to Greystones, and so, a friend collected Sinéad on Christmas Eve and drove her to her husband's safe house. Sinéad wrote that Dev would not see Greystones until the following July when he told her that in his pocket was a letter from Lloyd George proclaiming a truce. The war was over.

Sinéad described the months of the truce as happy ones, but then all changed following negotiations that December with the British government, for which Dev elected to stay home and sent over a contingent in his place that included Michael Collins and Arthur Griffith.

Sinéad read the treaty's terms as signed by Dev's representatives and the British government in a newspaper on 7 December and professed to being saddened by it, hoping that it would be reworked into something better. She met a friend, Father Rafter, who remarked that she did not seem to share everyone else's elation. When her son Vivion read the paper, he asked her if the treaty was a good one since he felt that 'Mick' would not have signed something that was not good. Meanwhile, her sister Bee denounced the treaty as partition.

The biggest upset caused by the treaty was what some viewed as the loss of the six northern countries from the republic of Ireland. Ireland was now in two parts, each with its own government, with the majority in the north preferring to maintain links with England in every way. That evening, when Sinéad's husband asked her what she thought of the treaty, she answered that though she knew that everyone else was delighted with it, she was not.

Christmas 1921 was far from jolly with Dev distracted by political events. Meanwhile, the household maid, Molly, went to visit her sister in England. Sinéad was left to do all the household chores and the cooking and child-minding which proved a distraction from Irish affairs. Following Dev's initial protests in the Dáil surrounding the treaty, tensions sprouted as conflicting feelings hardened, requiring one to choose a side and damn the cost in terms of friendships and family relations. Six months of bitter debate resulted in the first shots of the Irish Civil War ringing out on Tuesday, 28 June 1922, with the bombardment of Dublin's Four Courts by Collins's pro-treaty side. Ireland was at war once more but this time with herself.

Dev left Greystones for the foreseeable future and sent Sinéad a letter in which he wrote that he knew she would be brave – as if she had a choice. There were six children to be cared for and the same qualities that they benefitted from, her strength and independence, allowed their father to give himself entirely over to his professional life. In her memoir, she described her sorrow over former friends and colleagues turning on each other and she named some of the victims from both sides.

Sinéad not only had to be brave as a woman with young children in wartime, but also as the wife of Éamon de Valera she was a target, and where once she endured raids by English soldiers, her home was now invaded by Irish Free Staters. One of them told her that he was still a follower of Pearse, but she asked how he could claim that and still be raiding her house. She might have been thinking of Pádraig Pearse's mother Margaret (1857–1932) who was one of Dev's biggest supporters. Another one attempted to frighten her by telling her that Éamon best beware.

Once again Sinéad was coping with all whilst pregnant, giving birth to Terry, her seventh child, on 27 June 2022, a few weeks after her forty-fourth birthday.

She deals with three prominent deaths very swiftly in her memoir. She believed that the murder of Harry Boland, in July 1922, only increased the hatred between both sides. A few weeks later, Arthur Griffith died from natural causes and the very next week the butcher boy knocked on her door to tell her that 'Collins is gone'. One can argue that she would have been taken up with the new baby but there is hearsay to suggest that her feelings about Collins's death in an ambush were far stronger than she could admit to. She wrote that seven-year-old Brian was very fond of Mick, and that she had greatly admired Griffith as a girl, adding briefly that Mick was a friend of hers too.

This author has heard how a republican nationalist, and future politician, and ally of Dev, confided in mutual friends that Sinéad refused to share a bed with her husband after Michael Collins was killed. Of course, it cannot be proved today but it makes for an interesting conversation. Likewise, the entry about Sinéad in *Modern Irish Lives Dictionary of 20th Century Biography*, which mentions the rumour that she was actually pro-treaty, without providing any further detail.

In any case, when speaking about Collins in later years, Sinéad explained that she felt he was duped into signing the treaty through his inability to resist flattery, his 'Achilles Heel' as she saw it, which was gladly taken advantage of by the British. This flaw in Collins, she added, was not shared by men like Parnell or Dev.

Every new death must have increased Sinéad's anxiety about her husband.

Perhaps feeling vulnerable and isolated in Greystones, she decided to relocate to Dublin and was put in touch with a woman who had just bought 18 Claremont Road, Sandymount and was looking for tenants. On 2 November, Sinéad's friends rallied around her, taking the older children off her hands, while she moved herself and four-month-old Terry into the new house. The next day, they celebrated Rúaidhrí's sixth birthday.

Dev was in hiding a few miles away at 11 Mount Street, which was the closest that he had lived to his family in quite some time. Still, it was Sinéad who had to deal with continuous raids on the new house, while presumably hiding any fear from their seven children. Her strategy was to talk Irish to the raiders, and she told the children to do the same.

Things came to a head in the summer of 1923. From his hiding place, Dev called for a ceasefire which was not immediately embraced by the Free Staters. He received a request in July, from Sinn Féin delegates in Tipperary, to travel to Ennis and take his place as their number one choice in the imminent general election. This meant leaving his safe house.

Sinéad was at mass in Sandymount when she heard that Dev had been arrested in Ennis. This must have been a particularly frantic time as there was a band of extremist Free Staters, known as The Murder Gang, being incited to assassinate Dev in revenge for Collins's murder.

It took Sinéad a while to discover where Dev had been taken. Finally, on 23 August, she received a telegram informing her that he was being held in Arbour Hill. She wrote to Kathleen, his secretary, about going to the jail with a letter, cardigan and shirt and being told that the letter would only be given to Dev after it had passed the censors. Meanwhile, she was not allowed to see him, nor was he allowed to write to her. She planned to return to Arbour Hill with another parcel of his possessions the following day and urged Kathleen not to let anyone take any dangerous risks to rescue Dev. Clearly, she felt that enough blood had been shed on her husband's behalf.

In October, Dev was moved to solitary confinement in Kilmainham Gaol. Here, he attended to his books and studies, and he was now allowed to send out two letters a week. He asked Kathleen for his mathematics books and notebooks and began learning Gregg shorthand, with a view to compiling an Irish version until he heard it had already been done. We can be sure that Sinéad did not have that kind of time on her hands.

Dev was returned to Arbour Hill in the spring, where, by the end of June, Sinéad and one of her children were allowed to visit him. In another letter to Kathleen, Sinéad wrote that she was happiest when surrounded by her children, whilst regarding Dev, she could only hope for good news. Her patience was finally rewarded with his release on 16 July 1924. Dev had served his final prison sentence. For his first public meeting outside Dublin, Dev chose to speak in Ennis on the anniversary of his arrest. Sinéad refused to attend, preferring to spend the day exactly as she had the previous year, at Mass in Sandymount, praying that all would be well.

On Sunday, 9 February 1936, the de Valera family suffered a terrible loss. The day began with twenty-one-year-old Brian and his mother attending eight o'clock Mass. Brian was horse-mad and, after Mass, headed off to his riding school where, because his favourite horse was out, he saddled up an unfamiliar horse for his customary ride in the Phoenix Park. Quite quickly, the horse bolted, and it was all that Brian could do to cling on to its neck as it dashed in under tightly packed trees where a branch caught Brian on the back of his head, flinging him to the ground. He was rushed to the Mater Hospital, and someone rang the de Valera house around 1pm. Dev and Éamon Junior raced to the hospital, while Sinéad stayed home and sent Rúaidhrí, Emer and Terry to church to pray for their brother. Despite the great effort made by the Mater's staff, Brian died shortly before 3pm.

In his memoir, Terry de Valera wrote that twenty-three-year-old Máirín had to take her mother's place and receive the visitors that descended upon the house as Sinéad was completely inconsolable. It must have seemed such a dreadful wrong that the son who had sat beside her that morning in church was dead. How often over the coming months must she have replayed that precious hour in her mind, hearing his responses to the Mass, watching his head bowed in prayer as he received Holy Communion and made his way back to her side.

The funeral took place at Booterstown church, which proved too small for the huge number of mourners in attendance, and from there Brian was buried in the family's newly acquired plot at Glasnevin Cemetery. Messages poured in from across the world, from leading figures such as Mussolini, the Pope, King Edward VIII and the emperor of Ethiopia. Sinéad wore only black for the next two years and while she could never bring herself to see her son's grave, Dev visited it every single Sunday morning for the next few years.

When King Edward VIII (1894–1972) caused a sensation months later by abdicating from the throne to marry his lover, American divorcee Wallis Simpson (1896–1986), Sinéad, who abhorred divorce, could not help feeling sorry for him. Terry de Valera thought it was because of the personal telegram she and Dev received from the king when Brian died.

Terry de Valera describes his fourteen-year-old self meeting one of his heroes, aviator superstar Charles Lindbergh (1902–1974) and his wife Anne Murrow Lindbergh (1906–2001) in Dublin Castle, in November 1936. Lindbergh was being consulted as to the possibility of transatlantic flight routes from the west coast of Ireland, the forerunner of Shannon Airport. There is no mention of Sinéad being at the dinner which took place nine months after Brian's death. In hindsight, it is a pity if the two women did not meet, although, perhaps, they did, away from the flashbulbs and journalists. Anne Murrow documented her life in her published diaries and letters but makes no mention of meeting Sinéad in 1936. Of course, if they did meet, one can imagine Sinéad asking for it to be kept private. In time, these two wives would have a lot in common. Both hated being in the public eye but were married to famous men whose careers had to take precedence over anything else. Both were well educated and would go on to be bestselling writers. Both would have large families, and, by 1936, both had lost a son. The 1932 infamous kidnapping and murder of Anne's one-year-old son, Charles, had shocked the world.

Neither Sinéad's memoir nor Terry's mentions her writing career. It is almost as if a separate Sinéad wrote her children's books and plays. With her children full grown, she devoted more time to her writing, and maybe Brian's death acted as a catalyst, forcing her to confront herself and decide what was truly important to her, as well as writing providing an escape, a distraction, from her grief. Before her marriage, her life had been fuelled by passion for the Irish language, Irish literature and drama and now she returned to them.

When her husband became Ireland's third president in 1959, Sinéad was obliged to move into Áras an Uachtaráin, something she did reluctantly. Terry felt she was lonely in such grand surroundings, although she enjoyed her solitary walks in an area she nicknamed 'the wilderness', a wooded area on the north-western part of the grounds. She told him that she said her prayers as she walked, a plausible excuse to be left to walk alone. Presumably, she was also composing her stories and thinking of her son Brian who met his fatal accident nearby. One day when she was late returning, an *aide-de-camp* was sent out to look for her and found her 'chatting' to a buck deer. She had a great love for animals, as did Dev, and they willingly responded to her gentleness.

She certainly made a conquest of President John F Kennedy (*b.*1917) when he visited Ireland in June 1963, a mere five months before his assassination. It is not hard to imagine how this dashing young man who relished his Irish origins took to the eighty-five-year-old Sinéad. For one thing, he had had to leave his heavily pregnant wife Jacqueline behind. (The baby, Patrick, would live only thirty-nine hours following a difficult premature birth in August.) Furthermore, the American president and Sinéad shared a deep love for poetry. He spent an evening at Áras an Uachtaráin, where she recited a poem she had written about exile, which included the lines: *Thus returns from travels long, years of exile, years of pain, to see Old Shannon's face again* … Kennedy, whose great grandfather left Ireland during the Famine, was so taken with the poem that he took out an envelope and pen and scribbled down bits of it to be included in his departure speech the following day. That speech can be watched online. President Kennedy told the crowd how he spent the previous night sitting next to 'one of the most extraordinary women' he had ever met, 'who knows so much about Ireland and Irish history'. Then he recited the lines he had written down and fervently promised that he would be back to see Old Shannon's face again.

Terry de Valera quotes from the letter that the American President sent Sinéad when he got back to America, in which he tells her that sitting next to her at lunch and dinner would always be a highlight of both his trip to Ireland and his term in office.

She wrote in Irish and English, and translated and rewrote classic fairy stories, and with her love of the stage, it is no surprise that she also wrote plays for children. Her best-known works include *Coinneal na Nodlag agus sgéalta eile* (1944) and *Áilleacht agus an Beithidheach* (1946). This is the sort of work that allows the writer to remain elusive but perhaps Sinéad can be glimpsed here and there. For instance, in the story 'The Treacherous Waters', when a grateful young man tries to thank a widow and her son for saving his life, the widow assures him that he was 'as welcome as the flowers in May'. We remember Sinéad hearing those same words when she apologised for her numerous visits to the American embassy, following Dev's imprisonment after the Easter Rising. In another story, 'The Mountain Wolf', there is a Ruairi and a Sheila, while it is the young boy, Brian, whose bravery saves the day, both for his ailing mother and another mother who, thanks to his actions, is finally reunited with the son she had lost to an evil spell. However, Brian refuses to take all the credit, reminding his mother that Conn, the travelling man, and family friend, provided the crucial information that ultimately resolved the two situations. When their father must go away at a pertinent time, it is the travelling man that keeps the children company and solves the family's problems, singing songs, playing games and telling them stories – exactly what Michael Collins did for the de Valera children when Dev was in America.

In 'The Three Fires', the character Brian is described as 'the bravest and strongest' of his siblings and later on he is told that he has his mother's eyes. In 'The Haunted House', Brian, whose good deeds will rescue his mother from poverty, has a great way with animals who happily follow him on his journey.

Particularly poignant is 'The Spoiled Princess' where the character Brian is a brave young chieftain who is in a coma after being thrown from his horse. The princess must exchange her beloved dog for a magic potion that brings Brian back to life. And there are many more examples like this.

Dev's second term as president came to an end in June 1973. The day that he and Sinéad were leaving Áras an Uachtaráin, Terry found his ninety-five-year-old mother alone in the sitting room. On sighting him, she quoted the Irish writer and poet Thomas Moore (1779–1852), 'Our hearts, like thy waters, be mingled in peace.' Terry knew she was happy to leave, that the big house had never really been a home for her. He tested her memory, asking her to recite her favourite poem, Thomas Gray's (1716–1771) 'Elegy Written in a Country Churchyard' which she did, all thirty-two stanzas, without a stumble.

She and Dev moved to Talbot Lodge, which was attached to Linden Convalescent Home in Blackrock, County Dublin. Towards the end of 1974, the deterioration of her physical health saw Sinéad transferred to the Old Mater private nursing home and there she died on Tuesday, 7 January 1975, just one day short of her sixty-fifth wedding anniversary. Her funeral mass in the Pro-Cathedral drew huge numbers and she was brought to Glasnevin, where her family fulfilled her wish to be buried next to Brian. A few months later, on 2 September, the De Valera family returned to the cemetery for the state funeral for their father.

In 2016, Balbriggan's 1916 Commemorative Committee and Historical Society erected a plaque in memory of Sinéad de Valera – Daughter of Balbriggan – in Quay Street. The ceremony was attended by surviving family members, including Sinéad's grandson Éamon Ó Cuív and granddaughter Nora Ní Chuív.

Self-portrait of Margaret Clarke (1884–1961)

CHAPTER EIGHT

MARGARET CLARKE (1884-1961)

Wife of Harry Clarke, stained-glass artist

An article about Margaret Clarke, cleverly titled 'Treasured: Rediscovered artist shatters stained-glass ceiling', appeared in the *Irish Independent* on 22 February 2019. Margaret's work was having a moment, sales-wise, which, according to the writer, was well deserved for the artist whose reputation had been all but blotted out by that of her artist husband Harry (1889–1931). The writer acknowledged the splendour of Harry's work but argued that this should not diminish his talented wife, whose work was 'incisive, insightful and strong'. Margaret, the writer declares, was so much more than Mrs Harry Clarke.

The newspaper article concerned Margaret's painting 'Double Portrait of Two Girls', which was to be auctioned by Whyte's Irish and International Irish Art Auction on 4 March, and there was a story behind it. Previously, the painting had gone on sale in 2009, as part of the estate of Doctor Karl Mullen (1926–2009), consultant gynaecologist, who had captained the Irish rugby team and the British Lions on their 1950s tour to Australia and New Zealand. No name appeared on the painting but Mealy's Auctioneers, who were selling it, had reckoned on artist William Orpen's (1878–1931) involvement and, so, labelled it, 'Circle of Sir William Orpen'. In fact, Margaret was Sir William's favourite student at the Dublin Metropolitan School of Art. And some bidders recognised Margaret's work, driving up the price until it sold for €10,000, which was just a fraction of the payment, made in 2018, for her 1914 self-portrait, which went for €48,000.

In her essay in the *Irish Arts Review*, 'Darling Margaret: A Look at Orpen's Favourite Pupil', Hilary Pyle writes of the confusion surrounding Margaret Crilley's birthday. Margaret was born into a Catholic family in Newry, and later descendants provided Theo Snoddy with the birth date 29 July 1888 for his 1996 *Dictionary of Irish Artists*. However, thanks to the efforts of art historian Carla Briggs, we now know that Margaret was born four years earlier on 1 August.

Little is known about Margaret's mother, Ellen, who came from a local farming family, while her father, Patrick Crilley, was a hackler in the flax trade, which meant that he combed out and straightened, by hand, the fibres of flax, or hemp, to prepare them for being spun. The Crilleys and their six children lived at 17 Thomas Street in Newry, County Down, where Margaret was born, and a blue plaque, unveiled in 2007, marks the house today.

By the time of the 1901 census, Margaret and her family were living at 29 Kiln Street, in the Newry West Urban district, County Down. The original form is available online. In 1901, Patrick Crilly was sixty-four years old, while Ellen, his wife, was fifty-two. It is assumed that this spelling of Crilley was a clerical error. The form details: Fourteen-year-old Minnie (Mary), with an occupation of 'scholar'; sixteen-year-old Maggie (Margaret) was a teacher in a national school; twenty-one-year-old Terence, was also a teacher; twenty-two-year-old Michael was a storekeeper at Waterworks, while twenty-four-year-old Ellen was a housekeeper. Everyone was listed as having two languages, Irish and English, and, perhaps more tellingly, everyone, including both parents, could read and write.

Marie Hammond Callaghan, in her 1998 article about Margaret for the *Atlantis Journal*, described Patrick Crilley as an intelligent man who was known as the writer for his parish. He believed in the importance of a good education and ensured that *all* his children received one.

Hilary Pyle writes that Margaret had a gift for drawing and a love for learning that would have been encouraged by her parents. Certainly, the word 'scholar', chosen by whichever Crilley filled out the census form, to describe the occupation of fourteen-year-old Minnie (Mary), suggests a respect for books and learning. Margaret was already a teacher by trade but was ambitious to combine her enjoyment of teaching with her love of art. Her talent as a pianist had her briefly considering a career in music, but art won out, and when she was twenty-one years old, she started attending night classes at Newry Municipal Technical School.

The school, like other technical schools around Ireland, had been founded to meet the needs and demands of local industries. The night classes were relatively new, only coming into effect, in Newry, in January 1903, and quickly proved a success. The school was formally opened that September, in the presence of Sir Horace Plunkett (1854–1932), who championed education for improving agricultural practices, with 439 pupils studying a variety of subjects including carpentry, engineering, drapery, retail, art and so on. A photograph online shows a shorthand class, *c.*1900s, taking instruction from teacher Teddy Crilley, who also taught at Newry's Christian Brothers Grammar School. Two or three females are sitting in the front row while the rest of the students are male.

Hilary Pyle points out Margaret's good fortune in wanting to learn how to teach art at a time when it was considered an important component of the school curriculum. Margaret's commitment to this specific career indicates both that her family supported her ambition and that she was a gifted artist. Minnie Nagle was the art mistress in Newry, a talented artist who had won several awards during her student days at Cork's Crawford School of Art. In her 2016 essay about the Crawford School of Art, art historian Vera Ryan writes that Minnie Nagle received particular praise from artist Harold Rathbone (1858–1929) for her needlework which included a fan depicting peacocks and her design for a damask tablecloth. Presumably, Minnie encouraged Margaret towards the South Kensington Board of Education Art exams in 1905. An extremely detailed document, from 1905, numbering over fifty pages, sets out the regulations for the instruction and training of pupil-teachers. Margaret achieved first-class honours in Geometrical Drawing – the ability to create designs out of shapes like spheres and ellipsoid circles– and Drawing on the Blackboard – producing legible visual information in a classroom setting. The following year, she passed an exam in Light and Shade. She also studied Elementary Science and passed her Physiography exam – the study of physical features of the earth's surface – achieving a First Class in PP and S Geometry – the mathematics of shape. This sort of technical training would help her achieve an accuracy in later works such as her 1909 pencil study, 'A Girl's Head'.

Margaret had another ambition beyond teaching art and that was to leave Newry. Her granddaughter Sara Bourke told Marie Hammond Callaghan that she wanted to study in Dublin as she found her native town restricting and 'too parochial'. Bourke also described her grandmother as an intellectual who read widely and always had her own library of the most up-to-date novels, nonfiction and books of literary criticism.

Her commitment and hard work were duly rewarded when she won a scholarship for Dublin's Metropolitan School of Art (DMSA). She made the move from Newry to Dublin in 1907, to study painting under artist William Orpen (1878–1931) whilst pursuing her Art Teacher's Certificate. And she would not be living alone since the scholarship money allowed her to bring her younger sister Mary (Minnie) with her.

In 1877, the British government bought the art school's previous incarnation from the Royal Dublin Society and the school was renamed the Dublin Metropolitan School of Art (DMSA), which was supported by the Department of Art and Science. Then, in 1900, the school passed over to Horace Plunkett's new Irish Department of Agriculture and Technical Instruction though it was still funded by the British Treasury. A shake-up by its new owners saw an increase in craft courses, including stained glass, enamel and metalwork, along with life drawing with William Orpen. In 1924, the school was taken over by the Department of Education and, twelve years later, it became the National College of Art.

In their book *Irish Art 1920–2020*, writers Catherine Marshall and Yvonne Scott describe the school under Orpen's influence as preferring tradition over originality. Margaret became a favourite student of Orpen's who taught twice a year in the school, for a fortnight, in summer and autumn. He admired both her oil painting and life-drawing skills. Having already proved herself a winner of scholarships, Margaret went on to win both silver and bronze medals in the British Board of Education Art Competitions, for her still lives and nudes that showed off her mastery of the use of light.

Orpen, a well-known figure in Dublin's artistic society, was friends with the writer and surgeon Oliver St John Gogarty (1878–1957), whose memoir conjures up an image of Orpen as an affable partygoer who liked pretty women. Born in Stillorgan, Orpen was mostly based in London but was a frequent visitor to Ireland. He was a past pupil of DMSA, having enrolled there six weeks before his thirteenth birthday, and, from there, he went to study at the Slade School of Art in London, where he quickly made a name for himself as one of the most fashionable and sought-after portrait painters in Britain.

He bought one of Margaret's nude drawings and Hilary Pyle tells us that his comments on her work ranged from 'very good' to 'Darling Margaret', with Pyle adding that Orpen could penetrate Margaret's 'external gravity'. We remember the informal shortening of her name to Maggie, on the 1901 census form, which may have been her family's privilege. To Orpen and presumably her fellow students she was known as Margaret.

She modelled for Orpen, for several paintings including the undated *An Aran Islander*, in which a striking looking Margaret, with dark eyes and fine cheekbones, wearing a patterned shawl and flouncy dress that mirrors the navy tones of the landscape behind her, uses her left hand to gather both ends of the shawl about her neck while her right hand tips the brim of her hat at the

GREAT IRISH WIVES

viewer, if not exactly in welcome then at least in sporting acknowledgement.

Letters to Margaret Crilley in the National Library reveal her various addresses over the years before her marriage. In 1908, she is living at 40 Rutland Square and seven years later she is in Clontarf, at 6 St John's Terrace.

Hilary Pyle writes that Margaret's youthful appearance may have tempted

Margaret Clarke, modelling for William Orpen's painting An Aran Islander.

her to shave off some years from her age as most of her fellow students were four years younger than her. Nicola Gordon Bowe in her book *Harry Clarke: The Life and Work* describes Margaret as being short and intelligent looking with finely hewn features, brown hair and grey eyes that twinkled when she smiled and, indeed, the gaze of Orpen's Aran Islander gamely pierces the shadow thrown by the brim of her hat. Pyle describes Margaret as quiet but self-assured. Those extra four years, including her years as a full-time teacher, would have given her a maturity that stood her apart from the eighteen- and nineteen-year-olds in her class. Surely this is one of the reasons why Orpen favoured her, and the bonus was her prize-winning talent. Although he did need to tell her, in a letter, dated 28 February 1907, perhaps in response to her submitting a painting for a competition, to have no fear and refrain from describing her chances of succeeding as 'ghosts'. He assures her that doing her best will turn those chances into certainty. His writing is illegible in places, but he seems to warn against envying pompous people. So, Margaret was not always as self-assured as Pyle suggests. She had her moments of self-doubt and envy of other artists and was honest enough to share her misgivings with her teacher.

Margaret was likely doubly appreciative of her place at the Dublin school, having earned it through her own merit. The scholarship that allowed her through its doors was the first of many that sustained her studies over the next few years. There are two telegrams in the National Library from Orpen to Margaret, dated 2 October 1909 and 12 August 1910, to her Newry address, informing her that her scholarship had been renewed. Margaret was an independent woman, in every way.

Meanwhile, Orpen was not the only one she impressed. One of her fellow students, Harry Clarke (1889–1931) was a shy, self-conscious eighteen-year-old, who envied Margaret's self-confidence. Harry's father, Joshua, moved to Ireland from Leeds in 1877 after his family's thriving painting business had been given to two undeserving cousins. Joshua set himself up, in 1886, as an interior decorator for churches, who could also create artefacts and provide a cleaning service. He married a Sligo girl, Bridget MacGonigal, and they set up home on Dublin's North Strand until the following year when his flourishing business enabled them to lease 33 North Frederick Street, behind Parnell Square, and acquire a holiday home in Bray.

Bridget Clarke was consumptive, and, of her four children, it was the two boys, Harry and his older brother, Walter (*b*.1888), who inherited her weak chest, while their two sisters, Kathleen and Florence (Dolly) were luckier health-wise. Bridget's death, at the age of forty-six, on 11 August 1903 was a huge shock for her family. Fourteen-year-old Harry had just left school. As a schoolboy, he had helped out at his father's company, but when he got his first job, probably as a draughtsman, with architect Thomas F McNamara (1867–1947), his boss suggested that instead of being an architect, he should specialise in the art of stained glass.

Orpen and Margaret shared a passion for teaching art and Orpen was making great strides at reforming the profession at the DMSA, bringing nude models to the life-drawing classes that included both male and female students. Orpen sought to create an atmosphere that encouraged freedom in expression and believed in taking his students outside the classroom. His 1910 pencil and watercolour drawing, 'Life Class on the Beach', shows four students on Portmarnock Beach preparing to sketch a girl who is undressing for them. Margaret is thought to be the student in the centre of the drawing with three of her classmates, including portrait painter James Sleator (1885–1950) and Kathleen Fox (1880–1963), who would make a name for herself painting prominent figures of the Easter Rising throughout that fateful week of April 1916.

Margaret won a silver medal in 1911 for a nude she had submitted to the National Competition under the British Board of Education. Confirmation of the mutual respect shared between instructor and student was clear when in 1911, after she graduated, Margaret became Orpen's teaching assistant at the DMSA.

Two years later, in 1913, she took bronze in the same competition for a nude figure and the following year had three portraits on show at the RHA. One of her models was Harry's younger sister, Dolly. Hilary Pyle believes that Margaret's early portraits remain some of her best work, praising them for their vitality and magnetism. Meanwhile, Harry Clarke confirmed his recognition of Margaret's talent by advising his father to hire her to paint a series of gothic busts. Joshua Clarke, Nicola Gordon Bowe tells us, was proud, ever after, to call Margaret one of 'his' artists. Over the next forty years, all the way up to 1953, Margaret would have sixty paintings exhibited at the RHA.

The year 1914 was a significant one for Margaret, Harry and the world too. On 9 January, Harry sailed to Paris via London, for his Continental tour, having been awarded a travel scholarship the previous November by the Department of Agriculture and Technical Instruction. Planning to begin a recently won commission, to illustrate an edition of Hans Christian Andersen's *Fairy Tales*, for London publishers George G Harrap and Co., he arrived in Paris on 20 January. However, after happily examining stained-glass work in Chartres Cathedral, he caught a bad cold. Feeling unwell in a country where he hated the food and could not speak the language sent him running back to London to embark upon long days devoted to illustrating Andersen's stories. Margaret arrived in London on 13 February. It is difficult to discern the romance with their work dominating all. Harry rarely took breaks when working, but he did spend time with Margaret. One cannot be sure if they had discussed marriage at this time but, timing-wise, it would be hard to believe that the subject did not crop up over the weekend as they explored London, visited the galleries, and caught up with William Orpen. Margaret also made time to do a portrait of Harry during her visit. After she left, he returned to work but found himself missing Ireland and, possibly, Margaret too. He went home for the Easter break but was back in London in April and then sailed to Paris for a more successful visit in May where his father visited him in June.

Harry's life is well documented but, rather frustratingly, there are huge gaps when it comes to Margaret. As Orpen's assistant, she might have been teaching in the DMSA, in between his visits and, of course, she continued to make art.

An undated letter from Orpen, in the National Library, shows him giving her ideas for teaching art: she should ask her students to paint something that has appealed strongly to their eyes and minds, and is both dramatic and beautiful. Margaret may have taught Mainie Jellett (1897–1944) who started attending Orpen's class at the DMSA in 1914 since, having achieved her teacher's certificate in 1913, it was Margaret who took over Orpen's classes after he left to be a war artist in France in 1914. Orpen wrote to Margaret that November to tell her that history was being made, the result of which would be painted by artists like themselves.

Margaret's social life was made up of relatives and art-school friends, but she must also have been friendly with Harry's family after working successfully for his father and painting his sister Dolly. One of her good friends was stained-glass artist Ethel Rhind (1877–1952), who enrolled at the DMSA in 1902 after winning a scholarship to attend classes in mosaic technique. Once there, she embarked upon the craft of stained glass, showing an immediate affinity for the medium, with her student work being included at the 1907 Irish International Exhibition, the same year that Margaret arrived at the DMSA. After graduation, Ethel started work at artist and entrepreneur Sarah Purser's (1848–1943) glass workshop, *An Túr Gloine* (The Glass Tower), at 24 Pembroke Street, in 1907/8. Margaret's art-school friends were probably shared with Harry. Certainly, Harry and Ethel would have had lots in common. For instance, there is a postcard, in the National Library, that Ethel sent Margaret, in June 1908, describing her visit to Chartres Cathedral. Perhaps it was Ethel who encouraged Harry to go see it for himself.

Harry arrived back in Ireland in July and the following month travelled to Inisheer, an island off the coast of County Clare, with two artist friends, Austin Molloy (1886–1961) and Seán Keating (1889–1977). They were soon joined by Margaret, her sister Mary, Harry's brother Walter (*d.*1930) and Ethel Rhind. Margaret sketched Harry and also painted him in oil in a beautiful, sensual portrait that more than hints at the relationship between artist and sitter. The portrait is up close, with Harry gazing directly at her, filling

Margaret Clarke (standing at the back beside the skeleton) and fellow women artists at Dublin Metropolitan School of Art, c.1910.

much of the canvas, wearing a crumpled white shirt, that seems a little too big for him, and a slim dark tie. His head and shoulders are framed by a dark blue sky that suggests the intimacy of a late evening or night sitting.

Harry's photographs from this holiday were given to Ethel and are amongst her papers at the National Library.

Meanwhile, back in Dublin, Joshua Clarke was feeling the squeeze caused by the unreliability of supply ships in wartime. Shortages led to an increase in the price of lead, which was needed for ammunition. He sought to compensate for the decline in business by renting out the upper part of the Clarke house on North Frederick Street. His new tenants would turn out not to be strangers.

The Clarke family were most surprised when Harry announced that he was going to marry Margaret Crilley, suggesting that the romance was conducted out of sight, or at the very least was camouflaged by their love of art. They had known each other for six or seven years by this stage and it is natural to consider that their relationship had developed out of a genuine respect for each other's talent and commitment to their craft. We know from Orpen that Margaret was dedicated to her work and was likely impressed with Harry's work ethic – the long hours and the variety of commissions he was taking on.

The wedding took place on 31 October 1914, and the following day brought a new month and new beginnings when the couple moved into the Clarke family's newly renovated flat on North Frederick Street, after which Harry, at least, went right back to work. From now on, Margaret signed her work with her married name. Margaret's sister Mary (Minnie) moved in with the couple to keep house for them, and there would be yet another surprise for the Clarkes the following June when Walter, Harry's brother, announced his engagement to Mary.

Margaret and Harry finally went on a delayed honeymoon, leaving for the Aran Islands on 26 July 1915 and only returning on 1 September. In November, Oliver St John Gogarty performed a small nasal operation on Harry, who was busy illustrating such works as Samuel Taylor Coleridge's (1772–1834) 'The Rime of the Ancient Mariner' and the windows for Cork's Honan Chapel amongst other things.

The following year, Margaret's work, exhibited at the 1915 RHA Show, received a mention in May's edition of *The Studio*, the fine decorative arts magazine that was founded in 1893 to promote the work of new artists, designers and architects, and would prove hugely influential for early enthusiasts of the Art Nouveau and Arts and Crafts movements. This would not be her only mention in the popular magazine.

In April 1916, Harry was introduced to the barrister and art collector Thomas Bodkin (1887–1961) who wished to see Harry's progress on the Honan windows. This would be the start of a lifelong friendship, although, according to Nicola Gordon Bowe, Bodkin sought out the Clarkes only after visiting a mutual friend's house and seeing Margaret's portraits of his host's children on the wall.

April proved an explosive month for Dublin when schoolteacher Pádraig Pearse (1879–1916) and trade unionist James Connolly (1868–1916) led their men up Sackville Street, on a sunny Easter Monday, to take up an ill-conceived residence in the General Post Office (GPO) in their attempt to establish an independent Ireland. The ensuing battle with British forces threw the inner city into chaos. Joshua Clarke's studios, on North Frederick Street, were locked down by authorities who forbade any of the employees from leaving for four days. Joshua, now living in Shankill, could only pray that his studios had not been damaged, nor his sons killed. Fortunately, the studios were out of reach of both the gunboat *Helga* and the big guns trained on Sackville Street. That was the good news but there was plenty of bad news. The blocks for Harry's illustrations for *The Rime of the Ancient Mariner* were being stored at the publisher's, Maunsel and Co., 96 Middle Abbey Street, which succumbed to the flames that swallowed up Eason and the GPO, along with the RHA's purpose-built Academy House on Lower Abbey Street that housed portraits by Margaret. The latter was not the horrific loss that might be imagined as the RHA, and the building, had its critics, including Harry and Margaret's new friend Thomas Bodkin who likened it to a gloomy, dimly lit artist graveyard for pictures that had been forgotten about, while William Orpen seized upon the destruction of Academy House as an opportunity to resign his membership. In fact, after the war, Orpen would never visit Ireland again. Harry submitted a claim of compensation for the monetary loss of his work but received less than he asked for. At the end of June, he exhibited his stained-glass windows for Honan Chapel at his father's studio, thereby winning himself a commission for six more windows and glorious reviews from friends like Bodkin.

Probably because Walter and Mary, who shared North Frederick Street, had had a baby and needed more space, and maybe also wanting to escape the sight and smells of the charred remains of Sackville Street, and the strained atmosphere following the executions of the uprising's leaders in Kilmainham Gaol, Harry and Margaret decided to leave the city behind and head towards the sea, renting a house in Blackrock, at 36 Mount Merrion Avenue. Marie Hammond Callaghan quotes their granddaughter Sara Bourke, in 1996, who said that though Margaret knew the likes of Constance Markievicz (1868–1927), a talented artist as well as an activist, she avoided getting involved in politics. Sara surmised that both Margaret and Harry would have lamented the destruction of beautiful Dublin rather than championing the fighting rebels; she described them as 'armchair republicans' who opposed partition but preferred to concentrate on the Arts and Crafts Movement. Several art historians have noted that Margaret never joined *Cumann Na mBan*, the women's auxiliary of the Irish Volunteers.

Of course, this move might also have been motivated by the Clarkes wanting to start a family. Margaret would have discovered that she was pregnant in October or November. In any case, their new house had a fine garden which included a mews cottage that became Harry's studio. That Christmas must have been a time of celebration as, apart from Margaret's pregnancy, the Hans Christian Andersen's *Fairy Tales*, illustrated by Harry, released in September 1916, garnered huge acclaim for Harry and his work, though he would always advocate that, of the two of them, his wife was the real artist.

Margaret gave birth to Ann, the first of her three children, on 17 June 1917, and continued painting. The year was a busy one as, aside from becoming a mother, Margaret painted two portraits: one of her father-in-law and the other the result of a commission. Both were exhibited for the Royal Hibernian Academy at the DMSA, a temporary premises after the blazes of 1916. She also painted an allegorical work, entitled *Mary and Brigid*, using her sister and infant niece as models. Marie Hammond Callaghan writes that this picture signalled an important moment both for Margaret as an artist, and also, timing-wise, for an Ireland that was relying on a newfound appreciation for Irish history and culture to stimulate ardent nationalism. In her memoir *Today We Will Only Gossip*, Lady Beatrice Glenavy (1881–1970), an artist and friend of Margaret's, who had painted her interpretation of Kathleen ní Houlihan, describes visiting St Enda's College, post 1916, where one of the students spoke of his willingness to die for Ireland after seeing Margaret's painting. (Callaghan delivers a full analysis of *Mary and Brigid* in her article.)

Thomas Bodkin was a good friend and promoted Margaret as a portrait painter to acquaintances and friends. Margaret wrote to him in 1918, thanking him for securing her a commission for a Mrs Thompson for £21. Her love for children is apparent as she describes the subject as Mrs Thompson's 'little' son and professes her delight in painting the child. The following year, on 7 April 1919, Margaret gave birth to Michael.

In her book about Harry, Nicola Gordon Bowe includes a small photograph taken of Margaret some time that year in their back garden in Blackrock. Sitting in what might be a deckchair, she appears to be wearing what looks like a heavy blanket or heavy nightclothes. She could be a patient in convalescence except for the presence of her children, suggesting instead the exhaustion of motherhood. Baby Michael, sitting heavy in her lap, reaches for what might be a sheet of paper at his feet, while Ann holds out her hand to her brother. Only Margaret is looking at the photographer whose distance from the three figures makes one feel that the real purpose of the photograph was to capture Harry's studio, which dominates the frame. A portrait of the artist as mother in front of her husband's creative space. The following year, the last baby, David, arrived on 25 August.

After Joshua Clarke's death in 1921, Harry and Walter divided the running of his business, with Harry looking after the stained-glass side, while Walter managed the decorating services.

Three years later, in 1924, Margaret won gold, silver and bronze medals at the first Tailteann games, a Gaelic version of the Olympics, showcasing Irish sports and culture, that were established to celebrate Ireland's independence. This was the year that Jack B Yeats (1871–1957) won Ireland's first Olympic medal for his depiction of swimmers in the River Liffey. Margaret would win medals at the 1928 Tailteann games and again at the final games in 1932.

Margaret also held her first solo exhibition in 1924, at Dublin's St Stephen's Green Gallery, just months before Harry was elected into the Royal Hibernian Academy, a fitting acknowledgement of his status as an Irish artist. One of her most expensive paintings at this exhibition was her *Mary and Brigid*, priced at £50. When the exhibition was favourably reviewed by Thomas Bodkin, who was already a fan, Margaret wrote to him, taking issue with his shorthand description of her as Harry's wife and Orpen's student, hoping that in future he could respond to her work as an individual in her own right.

Whenever she could, she combined art and family. In 1925, she used her family and housekeeper, Julia O'Brien, as models for the painting *Bath Time at the Crèche*. Julia was also employed as a childminder, which undoubtedly allowed Margaret to produce some of her most important work. It is no coincidence that, that July, Margaret had taken the children on a seaside holiday to Kilcoole, County Wicklow, and they also spent time in Dalkey after dramatist Lennox Robinson (1886–1958) offered the use of his Sorrento Cottage. In August, she exhibited work alongside Harry's during Dublin's Horse Show Week. The exhibition was opened by President Cosgrave, and Harry was obviously the big draw, with folk invited to 'An Exhibition of Stained Glass Designed and Made by Harry Clarke and His Assistants'.

Aidan Dunne, writing in the *Irish Times*, in 2017, described Margaret as a high achiever but laments the extent of Orpen's influence on her work. Describing her allegorical painting *Strindbergian* as interesting, Dunne nevertheless finds its theatrics 'stilted' and 'arched'. However, he does compliment her storytelling, in particular her re-interpretation of the bible's Samson and Delilah in her *The Wife/The Haircut*, from 1927, for which Julia O'Brien and her brother modelled.

Margaret's reputation for portrait paintings soared, as evidenced by those who chose to sit for her. For instance, in 1926, her portrait of Abbey director and playwright Lennox Robinson was one of six paintings that opened the 1926 RHA Exhibition. At the time, Harry and Robinson were in Spain where Robinson worried about Harry's persistent headaches. The following year, the

Robinson portrait was included in the 'Irish Portraits by Ulster Artists' show at the Belfast Museum and Art Gallery. The accolades continued to roll in with Margaret being made a full member of the RHA, in 1927 – only the second woman in the Academy's history to be given this honour, after Sarah Purser in 1924. Margaret generously responds to Thomas Bodkin's letter of congratulations with a congratulations of her own about his new book, *An Approach to Painting*, telling him that she wanted to finish it before she replied to him.

The following year, she painted Éamon de Valera. There is a letter to Margaret in the National Library, confirming de Valera's consent to sit for her, from John JC Shelly in Winnipeg, Manitoba, who seems to have commissioned the work and wanted it for the 1929 RHA exhibition. It is a testament to her expertise that Margaret was Shelly's, and de Valera's, chosen artist, but also, we see how Shelly deferred to her about the details, agreeing to thirty guineas for her fee and an increase to £35 if Margaret deemed that was required.

Margaret could not afford to be complacent about earning money. It is hard to know if she suspected how soon everything would change. Harry's lungs and chest were in decline which necessitated his travelling to Davos, Switzerland, in 1929. She accompanied Harry and sent individual cheerful postcards home to twelve-year-old Ann, ten-year-old Michael and nine-year-old David. In one postcard to Michael, we glimpse her as doting mother, describing the overnight train journey from Calais to Basle as a nightmare which made her head 'hoppity-hoppity-hop'. She tells him that his daddy is fine and will be writing to him soon, signing off with 'love from Mammy.' Harry would remain there for the next twelve months.

On her return to Ireland, Margaret had a busy time ahead of her. She received a letter, dated 26 July, from John Dulanty, the Irish Commissioner for Trade for London, asking her if she would consider creating five posters for the Empire Marketing Board who would determine the subjects to be depicted and, if they liked her work, would pay her £250. This was the first time that an Irish artist had been approached for their posters. She discussed the commission with Harry and he wrote to her, from Switzerland, advising her to go to the National Library to research for this project and wished he could help her with them.

While Harry was away, Margaret visited Walter at the Clarke studios where she was obliged to field customer complaints about Harry's unfinished work. On 20 June she responded to Sister Bernard of the Assumption, at the Convent of Notre Dame in Sussex, who was losing patience and trust in Harry. Margaret's letter shows her staunchly defending her husband who she felt was under suspicion for no other crime than falling ill. She explained the situation in the hope of appeasing the nun, describing how Harry had ended up in a nursing home after contracting influenza, whereupon his doctor, becoming increasingly concerned about Harry's lungs, advised him to recuperate in a more congenial climate. Margaret confessed that they had both expected an improvement after six weeks, which had not happened. She explained how vitally important it was for Harry to rest and remain ignorant of any unpleasant worries created by business matters. Margaret asked Sr Bernard if she knew how conscientious Harry was about his work and his customers and she laid the blame for his breakdown on this very quality, that his inclination to worry could sometimes thwart his genius.

Margaret wrote about Harry in 1930, describing him as an artist whose success lay in his strength to concentrate and work for far longer hours than others in better health. The text is in pencil, in the National Library, and she crossed out the first half of her first sentence which had begun with the words, 'One of the most delicate men …'

In May 1930, Harry returned to Ireland to confront a huge backlog of work. Two months later, Walter Clarke's death, at forty-three, must have been a dreadful shock for his brother and sister-in-law. Harry managed another few months of work before worsening health forced him back to Davos in October. He planned to spend 1931 in Switzerland, but as the New Year began, he must have sensed that time was running out because he left Davos to make the journey home. Unfortunately, he only made it as far as Coire, or Chur, a small village about two hours away, where he died in his sleep on 6 January. He was just forty-one.

It is hard to imagine Margaret's feelings. Her husband died miles away from her, his last wish to be buried at Coire, leaving her with three young children to manage as well as the Clarke studios, while fulfilling her own commissions and artistic commitments. One piece of good news that year was that one of her Empire Marketing Board posters won the Publicity Club of London's prize for the most popular poster in England. Nine months after Harry's death came the news that fifty-two-year-old William Orpen had died in London.

In 1932, Margaret was asked to paint Saint Patrick by the Thomas Haverty Trust which was set up to buy art from Irish artists for institutions and public galleries. The commission, timed for that year's Eucharistic Congress in Dublin and also the 1,500th anniversary of the saint's arrival in Ireland was first shown at the RHA in April and then went on display during the congress and Tailteann Games in July. After that, Margaret's *St Patrick Climbs Croagh Patrick* spent several years in Dublin's Mansion House.

In 1938, she submitted work for an exhibition with the Society of Dublin Painters who undertook to bring modernism to Ireland by championing avant-garde work that was free of realism and accuracy. Mainie Jellett, exhibited with them in 1923.

New work by Margaret went on show at 7 St Stephen's Green in 1939. She was now much inspired by nature, as well as by her children, and this exhibition included her *Autumn at Davos*. In 1940, she submitted four different paintings of flowers to the RHA.

However, she was still in demand as a portrait artist. In 1943, she painted artist Dermod O'Brien (1855–1945), president of the RHA, and Catholic Archbishop John Charles McQuaid who wrote to thank her for the books she leant him. She had friends in high places. That same year, Margaret received a letter from Mainie Jellett about a new exhibition of Irish art that was being planned for the autumn as an alternative to the RHA. Jellett wanted Margaret's opinion on the matter and asked if she would like to take part in the exhibition. Margaret was immediately enthused, joining the executive committee and submitting her portrait of her daughter Ann with her cat for the first Irish Exhibition of Living Art.

Art historian Hilary Pyle describes Margaret growing more discontented over the years with her work. As director of the busy Harry Clarke Studios, Margaret likely felt that she lacked the necessary time and freedom to paint what she wanted to. The portraits paid the bills; she could not afford to be choosy. In 1950, she painted retired General Sean McMahon (1893–1955), who had been chief of staff of the Irish Defence Forces. That same year she heard that her painting *The Gael*, on exhibition in America, had been bought for the Irish College in Rome. So, she was still seen as a successful and relevant artist, but it was not enough and at some point, in the 1950s, Margaret gave up painting. However, she did not break with the art world. In 1957, she received a letter from the artist Anne King Harmon (1919–1979), thanking her for buying her painting *Cat at Night* and, the following year, she joined a committee to organise a posthumous exhibition of her friend Evie Hone's (1894–1955) work at University College, Dublin. Two years later, she started cataloguing the works of Mainie Jellett.

There is a short piece of text, undated, in Margaret's hand, in the National Library, in which she laments society's urge to know about an artist's life in order to appreciate their work. Perhaps this note offers an explanation as to why she gave up painting. She rails against irrelevant rhetoric churned out by gossipers who comment on pictures they have not actually seen. Similarly, it is wrong, she says, to judge a work after a single conversation with its creator who might be nervous or unwell and unable to articulate exactly what they mean. Should the artist stumble, however, the one sure thing is their art.

Margaret Clarke died on 31 October 1961 and is buried in the Redford Cemetery, Greystones, County Wicklow.

CHAPTER NINE

GEORGIE 'GEORGE' YEATS (1892-1968)

Wife of William Butler Yeats, poet

In his published journals, for 1948–1953, English poet Stephen Spender (1909–1995) describes meeting the widowed and 'elderly' George Yeats at a dinner party in Dublin on 13 March 1950. Earlier that day, he had been taken to meet Jack B Yeats (1871–1957), painter brother of William (1865–1939), who spoke at length about how his father, painter John Butler Yeats (1839–1922), made all his children learn how to paint and draw. The conversation must have made an impression since, that evening, Spender asked George about her father-in-law, and she explained why the old man sailed off to America, ostensibly for six months, after his wife died, but then refused to return to Ireland evermore, preferring to live an independent life and avoid any expectations that might be placed upon him by his family.

The use of 'elderly' is peculiar considering that George was only fifty-eight in 1950, seventeen years older than Spender. However, he counters it by emphasising George's vitality, calling her 'robust', 'alive', 'friendly' and 'extremely intelligent'. If their conversation strayed from her in-laws, Spender did not see fit to document it.

As usual, George was important only as a link to the males of the Yeats family. She was the wife, the sister-in-law and daughter-in-law … but there

Mrs W. B. Yeats, *by Edmund Dulac, exhibited at the Leicester Galleries, London, June 1920.*

was so much more to her. Before she became George, she was Georgie to all her friends.

She was born Bertha Georgie to militia captain (William) Gilbert Hyde-Lees (1865–1909) and his wife Edith Ellen, or Nelly, (1868–1942) on 16 October 1892, and had one sibling, Harold (1890–1963). At the time, the family were living in Fleet, Hampshire, and Gilbert Hyde-Lees was on his way to being an alcoholic, albeit a wealthy one thanks to a large inheritance from the uncle who had brought him up. Uncle Harold believed in enjoying life and his nephew followed suit. When Georgie was two, her father was promoted to major but then his name disappears from the army lists. The family moved to London where they settled at 17D de Vere Gardens in Kensington, seven miles away from Nelly's parents at 7 Southwell Gardens, which was of no benefit to anyone since Nelly had been banished and disinherited for talking openly about her mother's love affairs. Nelly was both the eldest of her mother's seven children and the only one that was definitely legitimate. In fact, her mother had told her second daughter that had she known more about birth control she would never have had any children, and declared, 'The Royal Family does not love their children. There is no reason why I should love mine.'

London was a huge change from Hampshire with busy, exotic shops like Harrods, while every Sunday, their governess walked Georgie and Harold around Hyde Park. Georgie loved to visit the zoo in Regent's Park, something she continued to do for the rest of her life. In the mammoth biography *Becoming George: the Life of Mrs W.B. Yeats*, Ann Saddlemyer records that there were over five hundred cinemas in London by 1912, not to mention the theatres, libraries, art galleries and a wide variety of bookshops, like Hatchard's of Piccadilly, where Nelly was a frequent customer and may have bought her copy of *The Wind Among the Reeds* by William Butler Yeats.

Thanks to their inheritance, the family travelled to Paris and Italy for extended stays. On their return to London, Georgie was sent off to a small boarding school in Somerset, perhaps because, Saddlemyer suggests, her father's drinking might have worsened, and her mother preferred to have her youngest child out of the way.

The next few years, as her father's health declined, the family moved several times, obliging Georgie to attend new schools. However, she discovered a love for books and study and began to build her own library, marking each new book with the date of its purchase. In 1902, the family moved to 4 Carlisle Mansions, Westminster, where one of their neighbours was the writer Somerset Maugham (1874–1965).

At some point, the Hyde-Lees marriage fell apart, with Gilbert and Nelly separating sometime between 1907 and 1908. Already shunned by her own family, Nelly may well have been trying to avoid the scandal of a divorce and needed Gilbert to pay the bills for herself and the children, now living in Kensington Palace Mansions, a stone's throw from her first marital home at de Vere Gardens.

Fifteen-year-old Georgie was unhappily attending St James's School for Girls, in West Malvern, where discipline was strict, and she was reprimanded for sneaking into the headmistress's garden in search of solitude. In July 1908, while Harold was preparing for Oxford University, Georgie began attending Miss Amabel Douglas's school for girls, where the curriculum embraced all the arts, and the girls enjoyed frequent visits to art galleries and the theatre.

Meanwhile, Nelly threw herself into the art world via afternoon teas and house parties where poets and musicians provided the entertainment. She was a close friend of English poet and playwright Olivia Shakespear (1863–1938) who introduced her to fellow poets, her former lover William Butler Yeats and American Ezra Pound (1885–1972), who was pursuing Olivia's daughter Dorothy (1886–1973), who would become a close friend of Georgie's.

Towards the end of 1908, Gilbert went into a private nursing home for alcoholics in London, and died the following year, in November 1909. Living with an alcoholic parent took its toll on both his son and daughter. Saddlemyer writes that Georgie exhibited typical traits found in children of alcoholics; she was a high achiever who determined to 'overly' cope with any situation by taking control of it. Her teachers remembered how she preferred her own company to anyone else's and complimented her striking maturity and wisdom. Whatever Gilbert's physical condition, at the time of his death, both Georgie and Harold were profoundly shocked at his passing, possibly resulting in a lifetime of nightmares and sleepwalking for his daughter.

Meanwhile, Harold's internal trauma over his father's death may have manifested in a poltergeist. Nelly and her children planned to spend the summer of 1910 in Hinxworth, forty-six miles from London, where they stayed in the spacious rectory house of Reverend Atkins. They were joined by Olivia Shakespear's brother Harry Tucker and young Dorothy, but the holiday was cut short after everyone was subjected to strange noises at night and having their hair pulled by invisible hands. Four years earlier, Harold had discovered that on holding a recently delivered, sealed envelope he could tell his mother who had sent it, and from where, providing so many personal details about the sender that Nelly was embarrassed into banning him from doing it again.

Nelly's literary friends dabbled in the occult which added bite to poetry readings. On being invited to a friend's house, one might hear Ezra Pound read his latest poem followed by some experimental play with the Ouija board and table-rapping. Conversation ranged from automatic writing to previous incarnations, with Olivia Shakespear, at least, believing that she had been Egyptian in a previous life. A party might also include members of the secret occult society the Order of the Golden Dawn.

Grief may have made Georgie curious about spiritual matters. Ann Saddlemyer provides a detailed account of how Georgie schooled herself in her chosen subjects, buying up book after book. She was a voracious reader and always open to prompts about new writers. For example, a reading of Ezra Pound's *The Spirit of Romance*, a book of essays on European literatures, in 1910, inspired her to embark upon a study of the poetry of philosophy of Dante Alighieri (1265–1321) in his native language. Apart from Italian, Georgie could also speak French, German and Spanish.

Similarly, the Italian psychologist Cesare Lombroso's *After Death – what?*

Spiritistic Phenomena and their Interpretation was a mere stepping stone, in 1909, for Georgie's exploration of spiritualism. In time, she would become a fan of writer Henry James's (1843–1916) philosopher brother, William (1842–1910).

On 1 February 1911, Nelly Hyde-Lees married Olivia's brother Harry Tucker and moved to Montpelier Square, while her eighteen-year-old daughter enrolled in the Heatherly School of Art, just off Oxford Street, alma mater of the likes of her future father-in-law John Butler Yeats, Edward Burne-Jones (1833–1898) and Dante Gabriel Rossetti (1828–1882).

Three months later, Georgie was formally introduced to William Butler Yeats in Olivia Shakespear's house. In fact, she had spied him that very morning when, instead of going to college, she had gone to the British Museum where he had dashed by her. Of course, as an avid theatregoer, and reader, she would have known who he was. And presumably she would have heard plenty about him from Nelly and Olivia Shakespear, whose on-and-off affair with the poet would be substituted by a lifelong solid friendship. Yeats was a frequent companion when the Tuckers and Shakespears holidayed together.

She obviously made an impression as a fourth member of the group as that December, when forty-six-year-old Yeats invited Ezra Pound and Dorothy to his flat at Woburn Buildings, nineteen-year-old Georgie was included in the invite.

Georgie's friendship with Dorothy Shakespear deepened after Nelly's marriage to Dorothy's uncle. The two young women shared a love for art, reading, clothes and beautiful hats and regularly took tea together with their mothers, which presumably meant being privy to the literary and occult gossip of the day. When the two families took short holidays together, Georgie and Dorothy would escape their relatives, to paint the landscape. In 1913, accompanied by Olivia, they travelled further afield, spending six weeks painting in Italy. They also attended lectures together. In 1912, Ezra Pound gave a lecture to the three-year-old Quest Society founded by historian, writer and translator George Robert Stow Mead (1863–1933) to promote the study of assorted religions via investigation and experience. Previously, Mead had spent two years working as private secretary to the Russian mystic and writer Madame Helena Blavatsky (1831–1891), who cofounded the Theosophical Society in 1875. That same year, Yeats gave a lecture to 'Questors' about his theories regarding the ghostly form. Saddlemyer suspects that Georgie and Dorothy were in the audience on both occasions, which led them to attending a course of Tuesday lectures given by Mead in Kensington Town Hall.

On their return from Italy, Georgie went to many more lectures. The Bengali poet and Nobel laureate Rabindranath Tagor (1861–1941) was visiting London at the time and being championed by Ezra Pound and Yeats, who got him invited to Olivia Shakespear's house. Georgie and Dorothy attended a month-long series of Tagor's lectures on Indian philosophy at Caxton Hall, Westminster.

Georgie's expanding library reflected her deepening interest in spiritual matters. In August 1913, she bought *The Spiritual Guide which Disentangles the Soul* by the Spanish priest and mystic Miguel de Molinos and two months later added Yeats's *The Celtic Twilight* to her collection. Alongside the philosophical and spiritual books, Georgie maintained her study of contemporary European literature, including Irish writers like James Stephens (1880–1950).

In the summer of 1913, the Tuckers rented a three-storey house, The Prelude, in East Sussex, where, according to Georgie, the surrounding woods were haunted. Yeats joined the family that August, along with Dorothy and Olivia, wanting to take rooms for himself and Ezra at a nearby farmhouse. Before he left for Ireland, Yeats told the group about the psychic Elizabeth (Bessie) Radcliffe, with whom he and their mutual friend, Eva Fowler, were exploring automatic and slate writing; he showed them the script that had resulted from sessions in May. Georgie offered to follow up on the identities of those mentioned in the writings to help Yeats avail of the messages given. For instance, one of the spirits that addressed him through the psychic was poet Anna Luise Karsch (1722–1791), an acquaintance of the writer Johann Wolfgang von Goethe (1749–1832). Following an operation for tonsillitis, which struck her down after Yeats left for Ireland, Georgie applied for a reading ticket for the British Museum and looked into the life and work of Karsch. Yeats benefitted from her fluency in German, and Georgie wrote to say that there was no evidence that Karsch ever belonged to any mystical society and that she kept herself to herself. There were three letters from Goethe to Karsch in the museum but nothing of particular interest.

At this time, grief propelled a collective interest in the occult and the spirit world in others around the world. The loss of life generated by the Crimean and the South African wars left many bereaved relatives wanting to believe that there was life after death. Séances and table-rapping sessions were also immensely popular amongst the likes of poet Elizabeth Barrett Browning (1806–1881), art historian and philosopher John Ruskin (1819–1900) and American president Abraham Lincoln (1809–1865), whose wife Mary used mediums following the death of their twelve-year-old son Willie from typhoid fever.

Georgie attended séances as part of her research into the supernatural, probably inspired by William James promoting experience over everything, and would have met mediums at the home of newspaper editor and spiritualist William Stead (1849–1912). Stead had created an office, 'Julia's Bureau', in his Wimbledon country house for grieving relatives wanting to be put in touch with mediums. Georgie went to a meeting there with New York medium Etta Wriedt (*c.*1859–1942) in 1911. Following a successful visit, the medium accepted Stead's invitation to return the following summer, and, in April 1912, the editor dutifully set sail for America to accompany her back to England. However, Stead was aboard *Titanic*, which hit an iceberg and sank, with the loss of most of the crew and passengers. A medium was later to channel Stead and wrote of his contentment in the afterlife in the book *The Blue Island*. It is possible that Georgie would have read this account.

Despite this tragedy, Etta Wriedt visited England again in May 1912 and in 1913, and both Georgie and Yeats attended her sessions in Julia's Bureau until Yeats was temporarily expelled for never being satisfied with the information provided. Although associated with Yeats, Georgie was still permitted to continue to see the medium, much to Yeats's annoyance.

In 1915, Georgie was one of the first 'customers' for a new medium Gladys Osborne Leonard (1882–1968), who would become famous after the book *Raymond* was published by Oliver Lodge, about the communication he received, via Leonard, from his son, Second Lieutenant Raymond Lodge, who had died in Belgium, in 1916.

On 20 April 1914, Georgie and Yeats were part of a small wedding party for Ezra Pound and Dorothy Shakespear. When the couple returned from their honeymoon, their flat was a frequent destination for Georgie. Colm Tóibín, in his book *New Ways to Kill Your Mother*, writes that her friendships with both Pounds would have expanded Georgie's learning and allowed her to witness a marriage between an intelligent, wealthy much younger woman and an older poet of questionable means.

Before the wedding, Georgie and Dorothy had taken one last Italian holiday together, with Olivia, where Georgie scoured the bookshops in search of astrology textbooks as part of her self-schooling on how to cast horoscopes. Being able to predict the future, both domestic and further afield, would allow her a better understanding of the workings of domestic and world events.

After the wedding, while Georgie continued her reading and explorations, Yeats sailed to Paris with his longtime unrequited married love, activist Maud Gonne (1866–1953), to visit several mediums. In the spring of 1914, Georgie and Yeats attended the opening of an art exhibition by three painters: Robert Gregory (1881–1918), William Orpen (1878–1931) and Augustus John (1878–1961). As Yeats stood with Georgie, her mother, and probably Olivia Shakespear too, Gregory's mother, the playwright Lady Gregory (1852–1932), approached them and Yeats introduced his great friend, with whom he had co-founded the Abbey Theatre in 1904. As Saddlemyer points out, Lady Gregory was probably too focused on her son to have taken much notice of young Georgie, which would explain why, when Georgie next saw the playwright, this time in Dublin's Abbey Theatre, Lady Gregory 'cut her', something that Georgie never forgot and possibly never forgave.

On 24 July 1914, at her request, Yeats was Georgie's sponsor when she joined the Hermetic Order of the Golden Dawn, the society he had been a member of for the last twenty-four years. Typically, she had studied diligently in advance, alongside practising astrology. In a way, she matched Yeats's obsession with the supernatural while cutting her own path through it. Others, like the new Mrs Pound, had grown tired of listening to Yeats obsessing about ghosts.

Membership of the Golden Dawn required a personal motto that reflected one's personality and aspirations, George chose '*Nemo Scit*' ('Let Nobody Know') which would prove very apt later on. Yeats's motto was typically more dramatic, '*Demon est Deus Inversus*' ('The Devil is the Converse of God'). Over the next few years, Georgie studied hard and attended society meetings. A more extensive rollcall of the books that she read can be found in Ann Saddlemyer's biography of Georgie. She passed all examinations and speedily moved up the chain of knowledge, almost matching Yeats's degree – a result of twenty-two years of study – within her first three years.

Treaties tied up millions of destinies together in 1914 when Germany invaded Belgium, obliging Britain and her allies, Russia and France, to declare war on Germany. Georgie's uncles joined up as did Lady Gregory's son, the painter Robert. England's population saw its first German Zeppelins in January 1915, and three months later, Georgie's thirty-eight-year-old maternal uncle Kenny died in action at Ypres. On 7 May 1915, RMS *Lusitania*, a Cunard ocean liner, was sunk by a German U-boat off the coast of Cork, with the loss of 1,197 lives, including Yeats's good friend and Lady Gregory's nephew Hugh Lane (1875–1915).

In a letter to his friend, the New York lawyer and art collector John Quinn (1870–1924), Yeats described the war as being 'merely the most expensive outbreak of insolence and stupidity that the world has even seen'. He refused to dwell on it any more than he had to.

Meanwhile, Georgie spent her summer hunting for books in London's antiquarian shops and compiling horoscopes for friends, including Yeats. Her twenty-third birthday in October meant that she was now old enough to apply to be a nurse in an army hospital and, in November, she signed up as a part-timer for the Voluntary Aid Detachment (VAD) Programme, Kensington Division, which meant attending lectures on cookery and hygiene and war rationing. She ended up working at the Endsleigh Palace Hospital for Officers, previously a grand hotel, which was practically next door to Yeats's flat. The VADs were specially selected from the middle and upper classes so that they were socially on the same level as the officers in their care. Georgie served her apprenticeship as a pantry orderly, serving food and doing the washing before being promoted to nursing assistant. The hours were long, and one had to run the gauntlet of fully qualified nurses resenting the barely trained newbies.

Georgie's life at this point is best summed up by her Golden Dawn notebook, in which she recorded her philosophical studies and books, and which included pages of recipes alongside lists of metallic poisons and diagrams depicting the inner workings of the heart. Not surprisingly, working amongst injured and dying soldiers stirred up an even greater interest in mediums and séances. Perhaps because she had lost her father, Georgie did seem very invested in the safety of her maternal uncles. Saddlemyer quotes from a table sitting with Gladys Leonard which focuses on George's uncle who, the voice declares via the medium, will go to India.

Meanwhile, Yeats was in want of a wife for Thoor Ballylee, the fifteenth-century Anglo-Norman castle that he was considering buying near Gort in County Galway.

In February 1916, Georgie went to work as a part-time nursing assistant at a smaller hospital in Berkeley Square, Westminster Division, which formally opened on 1 March. Here her duties increased, from general household duties to emptying bedpans and taking care of twenty-two officers. Once settled in, she was expected to administer treatment for conditions ranging from trench foot to the debilitating chills suffered by shell-shocked patients, while working the night shift meant being responsible for the entire ward. July's Battle of the Somme saw the return of thousands of horrifically wounded British soldiers. Georgie did not keep any personal records from this time, unlike nurse Vera Brittain's *Testament of Youth*, published in 1933.

The trauma of this time may well be reflected in how serious Georgie's sleepwalking became, necessitating her being tied to her bed. In later years, when her young daughter asked her to help her practise her first aid for the Girl Guides, George refused, saying it reminded her of the war.

Georgie used her free time to visit the British Museum, where she poured over books on early religions and the afterlife and saw Yeats at Golden Dawn meetings. The summer of 1916 was a challenging time for her. Ann Saddlemyer reckons that Georgie had become enamoured of William Butler Yeats as early as 1911 and most likely knew about his complicated love life, his affair with her mother's friend Olivia Shakespear and his love for Maud Gonne McBride. When Maud Gonne's husband, Major John MacBride (*b*.1868) was executed on 5 May 1916 for his part in the Easter Rising, Yeats visited several mediums to discuss proposing to the new widow. Meanwhile, Maud's daughter, Iseult (1894–1954), was in London and proving equally distracting.

At this time, Georgie became interested in compiling an A-Z book of horoscopes of notable Irish and international names. She sent a letter to the July issue of the *Occult Review* asking readers to provide the exact times, and proof, of famous births. She contacted Yeats for his help on the Irish personalities. Yeats was still pursuing Maud Gonne. He accompanied an unwell Iseult to her mother in Paris, where he proposed once more. When Maud Gonne rejected him again, he turned his attention to her twenty-two-year-old daughter, staying on in France in the hope of forging a relationship, a future, with Iseult.

Georgie next saw Yeats in London at the end of February 1917, when they attended a séance together and, for the first time in ages, Georgie's mother, Nelly, invited the poet to her house in Montpelier Square. Months later, he was still preoccupied by Iseult and Maud Gonne. It appears that several of his female confidents were trying to help him decide who best to marry. He had finally bought his derelict castle, which was in dire need of renovations and a wife to share it with. On 20 March, he raised the matter with Georgie, who was being championed by Yeats's former lover Olivia Shakespear as the best wife for him. Georgie believed that Lady Gregory preferred Iseult. It must have been an uncomfortable time. Georgie and Yeats shared an all-consuming absorption in spiritualism. Surely this sort of connection was enough for the poet.

Yet, even after discussing marriage with Georgie, he continued to ask the spirit world if he should be marrying Maud or Iseult Gonne. The fifty-two-year-old bachelor was lost in a tug-of-war between his heart and his head, and his ego. And it might be fair to say that perhaps a part of him feared the commitment to an actual proper wife. After all, look at how many brilliant poems had been created out of his misery. Might a wedding and a real live spouse affect his writing, his very self? Yeats removed himself from London for a bit, while Georgie did what she always did, distract herself by buying more books on astrology and art. An accident at work, burning the tips of her fingers with acid, proved a final straw regarding her demanding job, and she handed in her notice in August. Following a short holiday with her mother, she applied for a job at the Foreign Office, hoping her fluency in four languages would be useful.

That September, Yeats sailed back to London with the Gonne women and contacted Nelly about calling upon her. Incredibly, he was still dithering between Iseult and her mother but perhaps more so out of habit. He was also caught up in the Gonnes' being refused entry into Ireland under the Defence of the Realm Act, resulting in Maud taking a flat for six months in London. Yeats sent Lady Gregory a letter, telling her that he was going to visit Nelly Tucker to ask if Georgie would marry him. He also refers to Maud Gonne's growing conviction that Iseult might be his daughter, which he did not appear to believe. He had spent the night dreaming of pages of writing he could not read, wondering what the spirits were trying to tell him.

Georgie was still living in her mother's house when on 24 September Yeats arrived to ask for Nelly's blessing. Perhaps needing to process his request, Nelly waited until the following day to raise the matter with Georgie. In any case, at ten o'clock the next morning, Yeats proposed to Georgie. It took her twenty minutes to accept him. The biographer Saddlemyer supposes that those twenty minutes were spent discussing plans to travel and making a home out of Thoor Ballylee Castle. However, Yeats also admitted his feelings of responsibility for Iseult. Considering that he spent the previous year negotiating his various roles in Iseult's life as guardian, father and prospective husband, one can only imagine how he presented those feelings. Georgie would have expected her relationship with Yeats to be haunted by Maud Gonne, but it must have been a bit of a blow to realise that she would also have to make room for Maud's daughter, who was three years younger than her.

We know that, on 30 September, Georgie's mother, Nelly, wrote in secret, behind Georgie's back, to Yeats's great friend Lady Gregory, hoping that she would convince Yeats to break the engagement. In the letter, Nelly confessed she invited Yeats to call upon her but had little idea that he had designs on her daughter, believing that the pair only enjoyed their mutual interest in astrology, this belief being bolstered by Yeats telling her that astrology was 'a very flirtatious business'. Nelly professed her annoyance that a mutual friend – her sister-in-law Olivia Shakespear – had prodded Yeats in Georgie's direction. In Nelly's opinion, since he was so very anxious to marry, Georgie 'might do'. Nelly knew that Yeats was anxious to marry and she also knew he had been rejected by Maud and Iseult. She also referenced the sizeable age gap of thirty years between Yeats and Georgie, alongside Yeats's expertise at lovemaking which had, she believed, cast a spell over her daughter. At the same time, she proudly paid tribute to Georgie's strength of character, warning that if Georgie knew the real context of Yeats's proposal, she would have nothing to do with him – even if she only discovered it after getting married.

Two days later, Georgie and Yeats returned to London, where Georgie brought Dorothy with her to get the ten-shilling application for a licence to marry. According to her friend, Georgie was extremely nervous. The following day, her fiancé introduced her to his two loves, Maud and Iseult, and it seemed to have gone well, both women taking an instant liking to Georgie, although when a mutual friend wrote to John Quinn in New York about Yeats's engagement, he did mention that Maud laughed as she described the twenty-five-year-old who was, *of course*, rich.

Yeats left for Lady Gregory's big house in Coole, where his hostess, convinced by his genuine feelings for Georgie, sent an encouraging reply to Nelly who professed herself much reassured about the matter. Meanwhile, Georgie began to receive a string of ardent love letters from Yeats, telling her of Lady Gregory's happiness over their engagement. Georgie did not write back but did send a short note to Lady Gregory, thanking her for her kind thoughts. She must have experienced a giddy relief at these three giants in Yeats's life – the Gonnes and Lady Gregory – giving their approval.

The wedding date was chosen with the help of astrology. However, as soon as one was set, Yeats began to have doubts, believing once more that Iseult was the only woman for him. He arranged to see Iseult on 12 October, to talk things out. Iseult gave Yeats her blessing, telling him that from now on, he must prioritise Georgie's happiness. Yeats was elated and wrote to Lady Gregory that all was well once more and he knew he could make Georgie happy and, therefore, himself too.

The couple married on 20 October, three days after Georgie's twenty-fifth birthday, at the Harrow Road Registry Office in Paddington with just two witnesses, Georgie's mother and Ezra Pound. Afterwards, Georgie and her groom, who was feeling unwell, went back to his flat. It was two days before Yeats felt strong enough to head off on their honeymoon, travelling to the Ashdown Forest Hotel in Forest Row. It was not a happy time. Yeats's mood and health were out of sorts, as was the weather. Furthermore, they had to contend with hordes of marching soldiers from the nearby artillery camp. Then, relations were further strained when Yeats received a letter of congratulations from Iseult that plunged him into a depression. Instead of enjoying his wife's company, he wrote to Iseult to confess his guilt at betraying three people with his marriage, in other words, he regretted it. Georgie was reduced to a hapless bystander, as her new husband emotionally and mentally slipped away from her.

Four days after their wedding, with the atmosphere still decidedly wintry, Georgie and Yeats decided to cast individual horaries. Horary astrology is a complicated process whereby timing is of the utmost importance. Instead of consulting a natal chart, the seeker, the one in need of an answer, casts and interprets a horoscope for the precise moment they have realised their question. At 5.45pm, Yeats cast his, followed by Georgie at 6.40pm. Not surprisingly, they asked why they were unhappy and, both times, the planetary positions denoted tension, which is hardly an answer at all.

Understanding why Yeats was plagued by fatigue and neuralgia, Georgie briefly thought of leaving him, just as her mother had warned Lady Gregory. She could have panicked, she could have caused a scene but, instead, she fell back upon her strength of character. Sensing that a distraction, albeit a big one, might just fix their situation, she decided to try her hand at 'fake' automatic writing, just a couple of sentences, enough to assuage Yeats's anxiety over Iseult. Once his mood improved, she would make her confession. If we can imagine a drum roll, it might help us appreciate the importance of this moment in both their lives. Telling Yeats that she was experiencing déjà vu and an urge to write, she placed her loosely held pencil on a sheet of paper, continued to talk to him, and let her hand start writing. What appeared initially were two sentences in code reassuring Yeats that he had married the right woman. After that, Georgie silently asked when she might have peace of mind, to which her hand wrote that she would never regret her marriage. Expecting to stop there, having accomplished what she had set out to, Georgie was bewildered when her hand continued writing bits of sentences on a subject she knew nothing about.

Afterwards, Yeats wrote to Lady Gregory describing how his pains and fatigue disappeared after this 'miraculous intervention'. Of course, many biographers and historians have been distracted by that word 'fake', which Georgie herself used but only in relation to those first two sentences. Perhaps, an interest in spiritualism is required to understand why the word does her an injustice. For instance, her favourite medium, Gladys Leonard, only discovered her gift whilst playing at table-tipping with friends. One minute she is part of a group concentrating on a table, hoping to see it move, and the next moment she finds herself unexpectedly receiving messages from the afterlife. And, so, it was with Georgie. In that moment, with pencil poised, she accidentally presented her writing hand as a portal through which spirits could divulge messages – and thereby saved her marriage. For the rest of their honeymoon, they devoted an hour or two every day to automatic writing sessions.

In the introduction to her book *George's Ghosts: A New Life of W.B. Yeats*, Brenda Maddox is emphatic in her disbelief about George's mediumship. She believes that George was simply using the automatic writing as a more palatable way to insist that Yeats forget about Iseult. Writer Alison Lurie makes a similar point in her memoir about the American poet James Merrill (1926–1995) and his long-term partner David Jackson (1922–2001) when she suggests that their 'Ouija board years' were a desperate effort to save their relationship through an intellectual and emotional collaboration that excluded other people.

Ann Saddlemyer signals the flip side of that first writing session when she quotes what George, as she became known after her marriage, felt she had learned from the control, the spirit guiding their sittings. Yeats was told that he must use only George to ask his questions, whilst George was told she could not be both a psychic and an artist. Unwittingly, she had served herself up as her husband's instrument. From now on, she would devote herself, mentally and physically, to her poet and his art. Following the first dozen or so sittings with George, which resulted in pages of practically indecipherable fragments, Yeats asked if he was meant to spend his life explaining and piecing together the bits of sentences and received the answer, 'No, we have come to give you metaphors for poetry.' So, George's gift was made mandatory for her husband's creativity, declaring her both muse and secretary, albeit not in the usual sense.

In later years, George told biographer Richard Ellman that she found the long sessions of automatic writing gruelling. Twenty months later, following approximately 450 sittings, there were 3,600 pages of Yeats's questions and received answers in George's handwriting. The result was Yeats's book, *A Vision*, an intellectual discourse in philosophy, history, astrology and poetry, which was first published privately in 1925, followed by a revised version in 1932. Yeats and his medium disagreed on how much should be divulged as to the origins of the book, with George preferring to be a silent partner whilst Yeats wanted to show off how he received his inspiration. George told Ellman that the second edition caused the most serious row of their marriage as she determined to prevent Yeats from adding in a description of their sessions, his asking questions and her automatically writing out answers from the other world. At one point, she nicknamed him William Tell.

In the meantime, having passed the test regarding Yeats's female friends, there were two more women waiting to meet her. In March 1918, Yeats brought his new wife to Ireland to introduce her to his two sisters, Lily (1866–1949) and Lolly (1868–1940), and brother, Jack (1871–1957) and sister-in-law, Cottie (1869–1947). They all liked her very much with the sisters sending their father John, in New York, letters praising George's looks and manner. Both Yeats and his wife had decided that from now on, she would be known as George.

Colm Tóibín compliments George's patience and character for managing to remain on good terms with all these women in Yeats's life even as she kept them at a distance. For example, she cooperated with Yeats's attempts to help Iseult after her mother was locked up in London's Holloway Prison for anti-war activities. Iseult moved into Yeats's old flat, while George sent her money and fretted about her in letters to Ezra Pound.

Once married, George took over the renovations of Yeats's tower which meant embarking on a lengthy correspondence with the builder and footing his bills. The tower had consumed Yeats as much as his search for a wife to decorate and inhabit it, and now his dream had come true. George would create both a home in the tower and an environment conducive to writing, which is something she would do again and again, throughout their twenty-two-year marriage, and their multiple addresses, in Dublin, London and Rapallo in Italy. With every move, it was George who took up a paintbrush to paint whatever space she had designated to be her husband's workroom.

George's pregnancy in 1918 caused great excitement amongst the Yeats family, and Lily and Lolly would prove to be doting and devoted aunts. George and Yeats had rented Maud Gonne's house in Dublin, at 73 St Stephen's Green, with Yeats promising to vacate the property should Maud be allowed into Ireland after serving her sentence. Unfortunately, his promise proved impossible to keep after a heavily pregnant George contracted the infamous flu virus and Yeats feared that he might lose her. What happened next could be described as payback for what Yeats had put his new wife through on their honeymoon, regretting their wedding and pining for Iseult. Now, he found himself forced to prioritise George when Maud, her son Seán and Iseult, with assorted animals and lots of luggage turned up at number 73, demanding to be let in after Maud, disguised as a Red Cross nurse, travelled into Ireland illegally. One can imagine George wishing she could have witnessed the ensuing scene when Yeats refused the Gonnes entrance, explaining that not only was the house full of nursing staff, for the dangerously ill George, but he could not risk a raid by the authorities in search of the miscreant Maud and potentially endangering George's life.

A couple of months later, on 26 February, George gave birth to Anne Butler Yeats in a nursing home on Upper Fitzwilliam Street. Afterwards, she cast her baby's horoscope, which yielded a lacklustre future: that though she would be goodlooking and lucky, Anne would lack any significant talent. Two other horoscopes cast by friends proved much more interesting, mentioning Anne's future love for travel and her success in the art world; all of which turned out to be true.

George spent a month in the nursing home, bonding with her baby and resting as much as she could. Her proud husband visited from 4.30 to 7pm every day and relayed details about mother and infant back to his sisters who sent baby-themed letters off to their father and John Quinn in New York. Lily, in particular, was obsessed with the baby and appreciated George anew for her ability to handle her brother. She visited them one morning while they were having breakfast. When Yeats stood up from the table, complaining that his tea was cold, George ran and shook him for doing the neglected husband routine. Similarly, in later years, she could snap when he acted clueless about simple tasks like when she sent him to Lady Gregory's Coole Park with a paraffin lamp and he wrote back to ask her what type of oil he should put in it. Well, not olive oil was the gist of her exasperated reply.

While the War of Independence raged in Ireland, George and Yeats set sail for his American tour in January 1920, baby Anne left behind with her nurse and aunts. Yeats had lectured in America previously, while this would be George's first visit, during which she would finally meet her father-in-law and John Quinn who had organised this lecture tour to raise much-needed funds. A photograph of the couple, taken on their arrival, shows a rather bohemian-looking George gazing pointedly at the camera, eyes brimming with intelligence and perhaps a hint of scepticism, even scorn, while her husband looks his age and is slightly bloated about the face. With a cigarette in his left hand, he is caught mid-wave, bundled up in thick overcoat and cowboy hat against the cold. The trip was a busy one, involving his lectures and the many meals and gatherings held in his honour. There were also the sessions of automatic writing and visits to clairvoyants.

George was scathing about the women she met in New York, shrugging them off as social climbers whose conversation bored her. One can imagine these women mistaking George for being merely the devoted wife of a famous poet. Meanwhile, John Butler Yeats must have met with the same look that George gave the photographer on her arrival. Ann Saddlemyer quotes him about George's gaze being 'so searching' that he felt himself under minute observation until he realised that she was gazing at his expression to see what he thought of her. She sat for him in February, the pencil sketch showing

George and WB Yeats on arrival in America, 1920.

George to be perfectly relaxed, and she did confide in him about her father and grandfather being alcoholics. John Butler Yeats used the word 'genius' when describing her qualities and was impressed by how speedily she learned to navigate the train system and telephone, both of which were still beyond him as a resident.

The year 1920 marked the commencement of thirteen years of prohibition in America, which forbade the selling and drinking of alcohol. Attending a party at John Butler Yeats's patron's house, George smelled whiskey on Julia Ford's – her hostess's – breath and told her husband who remarked that plenty of desperate men would kiss a woman to inhale that very smell, but George assured him that regarding Mrs Ford, no man was that desperate.

So, George was not a saint and did not suffer fools gladly.

Their last weekend in New York, before Yeats delivered his first lecture, was marred by the poet collapsing just as they were to dine with some of

John Butler Yeats's more intellectual friends. John Quinn arrived at their hotel room to find Yeats lying awkwardly flat and felt that his wife should have propped him up against pillows. He also counted the three or four cigarettes she smoked while he was there. For a young woman, her husband's frequent illnesses may well have been frustrating.

In essence, George would spend the rest of her marriage nursing her husband and two children, after she gave birth to Michael on 22 August 1921 (*d*.2007), as the three of them fell hostage to a bewildering variety of illnesses. Her priority was always Yeats, so much so that when she believed the two-day-old Michael was dying from a rare natal disease, she kept it from his father, and arranged treatment with a doctor whereby the baby was injected with her blood, which saved him. She was nursemaid, mother, office manager and interior decorator, on top of being her husband's favourite medium and secretary. And, from time to time, it took its toll.

George and William Butler Yeats and their children, Anne and Michael.

In his 1969 essay about George, Curtis Bradford writes that the elderly George told him a story about taking the ferry from Dún Laoghaire to Holyhead, with the two children and lots of baggage, including a large box of manuscripts that Yeats and Lady Gregory wanted brought to England. On arriving at Holyhead, the customs official targeted the box of manuscripts and began leafing through the contents, but it must have been windy as the pages began to take flight, with George, the official and other passengers doing their best to catch them until George, suddenly overwhelmed by hopelessness, sat down and let them go. Bradford sensed the fatigue and misery she experienced as a young woman with too many responsibilities.

The family spent their first night in Ballylee Tower in April 1921, with Yeats boasting to John Quinn that George had transformed the ruined tower into 'a fourteenth-century picture'. In 1922, encouraged by George, Yeats accepted his appointment to the Irish Senate, and she delighted in his bravery. It was a dangerous time for any associates of the Free State government and George cast an horary on 6 January to ask if their house would be raided or burned down. That January and February, no fewer than thirty-seven houses, belonging to Irish senators, were burned to the ground.

At the height of the Civil War, George and a friend, on leaving a cinema one evening, found themselves in the middle of a battle that obliged them to sprint through machine-gun fire to take refuge at the Arts Club on Upper Fitzwilliam Street until the shooting died down hours later. When she finally got home, she found the servants crying and praying for her safe return. Yeats wanted her to leave Ireland, but she refused to, telling him that she felt no fear over the future; that if she did not fear for him, when he was her whole world, then surely, she was right not to be afraid for herself. Yeats's protests melted away in his happiness that she had described him so.

August 1922 was a pivotal month in Ireland's history. On 12 August, the fifty-one-year-old founder of Sinn Féin and President of Dáil Éireann, Arthur Griffith ($b.$1871) died from a cerebral haemorrhage, and ten days later, his Minister for Finance, and President of the Irish Republican Brotherhood

(IRB), Michael Collins (*b*.1890) was shot dead in West Cork. George, who liked Éamon de Valera, wrote a letter to her friend, English aristocrat Ottoline Morrell saying that Collins was the bigger loss of the two because he was better educated; he read the Ancient Greek poet Homer (*b. c.* 8th century BC) in Greek and was inspired by Homeric heroes, while Griffith, she felt, was too old and bitter to be a statesman.

In 1923, Yeats became the first Irish person to win the Nobel prize for Literature. By this stage, the family were living in 82 Merrion Square and George was becoming lifelong friends with Irish poet and future director of Ireland's National Gallery Thomas MacGreevy (1893–1967) and playwright and director Lennox Robinson (1886–1958). She was also involved with the Dublin Drama League, which dedicated itself to expanding the range of plays on offer. She and Robinson went to the races together, and to the cinema and theatre, and swapped hints on gardening and breeding canaries. They also drank a lot.

In 1926, George wrote that she was looking forward to three days of solitude in Ballylee. Two years later, Yeats released his book of poems *The Tower*, in February, and that signalled the end of days at Ballylee; neither George nor Yeats would ever stay in it again. As novelist Colm Tóibín writes, having been used to inspire poems now published, Ballylee had served its purpose.

Alongside their relinquishing a tower for a home, so too, it is believed, did they relinquish their sex life. Thirty-six-year-old George must be admired for taking this stance when she fulfilled her husband's wishes in every other way. After two children and at least two miscarriages, she may well have decided that enough was enough or she simply had no time to devote to new babies. She told American professor Curtis Bradford about her regret that 'some' of her pregnancies had ended in miscarriages and, that, as a girl, she had dreamt of having six sons. In any case, she relegated herself to carer and expanded her energies on keeping Yeats healthy, along with the two children. Her letters to confidants like Lennox Robinson and Thomas MacGreevy often included the instruction, 'Burn this when read', as she offloaded about her boredom, and echoed her maternal grandmother's words when she wrote that she would never have had a family had she known what was going to happen. Her sense of worthlessness is revealed in a letter to Robinson, telling him that if she ever disappeared, her family would easily replace her with a nurse, a governess, a secretary and a housekeeper and be the better for it.

However, she still had her sense of humour. As Lady Gregory succumbed to old age, Yeats spent a lot of time in Coole Park, while Lady Gregory, in turn, stayed with the Yeatses when visiting Dublin. Following a month-long visit by Lady Gregory, George wrote to Dorothy Pound, 'Christ how she repeats herself.' Lady Gregory wanted Yeats to come to Coole once more, and George hoped that he would go, marvelling that he seemed not to mind hearing the same stories on repeat as, 'Personally they send me nearer lunacy than anything I ever met.'

In March 1928, George took out a six-year lease on a large flat overlooking Rapallo Bay in Italy, close to where Ezra and Dorothy Pound were living and placed the two children in schools in Switzerland. Yeats's health was precarious, requiring constant care and, ultimately, they did not spend more than two winters there. Biographer Brenda Maddox writes of Yeats's total dependence on his wife. On being told that he needed a night nurse to allow George to rest, he burst into tears.

George's generosity of spirit saved her husband and her marriage in its final years, when her husband embarked on a number of love affairs, after a vasectomy in London, in April 1934, followed by a series of controversial injections to rejuvenate sexual desire, amongst other things. For Yeats, his sexuality was a viable necessity to creating poetry – not to have one was not to have the other. They returned to Rapallo on 5 June to hand over their flat to Ezra Pound's parents and pack up their furniture. Saddlemyer feels that George would have been unsettled by their friends' support for Benito Mussolini (1883–1945). By this stage of her life, George was already in pain from chronic rheumatism, and this would be the last time the Pounds and Yeatses saw each other as a foursome.

On their way back to Ireland, they stopped off in London, each to visit their own friends. George went to her mother's house where she enjoyed a long conversation with her cousin Grace, telling her that she had given up the occult because it was 'bad for the children', although she still practised astrology. She also voiced her worry over Yeats's health.

In early October, George and Yeats went to Rome, where he was to speak at a conference. George stayed on by herself to see the mosaics in Ravenna and returned to Ireland on 20 October. Meanwhile, the almost seventy-year-old Yeats went to London to consummate an affair with twenty-seven-year-old poet Margot Ruddock (1907–1951). There would be three more women after her.

When Yeats arrived back in Ireland, exhausted and coughing up blood, George wrote a letter to writer and surgeon Oliver St John Gogarty, asking about the possibility of Yeats having tuberculosis. It is an extraordinary letter, in which George explains that she does not want Yeats to be made an invalid. She wants him to die happy and explains about his London love affair so that Gogarty should understand why Yeats must go on living well.

Later on, George assured Yeats that when people wrote about his love affairs after his death, she would say nothing, knowing how proud he was of them. That is not to say that George was particularly happy at this time. When Michael went off to boarding school and Anne left home, she was often lonely and turned to alcohol as her own health declined.

However, as always, Yeats was her priority. She often accompanied Yeats on his frequent visits to England, travelling with him across the Irish Sea, assisting him through customs at Holyhead before boarding the boat home again. Irish literary critic and writer Mary Colum (1884–1957) described the journey, in her memoir *Life and the Dream*, as the world's most uncomfortable journey over the most agitated sea. However, in this way, George delivered Yeats safely to the other women and was available for good-natured instructions on how to care for him.

In writing about her husband's death in the south of France, in January

1939, Colm Tóibín applauds George's derring-do for arriving back in Ireland without a body. When Charles Stewart Parnell died (1846–1891), his English wife, Katharine (1846–1921), was obliged to hand over his body to the people of Ireland who wanted to bury him in style. George was blamed for her husband's French burial and curtly informed that various folk, from Maud Gonne to the Abbey Theatre, were demanding that Yeats's remains be returned to Ireland. However, as always, George was carrying out her husband's wishes. He wanted nothing to do with the nation's pomp and ceremony that he witnessed when George Russell (AE)'s (*b*.1867) body was returned to Ireland for his funeral in 1935; the streets were thronged with 500,000 people and his body lay in state. Two months after he died, George wrote to MacGreevy telling him how Yeats wanted to be buried in Roquebrune for twelve months, until the fuss had died down, and then be dug up and brought to Sligo. Those twelve months stretched out to nine years due to World War II.

Widowed at forty-six, George had another thirty years ahead of her, which were mostly filled by taking care of her husband's work and legacy. After Yeats's death, she moved to 46 Palmerston Park, which would also house Cuala Press. George had not just cared for their brother for the previous two decades, she had also provided money and support for his two sisters and their printing press, including their long-term staff. For example, when one employee, Mollie Gill (1891–1977), fell seriously ill, George paid her medical bills.

When American professor Curtis Bradford met George in 1954, she surprised him with her knowledge of American writers like Henry James and Ralph Waldo Emerson and impressed him with her generosity, intelligence and wit. On hearing that he was hoping to work with the Yeats manuscripts in her personal collection, she told him to ring her for an appointment, her number was in the phone book. This was her attitude to anyone wanting to see the manuscripts.

Over the years, she wrote plays and even started a novel, but she burnt all evidence of these works. Anne Yeats told Anne Saddlemyer that she remembered finding one of her mother's art portfolios, which then disappeared when she went looking for it a second time. And when Anne asked her mother if she could have the key to Thoor Ballylee in order to paint it, her mother gave her an emphatic no.

George's life from 1917 onwards was so completely entwined with that of her husband's wishes and ambitions – and her children's – that it is a challenge to locate her in the space between 'Mrs' and 'Yeats'.

Despite her loneliness, she always encouraged her son and daughter to be independent and to see the world. She became bound up with Anne's work in the theatre and voted for Fianna Fáil after Michael joined the party in 1943. Her last holiday outside Ireland was to her beloved Italy for eighteen days with Anne. Once the war was over, she had her own battle in the complications that arose regarding relocating her husband's remains to Sligo. She had to field aggressive interference from the likes of Yeats's mistress, journalist Edith Shackleton Heald (1885–1976) and her lesbian lover, the painter Gluck (1895–1978), who blamed her when the cemetery could find no records for Yeats's grave in Roquebrune. However, George had the receipts to prove all. Once she got the body back to Ireland, there was another problem when her brother-in-law declared that there would be no oration or address at Drumcliffe. It was George who had to tell writer Frank O'Connor (1903–1966) that he could not make his planned speech over the grave. She invited him to Drumcliffe anyway, all the while explaining that she, Michael and Anne felt they could not oppose Jack Yeats's wishes. Saddlemyer writes that George was likely mindful of Jack only losing his beloved wife, Cottie, the previous year, in April 1947.

In George's last years, so many scholars and biographers contacted her about her manuscripts and memories that she nicknamed summertime as her 'American season'. But she set standards for the seekers, having little time for those who professed not to believe in the occult or showed no interest in the supernatural in Yeats's work. She favoured biographer Richard Ellman but snapped at him when he responded negatively to her question on whether he believed in ghosts.

On 21 August 1968, Anne Yeats had her customary lunch with her seventy-six-year-old mother and left the house knowing that George was no longer well enough to continue living alone. Back at her flat, Anne fought a migraine for the next three days, as she tried to face up to the fact that she should move in with her mother, worrying whether she would have space and time to work. She rang her mother on Friday morning but there was no answer and at 3pm, her migraine suddenly disappeared; that same afternoon, Mollie Gill went to collect her wages and found George's lifeless body in the sitting room.

Her funeral took place on 26 August in Holy Trinity church, Rathmines, and from there George's coffin was driven to Sligo, and placed in her husband's grave.

In the weeks after her death, Anne Yeats felt the same chill she had experienced in the weeks after her father died, but each morning, on awakening, she felt comforted.

Beatrice and Brendan Behan

CHAPTER TEN

BEATRICE BEHAN (1925-1993)

Wife of Brendan Behan, playwright

Beatrice Behan's memoir, *My Life with Brendan*, begins with lines from a song by Brendan Behan (1923–1964), commemorating revolutionary hero Michael Collins (1890–1922) who was shot dead by anti-treaty rebels during an ambush in the west of Cork.

> My princely love, can ageless love do more than tell you
> Go raibh míle maith agat, for all you tried to do?
> For all you did and would have done, my enemies to destroy.
> I'll praise your name and guard your fame, my own dear laughing boy.

In a piece she wrote about her mother-in-law, Beatrice explained how Kathleen Behan (1889–1984) bumped into Michael Collins on O'Connell Street when she was pregnant with Brendan. Typically, Collins, who was wanted by the British, lingered to ask how she and her family were doing before pressing a ten-pound note into her hands. Thus, the song is Brendan's tribute to the man and his generosity and was, according to Beatrice, the first song written about Michael Collins.

Beatrice published her memoir in 1973, nine years after her husband's death and three years after she and the Behan family cooperated with Irish writer Ulick O'Connor (1928–2019) for his biography, *Brendan Behan*, which proved sensational with its allusion to Behan's alleged bisexuality. Beatrice, who never fell out with anyone, declared, 'I am never speaking to that man [Ulick O'Connor] again!' If ever she found herself in his company, she steered clear of him and told her children to ignore him. Apart from his book's claims, Beatrice was also hurt by the fact that she had given O'Connor original material which was never returned.

Perhaps wanting to sow seeds of doubt around O'Connor's controversial account, Beatrice alludes to, in her book, a satisfying sex life in the early years of her marriage. She also mentions Brendan's short-lived affair with another woman and even repeats the rumour that this woman might have been pregnant with his child, which, it turns out, was no rumour.

During one of the last conversations Beatrice had with her husband, as he lay dying in his Meath Hospital bed, he told her that she had only ever made one foolish mistake in her life and that was to marry him. Plenty may well have agreed with him. Her own friends had predicted the marriage would not last four months, and that she would never put up with him. However, Beatrice proved them all wrong and replied, 'I saw the two days, Brendan, and that is all that mattered,' the good days as well as the bad.

In fact, this exchange echoed one that took place between Brendan Behan's maternal grandparents, John and Kathleen Kearney, whose wealth had been lost through bad decisions. As John lay dying, he remarked to his wife, 'I could have done better.' She replied, 'Well, we saw the two days, one wet, one fine.'

Beatrice was widowed after nine years of marriage, her forty-one-year-old husband's body wrecked, inside and out, by alcohol and diabetes. Unbeknownst to them, time would always be of the essence; their courtship was a mere six weeks on meeting for the third time in 1955.

In photographs taken before and shortly after her marriage, the slim brunette, with shoulder-length hair and a shy smile, looks like the sort of girl who would never raise her voice or cause a fuss, yet Beatrice would prove time and time again that being the quietest person in the room did not suggest fragility. Beatrice was fiercely intelligent and a born survivor.

Ulick O'Connor is not alone in crediting Beatrice for her husband's success. Several of Behan's biographers believed that, without his wife, Brendan's career would have begun and ended with the tumultuous reception given to his play, *The Quare Fellow*. O'Connor praised her patience and 'her inexhaustible tolerance', which few could argue with. No doubt it helped that Beatrice was well experienced in dealing with both temperamental artists and alcoholics.

Beatrice's paternal grandmother was the poet, actor and dramatist Blanaid Salkeld (1880–1959), who was widowed seven years after marrying her husband Henry in 1902. They had been living in India, where Henry worked for the Indian Civil Service. On returning to Ireland with her son in 1909, Blanaid joined the Abbey Players. In 1933, she founded the Women's Writers' Club with fellow writer Dorothy McArdle (1889–1958) and befriended the big names of Dublin's literary set, from Brian O'Nolan/Flann O'Brien (1911–1966) to Kate O'Brien (1897–1974) and Patrick Kavanagh (1904–1967).

In 1937, Selkeld set up her own publishing press, The Gayfield Press, in her home at 43 Morehampton Road. Her poetry appeared in the likes of *The Spectator* newspaper and TS Eliot's (1888–1965) journal, *Criterion*, while Samuel Beckett (1906–1989) was a fan. Salkeld also translated Russian poets such as Anna Akhmatova (1889–1966) and Alexander Pushkin (1799–1837). In her essay about Salkeld, for volume 33 of the *Irish University Review*, Moynagh Sullivan laments that this woman has been largely forgotten about today and is mostly appreciated for being the mother of her son, artist Cecil Ffrench Salkeld (1903–69) and the grandmother of Mrs Brendan Behan.

In 1922, Cecil, a talented artist, left Dublin to continue his studies in Kassler, Germany, where he stayed with the Taeslers, a bohemian couple and their three daughters, Erica, Hedda and Irma. The mother had been a countess in her native Poznań, whilst the father believed in his daughters having a trade. Cecil fell for Irma who was studying domestic economy. They married, obliging Protestant Irma to convert to Catholicism, and Cecil brought her back to Ireland where they had two daughters, twelve years apart, Beatrice and Celia (1937–1984) who became an actress. Granddaughter Blanaid Behan-Walker (*b*.1963) believes that Cecil and Irma's marriage was complicated.

Cecil makes a controversial appearance in writer Joan de Frenay's memoir *Love in the Fast Lane*. She describes the married Cecil's persistence in persuading her to spend the night with him. When she refuses to risk a pregnancy, Cecil tells her it would be lovely to have a baby with her, as he did with his German lover, Carmella, whose son he delivered himself. The timeline of this pregnancy is not referenced, just that Carmella quickly exchanged Germany for America and Cecil never saw his son again. Meanwhile, Joan asked Cecil about his wife and two daughters, to distract him from herself, and is told that she, Joan, was the only one he loved. She finally gave in to Cecil after he threatened suicide. However, Joan's virginity remained intact after Cecil went out and drank all their money, possibly to stymie his guilt, forcing them to walk home the following day, from their Killiney hotel back to the city centre, fourteen miles all told.

The Ffrench Salkelds were not well off, obliging Irma to go out to work as a governess. Still, Beatrice attended the Catholic all-girls private school Loreto Convent at 53 St Stephen's Green, whose motto was, and continues to be, *Cruci Dum Spiro Fido* (While I live I trust in the Cross). According to the 1949 prospectus, annual school fees were £75 with supplementary charges for any student wishing to study extracurricular subjects like music, elocution, and dancing.

On finishing school, Beatrice enrolled at her father's alma mater, College of Art, formerly the Metropolitan School of Art, on Kildare Street. Cecil had attended the school in 1919 and studied under the likes of artist Seán Keating (1889–1997). Beatrice credits Cecil for encouraging her to be an artist. As a child, she loved to watch him work. But her mother Irma had painted too. Blanaid Behan-Walker found some of her grandmother's old watercolour landscapes, after she died, and thought them very fine. However, by the time Blanaid came along, Irma was almost blind from glaucoma.

Six months into her studies, the family's precarious finances obliged Beatrice, at her mother's behest, to reluctantly exchange her full-time studies for a full-time job and relegate college to the evenings. So, she entered the Civil Service, taking a clerical post, in the Office of Public Works, where she processed cheques for the lockkeepers of Ireland's inland waterways. A few years later, when the position of Technical Botany Assistant opened up in the Natural History Division of the National Museum of Ireland, Beatrice made a successful application, and this is where she met Assistant Keeper Mary (Maura) JP Scannell (1924–2011), who would become one of Ireland's leading botanists as well as a lifelong friend.

Cecil Ffrench Salkeld was also an alcoholic, and it is he who inadvertently set his eldest daughter on the road to raucous matrimony when, out drinking one afternoon in Davy Byrne's pub, he heard a young man in overalls solemnly announce, 'A job is death without dignity.' Cecil, whose talent and name attracted plenty of commissions for work, by this stage, preferred not to make a habit out of paid employment, and on recognising a kindred spirit, he invited the young man, Brendan Behan, back to his home on Morehampton Road, where he met the artist's seventeen-year-old daughter, Beatrice, doing her homework. Later on, Brendan Behan would accuse Beatrice of snubbing his 'Good evening', mistaking her schoolgirl shyness for rudeness. But Cecil frequently brought home all manner of folk. From an early age, Beatrice was used to some of Ireland's finest writers – and drinkers – turning up to visit her grandmother and/or father and, therefore, her father's newest drinking companion waxing lyrical about writing was nothing out of the ordinary. She served Brendan and her father scones and tea before returning to her books.

They bumped into each again once or twice over the next few years, mostly when Brendan was drunk and ill-tempered. However, by the time they were properly introduced, Brendan's star was rising thanks to rave reviews of the world premiere of his play *The Quare Fellow*, opening, in November 1954, at Dublin's Pike Theatre. Beatrice, having enjoyed an early performance, had returned to see it with her father and boyfriend Seán. By now, she was in her fifth year of employment as a botanical assistant in the Herbarium in the Museum of Natural History and presumably thinking of marriage.

Founded in 1847, the Herbarium's offices were on the top floor of the museum in Kildare Street until its move in 1970 to the Botanical Gardens in Glasnevin. Beatrice's responsibilities varied in providing technical assistance for the geology, zoology and botany sections, although it was the latter that she mostly dealt with, working alongside her friend Maura Scannell.

Today, Doctor Declan Doogue, botanist, ecologist, writer and teacher, who worked for Maura in the museum, remembers her fondly as a stern taskmaster who expected an awful lot from her technical assistants. For some, she was a phenomenal teacher, whilst others buckled beneath the burden of her expectation, and quit, evidence that Beatrice was no amateur. Back then, most women took a job to keep themselves until they married. The position of Technical Assistant was that type of job, a bottom-rung opportunity to cut your teeth upon before either leaving the civil service or, for male employees, springboarding up the ladder to better-paid positions. Doctor Doogue points out how Maura, who was goodlooking, single and ambitious, absolutely bucked that trend. She gave her all to her job and expected to see her commitment for natural history mirrored in her assistants.

One of Beatrice's main duties involved the processing of new plant specimens into the collection, drying them out, mounting and labelling them. Some days saw her out in the wilds, in search of new plants, where she combined her job with her membership and passion for the Dublin Naturalists' Field Club. Founded in 1886, for like-minded individuals to pool their knowledge and experience of Dublin's natural history, Beatrice had joined the club while still in school. As well as Dublin's outer regions, her work took her to Connemara, Westmeath, Wicklow and west Donegal. In the museum, she helped to stage special exhibitions for the zoological section, such as the earliest Irish botanical publications or plants collected in the west of Ireland.

Apart from Irish plants, Beatrice also mounted historic specimens from the colonies, for example India.

Personal opinions about her work life and politics are scant, but Beatrice mentioned how she was affected by a divided Ireland, complaining how at every border crossing she made for the museum, her boxes of botanical specimens were thoroughly examined for explosives.

There are a couple of photos from this time in the National Library collection. One photo, believed to have been taken in 1953, in the crypt of the museum, shows Beatrice and friends posing with a boar's head. Alongside Beatrice is Maura Scannell and Ireland's first professionally employed female archaeologist Ellen (Nell) Prendergast (1918–1999) and archaeologist Etienne Rynne (1932–2012) who would go on to excavate the Hill of Tara. Beatrice looks at ease amongst this group of heavy hitters and presumably could overcome social boundaries that might otherwise have curtailed the typical technical assistant, thanks both to her family's credentials and her own as an artist.

After the performance of *The Quare Fellow*, Brendan invited Cecil for a drink at the Eagle Bar, an early-house dockers' pub on the north quay, and Beatrice went too. The two men matched each other drink for drink, while Beatrice agreed to accompany Brendan to Leopardstown races on St Stephen's Day.

Brendan told her that as an artist she would be better off with him than with the civil servant (Seán). By 1954, Beatrice had successfully submitted three paintings, over three years, for exhibitions in the Royal Hibernian Academy (RHA) with *Spring in Wicklow* in 1948, *Another Sprint* in 1949 and *The Little Sister* in 1950, following in her father's footsteps. Cecil had first exhibited there in 1929. Working mostly in oils, Beatrice painted landscapes and the occasional portrait. Before that, she had provided line drawings for the 1945 children's book *Lisheen at the Valley Farm and Other Stories*, by Patricia Lynch, Helen Staunton and Teresa Deevy. Six years later, she illustrated a completely different book, *Of One Company: Biographical Studies of Famous*

Trinity Men, 1591–1951, which came out in 1951, and contains sixteen short essays on men such as former president of Ireland Douglas Hyde (1860–1949) and playwright Oscar Wilde (1856–1900). Beatrice provided seven half-page drawings, including botanist William Henry Harvey (1811–1866), whose chapter she illustrated with his namesake, the South African plant *Harveya capensis*.

That same year, 1951, saw her take part in a group exhibition at the Grafton Gallery, Harry Street, with ceramicist John ffrench (1928–2010) and artist and musician Michael Morrow (1929–1994), who had been in college with her. The exhibition was launched by family friend Seán MacBride (1904–1988), the Minister for External Affairs.

In her memoir, Beatrice described herself as being 'intensely religious', never skipping Sunday Mass. Brendan's biographer Michael Sullivan, who befriended Beatrice while studying at Trinity, interviewed her close friend Pauline Parker who remembered Beatrice praying whenever they holidayed together. The pair were members of An Óige, the Irish Youth Hostel Association. Possibly, her devout attachments alongside her father's addiction explain Beatrice waiting until she was twenty-one before drinking alcohol, while another three years would pass before she entered into a serious relationship.

There were four boyfriends before her marriage to Brendan Behan, including future sculptor Ian Stuart (1926–2013), son of Irish writer Francis Stuart's (1902–2000) and Maud Gonne's (1866–1953) daughter Iseult (1894–1954).

Years later, Maura Scannell explained to a colleague how everyone in the museum knew when Brendan was visiting as rather than venture up to her office on the top floor, he would take up position in the Centre Court, the ground floor, and simply roar 'BEATRICE' until she appeared. If Beatrice was too busy to leave work, she made do with joining him on the steps outside for a cigarette break.

When Brendan proposed to Beatrice in January 1955, during a night's drinking in Baggot Street, she turned him down because he had not proposed getting married, only 'shagging off' to the south of France for a 'trial marriage'.

She told him that they would not be going anywhere together unless they were married, because she said, 'It would not be right.' In other words, France was either a honeymoon destination or nothing at all. Brendan gave in immediately, telling her to pick a date in February, his birthday month. Then, in an instant, the tables were turned when she joked that she would have been more agreeable had he suggested getting married in a registry office instead. Now it was he who was affronted, telling her sternly that his was a Catholic family and that if there were to be a marriage it would only take place in a Catholic church.

We realise Beatrice was only joking when, later that year, she refused an invitation to appear as matron of honour at her brother-in-law Dominic Behan's (1928–1989) wedding because it was taking place in a registry office, something she disagreed with.

Beatrice shows strength in her defiance of her friends and sister Celia's sour opinions about a man whose preferred location was the pub. Brendan told her that he liked pubs because he liked people. This attitude to his fellow man was something she aspired to for herself. After he died, she wrote that his legacy to her was a new appreciation and understanding for people of all classes.

As the saying goes, beauty is in the eye of the beholder. There are many photographs of the couple, online and in books, but few flatter the playwright as many of them show Brendan looking bloated and overweight, his features contorted by drunkenness. Anyway, Beatrice thought him handsome and describes herself as being captivated by his voice and personality. Examining her attraction to him, for her memoir, she explained her attraction to Brendan who was widely perceived as a rebel and hard drinker. Instead, Beatrice appreciated him as a compassionate idealist with a great sense of humour.

Yet, with hindsight, she reflects that part of this attraction was her belief that he needed her more than any other man had. She never felt uncertain in his company, although he did expect her to keep drinking alongside him and listen to his stories. And if she did not want to do that, she would end up walking home alone.

In Maryann Burk Carver's (*b*.1940) memoir *What it Used to Be Like*, about her marriage to American writer, and alcoholic, Raymond Carver (1938–1988), she writes about having to go along with her husband and 'be a good sport' for fear that she would be left behind.

Nonetheless, it takes guts for a shy, young woman to persist with a socially unpopular partner. For one thing, Brendan was decidedly working class, a housepainter from inner-city Dublin, now residing in Kildare Road, Crumlin, whilst the Ffrench Salkelds considered themselves somewhere between upper-class and gentry.

Furthermore, aside from his tendency to get drunk and loud, and insult her friends at their parties, making her cry, Brendan was also a former jailbird. In his teens, he had done time in English and Irish prisons, as an enthusiastic member of the IRA (Irish Republican Army), for both carrying explosives and shooting at two police detectives, fortunately just damaging an overcoat and not actually killing either of them.

Of course, this would be the stuff of his best-loved works but also why Beatrice received few congratulations when it came to announcing her engagement. Not that she could announce it far and wide, Brendan wanted to keep their nuptials a secret but accepted that Beatrice needed to tell her father. After all, it was Cecil who had introduced them, and it was Cecil who understood Brendan's thirst.

With the wedding looming in secret, it must have been a shock to her colleagues when Beatrice decided to quit; the three weeks' notice as standard requirement by the Civil Service meant she had to move fast. She wrote her letter of resignation and made an appointment to see the museum's director, Doctor Anthony T Lucas (1911–1986). Beatrice described the encounter to Maura Scannell. Lucas, in his position less than a year, must have liked Beatrice as he did not hide his surprise when she handed in her notice. Instead, he asked her why she was leaving but Beatrice could only say that, for now, she was unable to provide an explanation, while assuring him that it was not out of dislike for the job. We can imagine Doctor Lucas taking a moment to digest this before asking her, 'Well, then, Miss Salkeld, I will ask you one question, are you bettering yourself?'

What else could Beatrice say, but yes.

Typically, Cecil was in bed when she broke the news. Beatrice thought of her father as one of the first 'dropouts', while Ulick O'Connor wrote that the bohemian Cecil took to his bed in 1957, only leaving it briefly in 1964 for Brendan's funeral. However, Cecil did make it to his daughter's wedding but not before asking her to be careful. Of course, he recognised Brendan's insatiable love for alcohol but he also thought Brendan to be rough. Gamely, Cecil reminded his daughter that she had already experienced life with a drinker, meaning himself.

In *Nobody's Business: the Aran Diaries of Ernie O'Malley*, the diarist recorded a conversation he had about Cecil with the artist Charles Lamb (1893–1964). When Lamb asserted that Cecil had two mothers, O'Malley understood that he was referring to Blanaid and Irma. He had visited the Ffrench-Salkeld house three days in a row to sit for Cecil, but nothing came of it because Cecil was 'sick' in bed. O'Malley knew the artist was hungover but refrained from contradicting Blanaid when she explained that poor Cecil had been working late the night before. Cecil managed to put in an appearance at 4pm, complaining of a sore throat. Neither Blanaid nor Cecil mentioned his drinking.

O'Malley was quite cruel about Irma, who vacated the room on his arrival, complaining that she lacked charm and resembled a sheep's head. It cannot have been easy for Irma to have to be the main breadwinner, married to an alcoholic who was doted upon by her enabling mother-in-law.

A woman of her time, aside from her full-time job in the Irish Sweepstakes office, Irma did all the housework, including climbing two flights of staircases to serve her husband all his meals in bed, and, furthermore, she refused to let her daughters help out in the kitchen. Her manner might have been considered severe in the eyes of O'Malley and other visitors but perhaps Irma felt isolated due to her German nationality. Throughout the 1940s and 1950s, Ireland was neutral during Hitler's war, though there may have been those who might have baulked at her German accent.

Not unexpectedly, Irma and Beatrice's sister, Celia, were appalled at Beatrice's announcement. Presumably her mother preferred her daughter to avoid the same mistake she made, in marrying a drinker, whilst Celia had heard about Brendan's drunken antics from her actor and artist friends. Only Beatrice's grandmother Blanaid was thrilled with the news. She loved hearing Brendan's stories about Dublin and the Republican movement.

Beatrice was less forgiving as a daughter than as a wife. Years earlier, when Cecil was still accepting work, he asked her to assist him on a mural for Jammet's, Dublin's famous French restaurant, in Nassau Street. She had already helped him with his most famous work, *The Triumph of Bacchus*, the 1942 three-part mural in Davy Byrne's pub, Duke Street, that still hangs there today. However, on arriving at Jammet's and finding Cecil too drunk to do anything, Beatrice marched out in embarrassment, and the commission was lost.

In his short memoir about his cousin Brendan, the writer and playwright Séamus de Burca remembers drinking with Brendan and Beatrice in McCabe's pub, beside the Olympia Theatre, on Dame Street, just after *Borstal Boy* was published by Hutchinson, in London, in 1958 and banned in Ireland. Brendan was on stout and in top form. He excused himself to go to the gents, as did de Burca, a minute or so behind him. When de Burca finished, he started back for their table but was waylaid by Brendan hiding in the snug with two glasses of whiskey, making a great play out of offering him one out of Beatrice's sight. When de Burca refused the whiskey, Brendan quickly drained the two glasses, and they returned to the lounge. It was obvious from Beatrice's expression, de Burca wrote, that she knew what had gone on, but she never said a word.

She did not question Brendan's secrecy over their wedding plans apart from briefly considering it a habit from his IRA days. Neither does she indicate what she felt about a wedding party that was solely made up of her parents, sister, friends and her mother's friends, or that she was marrying a man who spoke so fondly of his mother but had shown no interest in introducing her to Kathleen. Evidently, the religious Beatrice was prepared to accept unconventionality and ignore unnecessary details.

Meanwhile, Celia put aside her misgivings and agreed to be bridesmaid at the wedding of her twenty-nine-year-old sister to thirty-two-year-old Brendan Behan on 16 February 1955, at Donnybrook parish church. The bride had two stipulations before she would take her place in church. Firstly, her groom was to have his Confession heard the night before, in order to receive Holy Communion the next day and, secondly, Brendan was to have the wedding car drive by her house on Morehampton Road to let her know that he would definitely be there. Beatrice worried about his getting drunk and missing the wedding; however, this fear was put to rest at the sound of a car horn at 6.30am.

It was an early start for all, in order to outwit any curious journalists, the Mass beginning at 7.30am on a chilly but dry morning. Best man was bridesmaid Celia's boyfriend, portrait painter Reginald Gray (1930–2013), who carried the ring that Brendan had bought at the North City Pawn Office. Beatrice walked up the aisle on her father's arm and joined Brendan in the front pew, noting that he was all spruced up and nervous. Stepping outside the church afterwards as man and wife, Brendan was relieved, 'Thanks be to Jaysus that's over. Let's go and have a few jars.'

Maura Scannell, Beatrice's friend from work, had her camera with her but, to avoid attracting any attention, no photographs were taken at the church. Instead, the wedding party proceeded to Morehampton Road Hotel for their breakfast of bacon and eggs, and Maura was able to take the only photographs of the day. Beatrice's mother, Irma, stands out, with her ready smiles for the camera, and it is hard to reconcile her with Ernie O'Malley's cruel assessment that she lacked charm. One photo shows Irma and Beatrice framed by the doorway of the Morehampton and Irma looks positively giddy. The photograph of the couple surrounded by their guests accidentally captures what might have been a typical moment of the day. Brendan, cigarette in hand, has possibly said something untoward as Cecil, along with a few others, send perplexed looks in his direction, while Beatrice's head is bowed, leaving her mother almost alone in smiling – perhaps defiantly – at the camera. In fairness, Irma must have made peace with her daughter's choice of husband as the wedding party includes three or four women who worked with her in the Sweeps office. So, Irma is still working, and it is she that Brendan tells to pay for the food, whilst he takes care of 'the gargle'.

Without disclosing her feelings, Beatrice merely stated that there were no speeches, toasts or telegrams to be read out. Yet it cannot have been too sombre a day as Maura Scannell, who was due into work that afternoon, decided to stay on, obliging her to take an unscheduled half-day's leave.

Celia asked her sister where the Behans were and was told that this was what Brendan wanted. Not even his oldest friends knew he was getting married. Brendan had reasoned that his was a huge family and if they invited some, they would have to invite them all but that does not really explain the absence of his immediate family: his parents, brothers and sister.

Yet, maybe it was out of consideration for Beatrice that he did not summon his family to Donnybrook church. In his mother's memoir, *Mother of All the Behans*, Kathleen relates how Brendan and his brother Dominic, who had also been a house painter and was now a writer, were constantly clashing throughout the 1950s. She also mentioned that Brendan seldom got on with his father Stephen, who, she felt, might have been jealous of his famous son. For her part, she felt that Brendan owed his father credit for encouraging a love of books in his children by reading to them aloud and because Brendan only championed her, in his interviews and articles, she refused to agree with journalists that he was her favourite child.

One could understand Brendan wanting to avoid family tensions in front of his in-laws and Beatrice's girlfriends who he had, on occasion, drunkenly insulted with slurs about being 'bourgeois swine'.

In any case, after the bacon and eggs had been eaten, and the few guests departed, Brendan decided that now was the time to introduce Beatrice to his mother. His new father-in-law drove him, Beatrice, Celia and her boyfriend Reg to Crumlin where Brendan spied Kathleen heading for the shops. Hailing her from the car, he told her that they were heading to Kennedy's pub in Harold's Cross and for her to join them. She climbed in, asking who the young girls were, and laughed when Brendan introduced Beatrice as his wife. A few drinks later, in Kennedy's, she still did not believe he was married. Beatrice took to her mother-in-law, and father-in-law too, when she met him later on, recognising where Brendan got his spirit and energy from. She even wrote an appreciation of Kathleen which appears at the end of *Mother of All Behans*.

Thanks to the early start, Brendan and Beatrice fit a lot into their wedding day, including a tour of Brendan's friends in the afternoon so that he could tell them his news. At least this is what he told Beatrice. In reality, he was on the scrounge to secure money for their Parisian honeymoon. He hired a horse and cab and left Beatrice outside friends' houses and workplaces. Séamus de Burca remembers him arriving at his dress-hire shop and beckoning him to the basement. Intrigued, Séamus followed him and was shocked when his cousin said, 'To be honest, I was married this morning.' This was followed by a dramatic sigh which was then followed by more typical, 'Now, lend me a fiver.' He was gone by the time Séamus noticed that he had not been told the bride's name. Meanwhile, Beatrice had guessed the true natures of these brief and varied visits, acknowledging that they would not have been able to eat in Paris had it not been for these 'donations'.

Back in the city centre, Brendan realised that he had forgotten his passport, obliging them to take a taxi to his parents' house in Crumlin where, rather incredibly, he, once more, had Beatrice wait outside. She had still met only his mother but did not question his behaviour, accepting that Brendan's reluctance to have her meet the rest of the family was just part of who he was.

One person that Brendan did want her to meet was his oldest friend, Cathal Goulding (1923–1998). To do this, they had to go to Wakefield Prison, where Cathal was serving a sentence for his IRA activities. Cathal was delighted to meet Cecil Ffrench Salkeld's daughter. He told her that he remembered drinking with her father in McDaid's pub but never knew that Cecil had a family.

The similarities between Beatrice's father and husband were tenfold.

In her memoir, Beatrice professed surprise and disappointment at watching most of their Paris honeymoon funds being swallowed up by Brendan's 'prolonged bash' on Pernod. This was the first time she had seen him drink like this. It was only now that she began to perceive the insecure man beneath the boisterous entertainer. Then, one evening, her husband shocked her by bursting into tears. Beatrice had never seen a man cry before and begged to know what was wrong. He owned that he knew he was ruining their honeymoon and promised to make it up to her, and that one day he would buy her a house and diamonds and mink. She told him not to worry about money, that she was used to roughing it.

Beatrice receives praise from all of Brendan's biographers for being the calm, steady force in Brendan's life. Séamus de Burca admitted to Brendan Lynch that he could never have imagined a married Brendan, but when he finally met Beatrice, he really liked her and believed that with her family background she would be able understand and control Brendan.

Back in Ireland, with no savings nor home of their own, they moved in with Beatrice's family on Morehampton Road, but this could only be a temporary solution, and their next move was engineered through her mother's efforts to find them their own place. Irma only relaxed when she heard Brendan at his typewriter as, quite naturally, she feared that he would lead her husband astray and, consequently, banned all liquor in the house, which did not dint Brendan's enjoyment of being surrounded by Beatrice's family.

So, a flat was found and the newlyweds moved into 18 Waterloo Road. Rent was thirty shillings a week and their only income was the five pounds that Brendan earned for his weekly column for The *Irish Press* newspaper, which was rarely enough to survive on especially when Brendan went out drinking. In her memoir, Beatrice provided a complete and thorough account of Brendan's work and process but hardly mentioned her own endeavours. However, she did write that the need for more money pushed her to take a commission from the *Irish Times*, against her husband's wishes, to illustrate a horticultural feature. In vain, she asked the paper for two guineas per illustration but was forced to accept the thirty shillings on offer. Working as a commercial artist was a new experience and she struggled to produce art for a deadline, spending up to two or three hours on something that should have only taken her twenty minutes to do, adding that her drawings of grasses needed to be absolutely accurate.

She had to get used to a new routine as Mrs Behan. Brendan had started writing his autobiography *Borstal Boy*, about his prison experience, and was usually up before her. He did not drink every day, but when he did, he would take off for the pub late in the morning and not return until 3pm. Meanwhile, she and the lunch she had made for him could only await his key in the door. And just like his father-in-law, Brendan rarely returned alone, obliging Beatrice to quickly learn how to cook since her mother had never allowed her to help in the kitchen.

Beatrice provides a balanced portrait of her husband; it is one of the reasons that her memoir is so compelling. For instance, she writes that Brendan would paint houses all night so that she could buy herself a new dress for a party and then, in the very next paragraph, she writes that he did not care how she felt about his family and expected her to go out drinking with his parents every Sunday night in McDaid's as if she had known them for years. In fact, she forged a connection with her mother-in-law over a mutual friend, or acquaintance, when Brendan sent Beatrice to Crumlin with fish he had bought at the market. For Beatrice, this was an opportunity to spend time alone with Kathleen, away from the men, and find out more about this family she had married into. Brendan told Kathleen that Beatrice had known Maud Gonne MacBride, the beautiful actress turned republican and suffragette who was loved, in vain, by poet William Butler Yeats (1865–1939). She married Major John MacBride (1865–1916) in 1903, and their unhappy marriage was cut short by his execution in Kilmainham Gaol in 1916, for his part in the Easter Rising.

When her first husband died, leaving her penniless with two sons to raise alone, Kathleen Behan had approached 1916 rebel and politician Constance Markievicz (1868–1927) for help. Markievicz asked Maud Gonne to give Kathleen a job and she was hired as a receptionist in Gonne's house, answering the door and the telephone. Her duties were light and her wages tiny, but she got her meals for free.

Maud Gonne was a family friend through Blanaid Ffrench Salkeld's inner circle of republican activists, that also included republican and writer Ernie O'Malley (1897–1957) and Thomas MacDonagh (1878–1916), a signatory of the 1916 Proclamation. Beatrice spoke of her fondness for Kathleen's former employer and had cried on seeing the ailing, elderly Gonne in hospital after she broke her hip. A heavy smoker for years, Gonne assured Beatrice that she would stop smoking for Lent, although she could still smoke on Sundays as she did not consider the Lord's Day to be part of Lent.

Towards the end of 1955, Beatrice and Brendan moved again, this time to a ground-floor flat at 15 Herbert Street, which would be their home for the next two years. Beatrice told writer Brendan Lynch that their best days were in that flat. It was here that she would discover her husband's love for animals. On finding an abandoned kitten in Grafton Street, Brendan took him home. This might be Beamish that Beatrice refers to as sharing their flat. From now on, the couple would always have a cat.

Maura Scannell visited them and though Brendan was often drunk, Beatrice easily handled him by not making a fuss, suggesting that he might have 'a little rest' on the couch and letting him sleep for as long as he liked. Doctor Declan Doogue says Maura was good at spotting insincere people. Like Beatrice, she was also very religious but, to the surprise of those who knew her, she genuinely liked Brendan and defended him when her friends lamented his bad language. She believed that Brendan was a shy man whose sudden fame forced him into performing for the company he suddenly found himself in and, although his language was colourful, Maura never once heard him tell a smutty story. Brendan, she wrote, 'liked and admired women as persons'. She described how journalists would arrive from London, get him drunk and then gleefully describe his antics for their newspapers. And when museum colleagues asked her why a nice girl like Beatrice chose a man like Brendan, Maura explained that Beatrice's background enabled her to recognise his potential as a great writer.

And, of course, Beatrice was an artist too. Money was always tight, and she continued to participate in shows, including Conradh na Gaeilge's (the Gaelic League) Oireachtas Exhibition in 1957 and 1958, which attracted a thousand-strong crowds to see the Irish art and culture on offer. Then, Beatrice struck gold, albeit temporarily, when an American tourist paid £25 for her *Bin Day in Herbert Street*, in which she painted local cats foraging around her bin. This was a huge mark-up on the works she showed in the RHA, which were all priced around £10. In 1959, Beatrice exhibited at the annual Irish Exhibition of Living Art, set up in 1943 by abstract painter Mainie Jellett (1897–1944) as an outlet for those whose work would not be confined within the frames of the conservative RHA. We may surmise that Beatrice was continuing to develop as a painter, although, as usual, Cecil had been there before her, participating in the very first exhibition in 1943, and thereafter until 1949.

Rae Jeffs, the publicity manager at Hutchinson, entered the Behans' story in 1957. Her *Brendan Behan: Man and Showman*, published in 1966, is the first biography/memoir about Brendan and makes for a fascinating read as she worked closely with Brendan on his books and, some years later, considered giving up her job to work exclusively for him. She quickly became one of Beatrice's most trusted friends and stood as godmother to their daughter Blanaid. However, before all that, she was obliged to take part in a sometimes-gruelling situation that she termed 'the game of pandemonium', her description for life with the alcoholic playwright.

The Behans were in London for the radio broadcast of Brendan's play, *The Big House* and to deliver the almost finished first draft of his *Borstal Boy* to Hutchinson. Jeffs described her first encounter with Brendan and Beatrice in chapter one: Beatrice was sitting quietly in the corner while Brendan was holding court, singing ballads, dancing and telling stories. Jeffs tried to talk to

Beatrice, but it was impossible with her husband demanding all the attention in the room.

It was early days in Brendan's career, but he was already well known to English audiences. Following the successful London production of *The Quare Fellow*, he was invited to take part in a live interview for *Panorama*, BBC's current affairs programme, with journalist Malcolm Muggeridge (1903–1990). Even before the cameras started rolling, Brendan was incoherent, thus making him the first person to appear drunk on television – and a reputation was born.

The second time Jeffs met them, Brendan was in a temper and Beatrice was weeping in the corner. As Beatrice says, they saw the two days. Bookseller Mary King, who managed Parsons Bookshop, on Baggot Street Bridge, held the couple, who were regular customers, in high regard. When interviewed for Brendan Lynch's book *Prodigal and Geniuses: The Writers and Artists of Dublin's Baggotonia*, she declared that the Behans 'were closer than many married couples we knew'.

Later on, Beatrice confessed to artist Paul Hogarth (1917–2001) that her life was a demanding one. They were on the road for months at a time, to France, Germany, Spain, America and Canada, with Beatrice having to deal with the consequences of Brendan's drunkenness, from his getting into fights, to being arrested in France, and losing his typewriter, all the while straining to protect him from himself and his 'fans'.

Beatrice kept in touch with Maura Scannell with postcards from wherever she and Brendan happened to be. Her messages were bright and breezy, with no mention of literary events or escapades. Instead, she raved about beautiful flowers in San Francisco and feeding wildlife during a picnic in California's Big Basin Redwood State Park in 1961. In June 1959, she found Paris, Brendan's favourite city, oppressive in the heat following six days of sea breezes in the 'auld country', Germany.

In May 1963, her cheery New York postcard to Maura gave no clue as to the stressful situation she found herself in. She had had to follow Brendan, who was drinking heavily, to America after he left Ireland without telling her. She had remained in Ireland to complete her illustrations for Brendan's book *Hold Your Hour and Have Another*. At long last, Beatrice was pregnant and anxious to tell her husband. She sent word ahead of her arrival, but her husband was nowhere to be seen. So, she made her way to where he was staying, the famous Chelsea Hotel, where she announced herself as Mrs Behan. The receptionist looked embarrassed, with good reason as Brendan had told the staff that she was instituting divorce proceedings. She writes that she had managed to ignore rumours of another woman but on finding her hungover husband in bed, she demanded to know what was going on. He confirmed the rumours, adding needlessly that the girl was younger than Beatrice. There was also talk about the girl being pregnant.

Typically, Beatrice cobbled all her strength together and concentrated on the necessities, telling her husband they were to be parents, and determined not to lose him. It took her a while to understand how many of her friends knew about this affair and had failed to tell her. Brendan was sick and needed medical treatment. Meanwhile, there were huge hotel bills to be paid, and Beatrice had no money. And so on and so on.

One of her biggest frustrations was the fair-weather friends that Brendan attracted, who only wanted their bite of celebrity life, caring little about a vulnerable man who was unused to fame and having pockets full of cash. Rae Jeffs experienced this in New York when Beatrice did not feel up to a party they had been invited to and asked Jeffs to go in her place. When they made their entrance, the host, who wanted the famous writer at his party, informed Jeffs that Brendan was not to drink alcohol. Predictably, Brendan stormed off to get himself a whiskey, whereupon the host ordered them to leave.

It was Rae's idea that Beatrice illustrate Brendan's *Hold Your Hour and Have Another*. The book, published by Hutchinson in 1963, was a collection of his *Irish Press* columns. Beatrice's drawings, endearing and comical in turn, are in perfect alignment with her husband's amusing stories. The keen-eyed viewer will spot a cat in most of the pictures.

Beatrice had little time for art in the next couple of years. She gave birth to Blanaid in November 1963 and, five months later, she buried her husband. By the time she exhibited again, she was a widow and single mother of six-year-old Blanaid, and four-year-old Paudge (*b*.1965), whom she described in her memoir, as a companion she adopted for Blanaid. In fact, Paudge was the son she had with Brendan's friend Cathal Goulding.

At heart, Beatrice believed in preserving what mattered. She did it for a living before her marriage and she did it as a wife though the odds of a lifelong addiction were stacked against her, but it did not stop her trying to nurture the artist she knew Brendan to be.

After his death, she preserved his reputation as one of Ireland's finest writers, only ever speaking about him in the best of terms, describing him as, 'the most entertaining and most generous man I ever met'. She bequeathed his old typewriter to the Old Dublin Society in 1987, grateful to find a home worthy of the work that had been produced with it. And she had to preserve herself too. She was forced to rent out half her home after Brendan's death, to help pay off his income tax bill. The assumption that she was a rich widow brought strangers to her door for money owed to them by Brendan. Some claimed to be taxi drivers; others claimed to have paid for Brendan's drinks of an evening, whilst others claimed to have shares in his plays. It was a hugely stressful time, and Beatrice needed her old friends around her, from Maura Scannell to Cathal Goulding.

In October 2014, Paudge Behan gave an interview to the *Daily Mail* in which he described being told at twenty-one that Goulding was his father. Although his mother was a bohemian and a freethinker, she was, Paudge says, also consumed with Catholic guilt. Cathal had wanted the pregnant Beatrice to move in with him, but Beatrice could not bring herself to do so. One particularly poignant detail is that, following Paudge's birth, Beatrice continued going to Mass but considered herself forever more unfit to take communion.

Blanaid Behan-Walker believes the relationship between Goulding and Beatrice lasted several years and that her mother was in love. Goulding was a regular visitor to the house, and always there for birthdays and Christmases, frequently treating her mother, brother and herself to restaurant dinners. Then, when Goulding fell for feminist and social campaigner Doctor Moira Woods (1934–2023), in 1971, Beatrice felt betrayed and devastated.

She continued to travel around Ireland with the children, sending Maura postcards in English and Irish, looking out for interesting plants, and maintained a tight circle of friends that included her mother-in-law, Kathleen Behan. And she continued to paint. An edition of the Irish-American magazine *New York*, published 13 March 1972, in time for St Patrick's Day, contains an article about one of Brendan's favourite New York pubs, the Irish Pavillion, where barman Frank Conefrey remembered Brendan as a gentleman. The pub is known for selling authentic Irish goods and the list of stock includes Aran handknits, Galway crystal and paintings by Beatrice Behan.

Beatrice also took care of her ailing parents and her sister who died from motor neurone disease in 1984. Beatrice tended them all. Celia's death was particularly hard-hitting, so much so that Beatrice could never visit her grave.

When she could, Beatrice returned to her first love, art. Blanaid says her mother's easel was a permanent fixture in the kitchen and the house was awash with books and paintings and boxes of newspaper cuttings about her father. Beatrice was not a fastidious housekeeper, telling her daughter that the dust got no worse after three years.

In 1993, Beatrice bought herself a small house in Rathmullan, Donegal – a favourite place to visit. Thirty-year-old Blanaid was due home at the weekend, to help with the move, when she received a phone call from Cathal Goulding who cried as he told her that Beatrice was dead. For years, she had complained about a painful stomach, but she wasn't one for visiting doctors. Blanaid reckons that her mother did not bother cooking herself proper meals after her children moved out, though she continued to smoke and enjoy her daily vodka and tonic. On the night of 9 March 1993, the undiagnosed ulcer in her stomach ruptured, killing her. Cathal Goulding was one of her pallbearers and the large turnout for her funeral was testament to how much

Beatrice was loved by her friends and neighbours. She was buried in Glasnevin beside Brendan and her sister Celia.

In 1953, Beatrice made a Christmas card, a lino print of Our Lady with the infant Jesus in her arms. Mary gazes at her Son who is smiling at the viewer, both their expressions suggesting innocence of what would befall Him. Twelve years later, Beatrice made another lino print of a mother and child. The atmosphere is dark in this second print that is reminiscent of the 1942 *Stalingrad Madonna* drawn in charcoal by German doctor Kurt Reuber who endeavoured to communicate comfort to his fellow homesick soldiers during the dying days of Hitler's disastrous invasion of Russia. In 1965, the year she made this second card, Brendan is a year dead, and Beatrice is a mother second time around. Once again, the mother in the picture only has eyes for her baby and both are enclosed in a heavy cloak against the winter temperatures. In the background is a tree, alone, and bare. One feels that its thick branches have weathered many storms but understands that though the tree may sway and bend in the gales, it will continue to stand firm.

FURTHER READING

MATILDA TONE

Bartlett, Thomas (Ed.): *Life of Theobald Wolfe Tone: Memoirs, journals and political writings compiled and arranged by William T.W. Tone, 1826*, The Lilliput Press, Dublin, 1998.

Elliott, Marianne: *Wolfe Tone Prophet of Irish Independence*, Yale University Press, New Haven & London, 1989.

Jacob, Rosamund: *The Rebel's Wife*, The Kerryman Ltd., Tralee, 1957.

Keogh, Daragh & Furlong, Nicholas (Eds.): *The Women of 1798*, Four Courts Press, Dublin, 1998.

McNeill, Mary: *The Life and Times of Mary Ann McCracken, 1770–1866*, The Blackstaff Press, Belfast, 1988.

Ponsonby, Arthur: *Scottish and Irish Diaries from the XVIth to the XIXth Century*, Methuen & Co, London, 1927.

Essays

Kennedy, Maura: 'Politicks, Coffee and News: The Dublin Book Trade in the Eighteenth Century', *Dublin Historical Record*, LV111.1, pp.76–85, 2005.

Rendall, Jane, & Woods, CJ: 'Thomas Wilson (1758–1824) of Dullatur, the Scottish Second Husband of Matilda Tone: The Unravelling of a Mystery,' *Journal of Irish and Scottish Studies*, 6.1 pp.25–49.

MARY O'CONNELL

Bishop, Erin I: *'My Darling Danny': Letters from Mary O'Connell to her Son Daniel, 1830–1832*, Cork University Press, Cork, 1998.

Bishop, Erin I: *The World of Mary O'Connell 1778–1836*, The Lilliput Press, Dublin, 1999.

Cusack, Mary Francis: *Life of Daniel O'Connell, the Liberator*, Kenmare Publications, Cork, 1872.

Pierce, Nicola: *O'Connell Street, The History and Life of Dublin's Iconic Street*, The O'Brien Press, Dublin, 2021.

Essays

O'Connell, Maurice R: 'Daniel O'Connell: Income, Expenditure and Despair', *Irish Historical Studies*, Volume 17, Issue 66, pp.200–220, September 1970.

Brassil, Jim: 'The O'Connell vs D'esterre Duel, 1815', paper given to Naas Historical Society, 9 November 1995, and extracted in ardclough.wordpress.com/about/ardclough-history/oconnell-vs-desterre-duel/

CONSTANCE WILDE

Fitzsimons, Eleanor: *Wilde's Women: How Oscar Wilde Was Shaped by the Women He Knew*, Duckworth, London, 2016.

Moyle, Franny: *Constance, The Tragic and Scandalous Life of Mrs Oscar Wilde*, John Murray, London, 2011.

Pearson, Hesketh: *The Life of Oscar Wilde*, Penguin, London, 1954.

Wilson, TG, *Of One Company, Biographical Studies of Famous Trinity Men, 1591–1951*, Icarus, Dublin, 1951.

Essays

Clark Amor, Anne: 'Constantly Undervalued, a Centenary Appreciation of Constance Wilde', *The Wildean*, No 14, January 1999.

CHARLOTTE SHAW

Dunbar, Janet: *Mrs G.B.S. A Biographical Portrait of Charlotte Shaw*, George G. Harrap & Co. Ltd, London, 1963.

Holroyd, Michael: *Bernard Shaw*, Vintage, London, 1998.

Langner, Lawrence: *G.B.S. and the Lunatic*, Atheneum, New York, 1963.

Laurence, Dan H (Ed.): *Bernard Shaw: Collected Letters, 1911–1925*, Viking Penguin, USA, 1985.

MacKenzie, Norman and Jeanne (Eds.): *The Diaries of Beatrice Webb*, Virago, London, 2000.

Oakley, Ann: *Forgotten Wives: How Women Get Written Out of History*, Bristol University Press, Bristol, 2021.

Patch, Blanche: *30 Years with G.B.S.*, Victor Gollancz Ltd, London, 1951.

EMILY SHACKLETON

Bound, Mensun: *The Ship Beneath the Ice: The Discovery of Shackleton's Endurance*, Pan Books, London, 2023.

Heacox, Kim: Shackleton: *The Antarctic Challenge*, National Geographic Society, Washington D.C., 1999.

Herbert, Kari: *Polar Wives: The Remarkable Women behind the World's Most Daring Explorers*, Greystone Books, Canada, 2012.

Huntford, Roland: *Shackleton*, Abacus, London, 1989.

Mill, Hugh Robert: *The Life of Sir Ernest Shackleton*, William Heinemann, London, 1924.

Nugent, Frank: *Seek the Frozen Lands: Irish Polar Explorers 1740–1922*, Collins Press, Cork, 2013.

Pierce, Nicola: *Titanic: True Stories of Her Legacy, Crew and Passengers*, The O'Brien Press, Dublin, 2018.

Rosove, Michael: *Rejoice My Heart, The Making of H.R. Mill's 'The Life of Sir Ernest Shackleton' (The Private Correspondence of Dr. Hugh Mill and Lady Shackleton, 1922–33)*, Adélie Books, California, 2007.

Young, Louisa: *A Great Task of Happiness: The Life of Kathleen Scott*, Hydraulic Press, London, 2011.

Websites

greatbritishlife.co.uk/magazines/sussex/22579381.edwardian-explorer-sir-ernest-shackletons-life-sussex/

womenofeastbourne.co.uk/influential-women/lady-emily-shackleton/

ANNETTE CARSON

Fingall, Countess of, Elizabeth: *Seventy Years Young*, Lilliput Press, Dublin, 1991.

Hyde, H Montgomery: *Carson*, Constable, London, 1974.

Jackson, Alvin: *Judging Redmond & Carson*, Royal Irish Academy, Dublin, 2018.

Lewis, Geoffrey: *Carson: The Man Who Divided Ireland*, Hambledon and London, London and New York, 2005.

Essay

Envers, Theresa: 'Edward Carson, A Family Man' accessed at https://athenry.org/record/edward-carson-a-family-man-441/

Websites

athenry.org/record/edward-carson-a-family-man-441/
stmargaretschurchyard.com/churchyard-guide/12

Newspapers

Listed in chronological order
Berrow's Worcester Journal – 5 December 1885
The Times – 24 August 1901
The Cornishman – 22 August 1901
Evening Irish Times – 7 April 1913
Lincolnshire Echo – 7 April 1913
Liverpool Daily Post – 7 April 1913
Brighton Gazette – 12 April 1913
Gloucestershire Echo – 18 October 1923
Reynolds Illustrated News – 11 May 1930
Newry Reporter – 19 September 1914
Western Times – 19 September 1914
Belfast News Letter – 12 September 1936
Manchester Evening News – 19 October 1923
Edinburgh Evening Newspaper – 20 December 1922
Hull Daily Mail – 18 October 1923
Leamington Spa Courier – 9 February 1917
Leicester Evening Mail News – 2 March 1946

SINÉAD DE VALERA

Brady, Anne M. & Cleeve, Brian: *A Biographical Dictionary of Irish Writers*, The Lilliput Press, Dublin, 1985.
De Valera, Sinéad: *The Enchanted Lake*, Currach Books, Dublin, 2020.
De Valera, Sinéad: *The Magic Girdle and Other Stories*, Fallons, Dublin, 1964.
De Valera, Sinéad: *The Verdant Valley and Other Stories*, Fallons, Dublin, 1965.
De Valera, Terry: *A Memoir*, Currach Press, Dublin, 2004.
Ferriter, Diarmaid: *Judging Dev: A Reassessment on the Life and Legacy of Eamon de Valera*, Royal Irish Academy, Dublin, 2007.
Longford, Earl of & O'Neill, Thomas P: *Eamon de Valera*, Hutchinson, London, 1970.
McRedmond, Louis (Ed.): *Modern Irish Lives: Dictionary of 20th-century Biography*, Gill & Macmillan, Dublin, 1995.

Murray, Patrick and Paul: *The Life and Times of Kathleen O'Connell*, De Búrca Books, Dublin, 2022.

MARGARET CLARKE

Gordon Bowe, Nicola: *Harry Clarke: The Life & Work*, The History Press, Ireland, 2012.

Hughes, Andrew: *Lives Less Ordinary: Dublin's Fitzwilliam Square, 1798–1922*, The Liffey Press, Dublin, 2011.

Marshall, Catherine & Scott, Yvonne (Eds.): *Irish Art 1920–2020: Perspectives on Change*, Royal Irish Academy, Dublin, 2022.

Ó Céirín, Kit & Cyril: *Women of Ireland: A Biographical Dictionary*, Tír Eolas, Ireland, 1996.

Robinson, Lennox: *Curtains Up: An Autobiography*, Michael Joseph, London, 1942.

Rooney, Brendan (Ed.): *Creating History: Stories of Ireland in Art*, Irish Academic Press, Dublin, 2016.

Snoddy, Theo: *Dictionary of Irish Artists: 20th Century*, Merlin, Dublin, 2006.

Essays

Briggs, Carla: 'Out of the Shadows', *Irish Arts Review*, Volume 34, No. 2, Summer 2017, pp.132–166.

Callaghan, Marie Hammond: 'Margaret Clarke's Mary and Brigid, 1917: Mother Ireland', *Atlantis*, Volume 22, No. 2, Spring/Summer 1998.

Dunne, Aidan: 'Margaret Clarke's portrait work steps out of the stained-glass shadows', *The Irish Times*, 9 May 2017.

Pyle, Hilary: 'Darling Margaret: A Look at Orpen's Favourite Pupil', *Irish Arts Review*, Volume 24, No. 1, Spring 2007, pp.86–91

Websites

crawfordartgallery.ie/wp-content/uploads/Made-in-Cork-1.pdf

dib.ie/biography/rhind-ethel-a7651

independent.ie/life/home-garden/treasures-rediscovered-artist-shatters-stained-glass-ceiling/37835558.html

nationalgallery.ie/art-and-artists/exhibitions/past-exhibitions/margaret-clarke-independent-spirit/

online.newry.ie/newry-100-years-ago/newry-municipal-technical-school

ulsterhistorycircle.org.uk/margaret-clarke/

GEORGIE 'GEORGE' YEATS

Colum, Mary: *Life and the Dream*, The Dolmen Press, Dublin, 1966.

Ellman, Richard: *Four Dubliners: Oscar Wilde, William Butler Yeats, James Joyce, Samuel Beckett*, Sphere Books, London, 1988.

Lurie, Alison: *Familiar Spirits: A Memoir of James Merrill and David Jackson*, Penguin, London, 2001.

Maddox, Brenda: *George's Ghosts: A New Life of W.B. Yeats*, Picador, London, 2000.

Saddlemyer, Ann: *Becoming George: The Life of Mrs W.B. Yeats*, Oxford University Press, London, 2002.

Saunders, Norah & Kelly, AA: *Joseph Campbell: Poet & Nationalist, 1879–1944*, Wolfhound Press, Dublin, 1988.

Spender, Stephen: *Journals 1939–1983*, Faber, London, 1985.

Tóibín, Colm: *New Ways to Kill Your Mother: Writers and Their Families*, Penguin, London, 2012.

Essays

Bradford, Curtis B: 'George Yeats: Poet's Wife', *The Sewanee Review*, Volume 77, No. 3, Summer, 1969.

BEATRICE BEHAN

Behan, Beatrice: *My Life with Brendan*, Leslie Frewin, London, 1973.

Behan, Kathleen: *Mother of All The Behans*, Arrow Books, London, 1984.

Carver, Maryann Burk: *What It Used To Be Like: A Portrait of my Marriage to Raymond Carver*, St Martin's Griffin, New York, 2007.

De Burca, Séamus: *Brendan Behan: A Memoir*, Proscenium Press, USA, 1971.

De Frenay, Joan: *Love in the Fast Lane*, Trafford Publishing, North America, 2008.

Jeffs, Rae: *Brendan Behan: Man and Showman*, Hutchinson, London, 1966.

Lynch, Brendan: *Prodigals & Geniuses: The Writers and Artists of Dublin's Baggotonia*, The Liffey Press, Dublin, 2011.

Mikhail, EH (Ed.): *Brendan Behan: Volume 1*, Gill & Macmillan, Dublin, 1982.

O'Connor, Ulick: *Brendan Behan*, Black Swan, London, 1970.

O'Malley, Cormac & Kennedy, Róisín (Eds.): *Nobody's Business: The Aran Diaries of Ernie O'Malley*, Lilliput Press, Dublin, 2017.

O'Sullivan, Michael: *Brendan Behan: A Life*, Blackwater Press, Dublin, 1997.

INDEX

A

Abbey Theatre, Dublin 109, 171, 217, 235
  director 204
  Players 241
Act of Union 48, 63
Adey, William More 89
Aestheticism 68, 69, 70–9
Ainslie, Douglas 72–3
Ainslie, Grant Duff 72
Akhmatova, Anna 241
Alexandra, Queen 121, 127, 129, 137
Alighieri, Dante 213
Amor, Anne Clark 84, 88
Amundsen, Roald 130, 133, 134
Andersen, Hans Christian 197, 202
Anderson, Mary 73
Arbour Hill prison 182, 183
Archer, William 108
Archer-Shee, George 151, 159
Arran Quay, Dublin 170, 172
Arthur, Prince, Duke of Connaught 127
Asquith, Herbert 134
Atkins, Reverend 213
Atkinson, Ella 70
Atkinson, John 65, 71, 74, 75
Atkinson, Mary 65, 70, 74, 75

B

Baggot Street, Dublin 168, 246, 258
Balbriggan, County Dublin 165, 167, 168, 174, 175, 179, 187
Barrett Browning, Elizabeth 216
Beardmore, Elspeth 158
Beardmore, William 124, 125, 138
Beckett, Samuel 241
Begbie, Harold 140
Behan family 240, 252
Behan, Beatrice *238*, 239–62
  Background 241–2
  birth of daughter 259
  birth of son 260
  Brendan proposes 246–7
  death of Brendan 240, 259
  Eagle Bar with father and Brendan 245
  enrolment in College of Art, Kildare Street 242
  exhibits at Grafton Gallery, Dublin 246
  exhibits at Irish Exhibition of Living Art 257
  exhibits at Oireachtas Exhibition 257
  exhibits at RHA 245
  father invites Brendan home 243
  first homes as a newlywed 254, 256
  illustration work for *The Irish Times* 254–5
  illustrates *Hold Your Hour and Have Another* 259
  introduction to Brendan's mother 252–3
  job in Herbarium, Natural History Museum 243–5, 248
  memoir 239–40, 246, 247, 254, 255, 260
  move to Donegal 261
  on tour with Brendan 258
  relationship with Cathal Goulding 260
  wedding 250–53
Behan, Brendan *238*, 239, 241, 243–62
  Borstal Boy 250, 255, 257
  child with other woman 240
  death 240, 259
  house painting 255
  The Quare Fellow 13, 241, 243–4, 245, 258
  Ulick O'Connor's biography 240, 241, 249
  wedding 250–53
Behan, Dominic 247, 252
Behan, Kathleen, 239, 250, 252, 253, 255–6, 261

Behan, Paudge 260–61
Behan, Stephen 252, 253, 255
Behan-Walker, Blanaid 242–3, 257, 259–61
Belfast 22, 23, 24, 26, 27, 28, 29, 143, 144
Belfast Museum and Art Gallery 205
Belt, Richard Claude 69–70
Beresford, Blanche Elizabeth Adelaide (née Somerset), Marchioness of Waterford 100
Beresford, John Henry de la Poer, fifth Marquess of Waterford 100
Bernhardt, Sarah 76
Bishop, Erin 46, 47, 49, 58, 60
Black, William 157
Blackrock, County Dublin *176*, 187, 202, 203
Blavatsky, Helena 215
Blythe, Ernest 170
Bodkin, Thomas 200, 201, 203, 204, 205
Boland, Harry 177, 178, 181
Bonaparte, Napoleon 31, 35–6, 37
   Russian campaign 37
Bonar Law, Andrew 159
Bosie *see* Lord Alfred Douglas
Bossi, Luigi Maria 88, 91
Boulton, Sidney 120, 136–7

Bound, Mensun 136
Bourke, Sara 192, 202
Bowers, Lieutenant Henry 135
Bowles, George 155
Bradford, Curtis 230–1, 232, 235
Brémont, Anna, Comtesse de 80
Brieux, Eugène 109, 110, 111
Briggs, Carla 90
British Museum 120, 214, 216, 220
Brittain, Vera 220
Brook, Lady Margaret, Ranee of Sarawak 88
Browning, Elizabeth Barrett, *see* Elizabeth Barrett Browning
Browning, Robert 117, 119, 131
Burke, Alexander 58
Burke, John 58
Burne-Jones, Georgiana, née MacDonald 157
Burne-Jones, Sir Edward 157, 214
Burnette, Frances Hodgeson 80
Byrne, Kate 167, 174, 176
Byron, Alfred, Lord 69, 169

C

Callaghan, Marie Hammond 190, 192, 202, 203
Campbell, Mrs Patrick 76

Canada 119, 130, 132, 133, 162, 179, 258
Carson family 150, *151*
Carson, Aileen 145–6, 150, *151*, 152, 153, 159, 160, 161, 164
Carson, Annette *142*, 143–64, *151*
   birth 144, 153–4
   births of children 145, 146
   death 154
   death of father 146
   death of mother 144
   emigration of Harry 147, 151–2
   failing health 150, 154
   fate of children 161–4
   final years 153, 157–8
   first meets Edward 144
   funeral 155–6, *156*
   High Wycombe attack 146
   Ill-health of Gladys 152
   marriage of Aileen 152
   move from Dublin to London 147
   mugging and court case 148–9, 155
   nurses Edward through diphtheria 146
   Walter joins Navy 152
   wedding 144–5
Carson, Annette (granddaughter) 163
Carson, Bella 145, 148, 157
Carson, Edward 143–53,

INDEX

151, 155, 156, 157–64
death of father 145
defence of George Archer-Shee 151, 159
first meets Annette 144
first meets Ruby 158
first wedding 144–5
meets Lady Londonderry 147
second marriage 159, 160
visit to Belfast with Ruby 143–4,
Carson, Edward (son of Edward and Ruby) 164
Carson, Edward Henry, Senior 144–5
Carson, Edward (grandson) 152, 160
Carson, Gladys Isobel 146, 150, *151*, 152, 153, 161
Carson, Harriet May 152, 160, 161, 162
Carson, Harry (William Henry Lambert) 145, 147, 150, *151*, 151–2, 153, 157, 160–63, 164
Carson, Ian 152, 160
Carson, Ruby, née Frewen 143–4, 158–61, *158*, 163, 164
Carson, Violet, née Taswell Richardson 163
Carson, Walter Seymour 146, 150, *151*, 151, 152, 153, 160, 163, 164
Carson, William Henry Lambert *see* Harry Carson
Carver, Maryann Burk 248
Carver, Raymond 248
Casement, Roger 130, 175
Catholic Emancipation 48, 49, 50, 58, 59, 60
Charles II, King 16
Charles V, King 35
Chesterman, Gerald William 150, 152
Cholmondeley, Hugh Cecil 98, 99
Churchill, Lord Randolph 155
Churchill, Winston 155
Civil War, Irish 12, 180, 231
Clarke family 199, 200, 203, 205
Clarke, Ann 202, 203, 205, 208
Clarke, Bridget, née MacGonigal 196
Clarke, David 203, 205
Clarke, Florence (Dolly) 196, 197, 198
Clarke, Harry 189, 195–207
blocks for illustrations destroyed during Easter Rising
commission to illustrate Hans Christian Andersen's *Fairy Tales* 197
death in Switzerland 207
death of father 203
death of mother 196
death of Walter 206
elected to RHA 204
failing health 205–6
introduction to Thomas Bodkin 201
stained glass for Honan Chapel, Cork 200, 201
visits Chartres Cathedral 197
wedding 200
Clarke, Joshua 195–6, 197, 199, 201, 202, 203
Clarke, Kathleen 196
Clarke, Margaret, née Crilley *188*, 189–208, *194*, *199*
accompanies ailing Harry to Switzerland 205
becomes Orpen's teaching assistant 196
begins studies under Orpen 192
birth 190
births of children 202, 203
commission to create marketing posters 205
Crawford School of Art, Cork 191
death 208
death of Harry 207
death of Joshua 203
death of Orpen 207
director of Harry Clarke Studios 207–8
exhibits at RHA 197, 200, 205, 207
first solo exhibition 204

full membership of RHA
205
hired by Joshua Clarke
197
meets Harry 195
models for Orpen 195
night classes in art,
Newry 191
organises posthumous
exhibition of Harry's
work 208
prize-winner at Tailteann
games 203
prize-winner in National
Competition, British
Board of Education 196
scholarship to Dublin
Metropolitan School of
Art 192, 195
takes over Orpen's classes,
1914 198
wedding 200
Clarke, Mary *see* Mary
(Minnie) Crilley
Clarke, Michael 203, 205
Clarke, Walter 196, 198,
200, 201, 203, 206
Clery, General 100
Clonakilty, County Cork
93, 97, 99
Clongowes Wood College
58, 60
Clontuskart, County
Galway 144, 154
Coholan, Judge Daniel 178
Coleridge, Samuel Taylor
200

College Green, Dublin 15,
24, 54
Collins, Churton 119
Collins, Michael 177, 178,
179, 180, 181, 182, 186,
231–2, 239
Collins, Mr, tutor to
Constance Wilde 66
Colum, Mary 234
Conefrey, Frank 261
Connolly, James 173, 201
Cosgrave, William T 175,
204
Cotter, Bee *see* Bee Flanagan
Cotter, Dick 178
Cotterill, Erica 111
Courtenay, Ellen 61, 62
Crean, Tom 141
Crilley, Ellen 190
Crilley, Margaret *see*
Margaret Clarke
Crilley, Mary (Minnie), later
Clarke 190, 191, 192,
198, 200, 201, 202
Crilley, Michael 190
Crilley, Patrick 190
Crilley, Terence (Teddy)
190, 191
Crumlin, Dublin 248, 252,
253, 255
Curtin, Nancy J 18, 28, 38
Cusack, Sister Mary Francis
44, 48, 51, 52, 63

D

Dalkey, County Dublin 146,
204

Davitt, Michael 171
de Burca, Séamus 250, 253,
254
Deevy, Teresa 245
D'Esterre, John 50–51
de Frenay, Joan 242
de Valera, Brian 172, 174–5,
176, 177, 181, 183–4,
187
de Valera, Éamon 165,
171–87, *176*, 205, 231
arrest in 1918 175
arrest in 1923 182
becomes President, 1959
185
death 187
escape from Lincoln
Prison 177
release in 1924 183
reprieve 174
solitary confinement 182
takes part in Easter
Rising 172–4
wins Clare by-election
175
de Valera, Éamon, Junior
172, *176*, 183
de Valera, Emer *176*, 176–7,
183
de Valera, Máirín 172, 173,
174, *176*, 176, 183
de Valera, Rúaidhrí 175,
176, 177, 182, 183
de Valera, Sinéad 12, 16,
165–87, *166*, *176*
acts in Hyde's *The Tinker
and the Fairy* 170

becomes involved with Gaelic League 169
begins to teach Irish 170
birth 165
births of children 172, 174, 176, 181
death 187
death of father 177
death of Michael Collins 181
death of mother 175
death of sister 174
death of Brian 183, 184, 185–6
Easter week, 1916 172–4
meets Éamon 171
move to Áras an Uachtaráin 185
release of 1916 prisoners 175
Spanish flu 176–7
teacher training 168
Treaty talks 179
trip to America 178–9
visit of John F Kennedy 185
visits Éamon in prison 182
wedding 172
writes fairytales 186–7
de Valera, Terry 15, 165, 168, *176*, 178, 181, 182, 183, 184, 185, 186, 187
de Valera, Vivion 172, 174, *176*, 176, 178, 179
de Valera family 172, *176*, 178, 180, 183

Derry House 94, 97, 100
Derrynane, Caherdaniel, County Kerry *40*, 41, 42, 44, 54, 58, 59, 62, 63
Devoy, John 178
Dickens, Charles 169
Discovery expedition 121, 122, 123, 127
Disraeli, Benjamin 155
Doogue, Declan 244, 256
Dorman, Reverend Arthur 123, 125
Dorman, Charles 117, 118, 120, 122, 135–6
Dorman, Jane (Janie), née Swinford 117
Dorman, Julia 125
Douglas, Lord Alfred (Bosie) 84, 85, 86, 88, 90
Dublin Castle 97, 184
Dublin Metropolitan School of Art (DMSA) 192, 193, 196–8, *199*, 202
Dulac, Edmund *210*
Dulanty, John 205
Dún Laoghaire 230 *see also* Kingstown
Dunbar, Jane 94, 95, 96, 97
Duncan, Mr (teacher at Clongowes Wood College) 60
Dunne, Aidan 204
Duret, Alexander 148

E

Easter Rising, 1916 12, 169, 172–3, 175, 186, 187, 196, 201, 202, 203, 220, 255, 256
executions 173–4, 175, 202, 220
Edward VII, King 121, 122, 130, 137
Edward, VIII, King 184
Edward, Prince (1894–1972) 127
Eliot, George 169
Eliot, TS 241
Elizabeth, Queen 77
Elliott, Marianne 15, 18, 19, 23, 24
Ellman, Richard 225, 226, 236
Ely Place, Dublin 65, 74, 170
Emerson, Ralph Waldo 235
Emmet, Robert 34
Envers, Theresa 146
Ervine, Leonara 111
Ervine, St John Green 111
Evans, Edward (Terry) 128
Evans, Hilda 128

F

Famine, 1845–7 95, 165, 185
Fanning, Reverend Edward 16, 17, 18, 21, 23
Ferguson, Helen Mary 153
Feodorovna, Maria, Dowager Empress of Russia 137
Ferriter, Diarmaid 165
ffrench, John 246
Ffrench Salkeld family 242,

248, 249
Ffrench Salkeld, Blanaid 241, 249, 250, 256
Ffrench Salkeld, Cecil 241–2, 243, 245, 248, 249, 250, 251, 252, 253, 257, 261
Ffrench Salkeld, Irma, née Taesler 241–3, 249–52, 254, 261
Finn, Alicia, née O'Connell 55
Finn, Reverend 44
Finn, William 55
Fitzpatrick, PV 60
Fitzsimon, Christopher 59
Fitzsimons, Eleanor 73, 77, 84, 88, 90, 154
Fitzroy, Henry, Duke of Grafton 16
Flanagan family 165, 168
Flanagan, Brigid 168
Flanagan, Bee 173, 174, 176, 178, 180
Flanagan, Jane *see* Sinéad de Valera
Flanagan, Kitty 179
Flanagan, Laurence 165, 166, 167, 174–5, 177
Flanagan, Larry 168, 179
Flanagan, Margaret, née Byrne 167, 169, 175
Flanagan, Mary 174
Ford, Julia 229
Fowler, Eva 215
Fox, Kathleen 196
French Revolution 23, 51

G

Gahan, Miss (O'Connell governess) 61
Galway 144, 155, 219
George V, King 141
Giauque, Jean Frederic 30, 33
Gill, Mollie 235, 237
Gladstone, William 82
Glangeld, George 148–9
Glasnevin Cemetery 63, 168, 184, 187, 261
Glenavy, Lady Beatrice 202–3
Gluck, Christoph Willibald 236
Godwin, Edward William 77
Goethe, Johann Wolfgang von 215, 216
Gogarty, Oliver St John 193, 200, 234
Gonne, Iseult 220–27, 246
Gonne, Maud 170, 217, 220–23, 227, 235, 246, 255–6
Gordon Bowe, Nicola 195, 197, 200, 203
Goulding, Cathal 253, 260, 261
Grafton Street, Dublin 15, 16, 17, 18, 21, 35, 37, 39, 51, 256
Gray, Reginald 251, 252
Gray, Thomas 187
Gregory, Augusta (Lady Gregory) 217, 218, 221, 222, 223, 224, 228, 231, 233
Gregory, Barnard 62
Gregory, Robert 217, 218
Greystones, County Wicklow 175, 176, 177, 178, 179, 180, 181, 208
Griffith, Arthur 169, 171, 179, 181, 231, 232
Gubbins, John 41, 48

H

Hall, Reverend Frank 145
Hands, Patrick 49
Harberton, Viscountess 79
Harmon, Anne King 208
Harrison, Mrs (O'Connells' landlady in Bordeaux) 55
Hart, Charles 39
Harvey, William Henry 246
Heacox, Kim 136
Heald, Edith Shackleton 236
Heard, Gerald 113
Hemphill, Charles Hare 65, 70
Hemphill, Eliza (Lizzy) 75
Hemphill, Stanhope 66, 70, 74
Henry, Augustine 105–6
Herbert, Kari 117, 120, 125
Herbert Place 145, 146
Herbert Street 256, 257
Hermetic Order of the Golden Dawn 83, 213, 218, 219, 220
Hickson, John 54

INDEX

Hogarth, Paul 258
Holland, Cyril *64*, 79, 80, 85, 87, 89, 90
Holland, Merlin 91
Holland, Vyvan 80, *85*, 85, 87, 89, 90, 91
Holroyd, Michael 103, 114
Home, John 18
Home Rule 82, 165
Hone, Evie 208
House of Commons 22, 148 *see also* Westminster Parliament
Howe, Julia Ward 73
Howe, Maud 73
Hugo, Léopoldine 78
Hugo, Victor 78
Humphreys, Arthur 85
Huntford, Roland 120, 130, 132, 136, 137
Hutchison, Nellie 74, 80
Huxley, Mr 72
Hyde, Douglas 170, 171, 246
Hyde, H Montgomery 144, 145
Hyde-Lees, Bertha Georgie *see* Georgie 'George' Yeats
Hyde-Lees, Edith Ellen (Nelly) 211–4, 215, 220, 221, 222, 223, 233
Hyde-Lees, (William) Gilbert 211, 212, 228
Hyde-Lees, Harold 211, 212, 213
Hyde Park 84, 211

I

Ibsen, Henrik 108
Incorporated Stage Society 109, 110, 111
Inghínidhe na Éireann 170
Irish Volunteers 172, 202

J

Jacob, Rosamond 15, 16, 20, 37
Jackson, Alvin 145, 147
Jackson, David 225
Jackson, Reverend William 25–6, 32
James II, King 35
James, Henry 214, 235
James, William 214, 216
Jeffs, Rae 257, 258, 259
Jellett, Mainie 198, 207, 208, 257
John, Augustus 217

K

Karsch, Anna Luise 215–6
Kassler, Germany 241–2
Kavanagh, Patrick 241
Kearney, John 240
Kearney, Kathleen 240
Keating, Seán 198, 242
Keats, John 169
Kennedy, Jaqueline 185
Kennedy, John F 185–6
Kennedy, Máire 16
Kennedy, Patrick 185
Kennedy, William 169
Kenney, Father Peter 58
Kensington, London 69, 192, 211, 212, 215, 219
Kent, England 62, 117, 118
Kildare 17, 19, 24, 25, 60, 118, 165
Kildare Street, Dublin 242, 244
Kilmainham Gaol 182, 202, 255
King, Mary 258
Kingsford, Anna 83
Kingstown 22, 144, 173 *see also* Dún Laoghaire
Kipling, Alice, née MacDonald 157
Kipling, Rudyard 102, 157
Kirwan, Ann, née Foster 144, 145
Kirwan, Henry Persse 144, 145, 146, 153, 155
Kirwan, John Joseph 145
Kirwan, Sarah Annette *see* Annette Carson
Kitchener, Field Marshal Horatio Herbert 100

L

Lamb, Charles 249
Lambert, William Henry (Harry) 145
Lancaster Gate, London 66, 67, 69, 70, 74, 75, 77
Lane, Hugh 218
Langner, Lawrence 110
Laslett, Mike 153
Lawes, Charles 69
Lawrence, Thomas Edward 96, 99, 111–2

Leonard, Gladys Osborne 217, 219, 224–5
Leopold II of Belgium 130
Lewis, Geoffrey 146–8, 150–2, 157, 159
Lincoln, Abraham 216
Lincoln, Mary 216
Lincoln, Willie 216
Lindbergh, Anne Murrow 184
Lindbergh, Charles 184
Lindbergh, Charles, Junior 184
Lloyd, Adelaide (Ada) 65–71, 75, 82
  remarriage 67–9
Lloyd, Emily 69, 70, 77
Lloyd, Horace 65–67, 69, 77
Lloyd, John Horatio 66, 67, 68, 70, 74, 75, 76, 77
  end of stipend to Ada 63
Lloyd, Otho 66–75, 77, 80, 82, 87, 88, 91
Lloyd George, David 173, 179
Lloyd siblings 73
Lodge, Oliver 217
Lodge, Raymond 217
Lombroso, Cesare 213
Longford, Lord *see* Packenham, Frank, seventh Earl of Longford
London School of Economics and Political Science 102
London School of Medicine for Women 106
Londonderry, Lady *see* Theresa Vane-Tempest Stewart
Londonderry, Lord *see* Vane-Tempest Stewart, Charles, sixth Marquess of Londonderry
Longhurst, Cyril 123
Lucas, Anthony T 248
Lucy, Emily Anne, née White 133
Lucy, Sir Henry 133–4
Lurie, Alison 225
Lynch, Brendan 254, 256, 258
Lynch, Patricia 245

M

McArdle, Dorothy 241
MacBride, Major John 220, 255
MacBride, Seán 227, 246
McCracken, Mary Ann 26
MacDonagh, Thomas 256
MacGonigal, Bridget 196
MacGreevy, Thomas 232, 235
McMahon, General Sean 208
McNamara, Thomas F 196
MacNeill, Eoin 173
McQuaid, Archbishop John Charles 207
McVeigh, Miss (teacher of Sinéad de Valera) 167
Maddox, Brenda 225, 233

Malone, Michael 172
Markievicz, Constance 175, 202, 255
Marshall, Catherine 193
Martin, Eliza 18
Martin, Father 172
Martyn, Edward 171
Maugham, William Somerset 212
Mead, George Robert Stow 214–5
Mealy's Auctioneers 189
Merchant Navy 119, 120
Merrill, James 225
Merrion Square, Dublin 41, 47, 48, 52, 57, 59, 61, 65, 66, 97, 146, 147, 232
Mill, Hugh Robert 119–21, 124, 125, 126, 129, 130, 132–3, 134, 135, 137, 138, 139–41
Mills, Ivor 143
Mills, James Porter 112–3,
Mitchel, John 167
Molinos, Miguel de 85, 215
Molloy, Austin 198
Moran, Mrs (school principal in Edenderry) 168, 169
Morehampton Road, Dublin 172, 241, 243, 251, 254
Morgan, Detective Sergeant 149
Moore. George 12, 170, 171
Moore, Thomas 187

Morrell, Ottoline 231–2
Morris, Jane 68
Morris, William 68
Morrow, Michael 246
Moyle, Franny 67, 74, 78, 83
Muggeridge, Malcolm 258
Mullen, Karl 189
Munthe, Axel 93, 100–2, 105
Murray, Daniel, Archbishop of Dublin 51
Murray, Patrick 178
Murray, Paul 178
Mussolini, Benito 184, 233

N

Nagle, Minnie 191
Napper Tandy, James 31
National Antarctic Expedition *see Discovery* expedition
National Museum of Ireland Natural History Division 243–4
Nettleship, Adeline (Ada) 76, 77
Nettleship, John 76
Newcombe, Bertha 104
Newry, County Down 159, 190–92, 195
Ní Chuív, Nora 187
North Frederick Street, Dublin 196, 199, 200, 201
Nugent, Frank 122, 126

O

Oakley, Ann 101
Oates, Caroline 135
Oates, Lawrence (Titus) 128, 135
O'Brien, Dermod 207
O'Brien, Flann *see* Brian O'Nolan/Flann O'Brien
O'Brien, Julia 204
O'Brien, Kate 241
O'Connell, Catherine (Kate) 46, 60
O'Connell, Count Daniel (The General) 52, 54, 56, 57, 59
O'Connell, Daniel 41, 42–63, 96, 167
 accusations by Ellen Courtenay 61–2
 death of father 47
 death of Mary 63
 death of uncle (Hunting Cap) 58
 duels 50–52
 inherits Derrynane House 58
 joins Catholic Committee 48
 revelation of marriage to his uncle (Hunting Cap) 44
 secret engagement 42–3
 speech at Royal Exchange, 1800 48
 takes seat at Westminster 60
 uncle (Hunting Cap) changes will to favour John 45–6
 wins Clare by-election 59
 wedding 44, 65
O'Connell, Daniel (son of Mary and Daniel) 42
O'Connell, Daniel (Splinter) 43
O'Connell, Edward 47
O'Connell, Elizabeth (Betsey) (sister of Mary) 48, 60
O'Connell, Elizabeth, née Coppinger 45
O'Connell, Ellen, née Tuohy 42
O'Connell, Ellen (sister of Daniel) 54
O'Connell, Ellen (daughter of Mary and Daniel) 46, 55, 56, 59
O'Connell, James 43, 53, 54, 57, 58, 59
O'Connell, John (brother of Daniel) 44, 45, 46, 58, 59
O'Connell, John (son of Mary and Daniel) 48, 54, 62
O'Connell, Kathleen 178, 182, 183
O'Connell, Kitty 46
O'Connell, Mary *40*, 41–63
 accusation by Ellen Courtenay 61–2
 birth 42
 births of children 42, 45,

46, 47, 48, 54
childhood encounters with gaoler 49
death 63
deaths of children 42, 47, 48, 54
death of father 42
lives in France 54–6
moves to Cahersiveen to live with in-laws 45
moves to Derrynane House 58–9
moves to Dublin 46
moves to Southampton 56
political tour with Daniel 62
pregnancies 44–7
returns to Ireland 57
secret engagement 42–3
wedding 44, 65
O'Connell, Maurice (Hunting Cap) 42, 43, 44, 45, 46, 53–9
O'Connell, Maurice (son of Mary and Daniel) 45, 55
O'Connell, Maurice R 57, 58, 59
O'Connell, Morgan 45, 46, 47
O'Connell, Ricarda (Ducky) 54
O'Connell, Rickard 43
O'Connell, Thomas 42
O'Connell Street, Dublin 11, 169, 239 *see also* Sackville Street, Dublin

O'Connor, Betsey, née O'Connell (sister of Mary) 42, 43, 44, 47
O'Connor, Frank 236
O'Connor, James 42, 43, 44
O'Connor, Ulick 240, 241, 249
Ó Cuív, Éamon 187
O'Leary, James 53–4
O'Malley, Ernie 249, 251, 256
O'Neill, Thomas P 174
O'Nolan, Brian/Flann O'Brien 241
O'Rahilly, Michael Joseph (The O'Rahilly) 173
Orpen, William 189, 190, 192–8, *194*, 200, 201, 204, 207, 217
Ouspensky, Pyotr Demianovich 113
Oxford University 67, 68, 212

P

Packenham, Frank, seventh Earl of Longford 174
Parker, Pauline 247
Parnell, Charles Stewart 165, 168, 181, 234–5
Parnell Square 196
Parnell, Katharine 235
Patch, Blanche 107
Payne-Townshend, Mary Stewart (Sissy) 95, 96, 98, 99
Payne-Townshend, Mary Susanna 94–8, 99, 107, 111, 114
Pearse, Margaret 180
Pearse, Patrick (Pádraig) 169, 173, 180, 201
Peel, Sir Robert (1750–1830) 52, 53
Peel, Sir Robert (1788–1850), Chief Secretary of Ireland 52
Piccadilly, London 81, 163, 211
Pickering, John 149
Pike Theatre, Dublin 244
Pines, John 148–9
Platt, Peter 148–9
Plunkett, Elizabeth, née Burke, Countess of Fingall 112, 160
Plunkett, Sir Horace 191, 192
Ponsonby, Arthur 63
Pound, Dorothy *see* Dorothy Shakespear
Pound, Ezra 212, 213, 214, 215, 217, 223, 226, 233
Prendergast, Ellen (Nell) 245
Primrose, John 62
Purser, Sarah 198, 205
Pushkin, Alexander 241
Pyle, Hilary 190, 191, 193, 194, 195, 197, 208

Q

Queen's Gate, London 97, 100

INDEX

Queensbury, Marquis of 85, 86, 90
Quinn, John 218, 223, 227, 228, 229, 231

R

Radcliffe, Elizabeth (Bessie) 215
Rafter, Father 179
Rathbone, Harold 191
Rattigan, Terence 159
Rawdon, Francis, second Earl of Moira 25
Redmond, Willie 175
Reubell, Henrietta 77
Reuber, Kurt 262
Reynolds, Harriet, nee Witherington 32, 33
Reynolds, Thomas 32
Rhind, Ethel 198, 199
Rhodes, Cecil 152
Robins, Ashley H 91
Robinson, Lennox 204–5, 232–3
Rodin, Auguste
  bust of George Bernard Shaw 111
Ross, Robbie 86, 87, 89, 90
Rossetti, Dante Gabriel 68, 214
Rottingdean 147, 150, 153, 155, 156, 157
Royal Geographical Society 122, 126
Royal Hibernian Academy (RHA), Dublin 197, 200, 201, 204, 205, 207, 245, 257
Ruddock, Margot 234
Ruskin, John 80, 216
Russell, George (AE) 235
Russell, John 22
Russell, Margaret 24
Russell, Thomas 22, 23, 24, 26, 27, 28, 29, 34
Rutland Gate, London 147, 148
Ryan, Vera 191
Rynne, Etienne 245

S

Sackville Street, Dublin 16, 201 *see also* O'Connell Street, Dublin
Saddlemyer, Ann 211, 212, 213, 215, 217, 218, 219, 220, 222, 225, 228, 233, 235, 236
Salkeld, Blanaid *see* Blanaid Ffrench Salkeld
Salkeld, Cecil *see* Cecil Ffrench Salkeld
Salkeld, Celia 242, 247, 250, 251, 252, 252, 261
Salkeld, Henry 241
Sandymount, County Dublin 168, 181, 182, 183
Sampson, Catherine 37–8
Sampson, William 38
Sandhurst, Lady Margaret 82
Sartorio, Giulio Aristide *92*, 101, 102, 115
Scannell, Mary (Maura) JP 243, 244, 245, 246, 248, 251, 252, 256, 258, 260
Scott, Robert Falcon 114, 121, 122, 123, 124, 126, 128, 133, 134, 135, 136, 141
Scott, Kathleen 114, 128, 135
Scott, Peter 128
Scott, Yvonne 193
Scottish Geographical Society 123, 124
Scully, Denys 58
Shackleton, Aimee 139, 140
Shackleton, Alexandra 141
Shackleton, Cecily 125, 129, 132, 133, 136, 137, 139, 140, 141
Shackleton, Edward 133, 136, 137, 139, 140, 141
Shackleton, Eleanor 119, 133
Shackleton, Emily 12, *116*, 117–41, *131*
  birth 117
  births of children 124, 125, 133
  co-operates with Hugh Robert Mill on biography of Ernest 139–41
  co-writes *The Corona of Royalty* 122
  death 141
  death of father 122
  death of mother 117
  death of Ernest 139

engagement 121–2
Ernest returns from Imperial Trans-Antarctic Expedition 138
Ernest sets off to join *Nimrod* 127
establishes Memorial Fund 139, 140
family move to Tidebrook, Sussex 117
honeymoon to Peterborough 124
introduction to Ernest 118–9
learns to play golf 124
marital problems 138
reunited with Ernest at Dover, 1909 129
tour of Europe with Ernest 130
tour of US and Canada with Ernest 130–33
wedding 123
wins government grant for Ernest 133–4
Shackleton, Ernest 13, 117–41, *131*
applies to join National Antarctic Expedition 121
death and burial in South Georgia 139
death of father 139
embarks on final expedition on *Quest* 139
family move to England 118
honeymoon to Peterborough 124
Imperial Trans-Antarctic Expedition 136–8
knighted 130
learns to play golf 124
meets Emily 119
plans for expedition to South Pole 125–7
return from Japan 119
returns from South Pole expedition, 1909 129
secretary of Scottish Geographical Society 122–4
sent home by Scott 122
tour of Europe 130
tour of US and Canada 130–33
turns back 97 miles from South Pole 129
turns down Congo medal 130
wedding 123
writes first book 121
Shackleton, Ethel 117–8, 119
Shackleton, Frank 138
Shackleton, Henrietta, née Gavan 118, 139, 140
Shackleton, Henry 118–9, 121, 129
Shackleton, Kathleen 119
Shackleton, Raymond 124, 129, 132, 133, 136, 137, 139, 140, 141
Shakespear, Dorothy 212–5, 217, 218, 222, 233
Shakespear, Olivia 212–5, 217, 220, 221, 222
Shannon, James 144–6
Shand, Alec 70
Shaw, Charlotte 12, 13, *92*, 93–115, *113*
annuity for mother-in-law 107–8
birth 95
childhood 95–6
Clonakilty and Rosscarbery Railway 99, 114
completion of first-aid course 98
death and will 114
death of father 99
death of mother 99–100
decision never to marry 97
engagement 107
first meeting with Shaw 103
friendship with Webbs 102–4, 105, *113*
introduction to Fabianism 102
marriage proposals 93, 100
meets Shaws at their home 106–7
move to London 97
Paris for International Expedition of Electrical Apparatus 98
Paris with her father and Edith Somerville 98–9

philanthropy 106, 114–5
portrait by Giulio
 Aristide Sartorio *92*,
 101–2, 115
relationship with Axel
 Munthe 93, 100–2, 105
support for writers
 including TE Lawrence
 111–2
tours France and Spain
 with father 98
translates Eugene Brieux's
 plays109–10
travels following death of
 mother 100–1
travels to South Africa,
 China and Russia 112,
 113
wedding 107
Shaw, George Bernard 11,
 12, 93, 103–15, *113*
approach by translator
 Siegfried Trebitsch 108
break-up with Bertha
 Newcombe 104, 105
correspondence with
 Charlotte 104–5
first meeting with
 Charlotte 103
John Bull's Other Island
 rejected by Yeats 109
The Devil's Disciple
 produced in Vienna
 108–9
wedding 107
Shaw, Lucinda Elizabeth
 (Bessie) 106, 107, 108

Shelley, Percy Bysshe 66
Shelly, John JC 205
Sherard, Robert 87
Siddal, Elizabeth 68
Simpson, Henry 61, 62
Simpson, Wallis 184
Sleator, James 196
Smith, Michael 118, 120, 122
Snell, Thomas 148–9
Snoddy, Theo 190
Spender, Stephen 209
Speranza *see* Lady Jane Wilde
St Stephen's Green, Dublin 15, 173, 204, 227, 242, 245
Staunton, Helen 245
Stead, William 216
Stephens, James 215
Stuart, Francis 246
Stuart, Ian 246
Sullivan, Michael 246
Sullivan, Moynagh 241
Sussex, England 117, 134, 141, 152, 206, 215
Sussex Gardens, London 66, 76
Swinburne, Algernon Charles 134
Swinburne-King, George 67, 68, 69, 71, 75, 82
Sydenham, Kent 117, 118

T

Taesler family 241–2
Taesler, Erica 241

Taesler, Hedda 241
Tagor, Rabindranath 215
Talleyrand-Périgord, Charles Maurice de, Prince of Benevento 36
Taylor, John Henry 124
Tenterden, Emma 156–7
Terry, Ellen 76, 103, 105
Theosophical Society 83, 215
Thompson, Mrs 205
Thoor Ballylee 219, 222, 231, 232, 235
Tidebrook, Sussex 117, 129
Tóibín, Colm 217, 226, 232, 234
Tone, Arthur 19, 26, 28, 33
Tone, Fanny 19, 25
Tone, Francis Rawdon (Frank) 25, 31, 33, 34, 37
Tone, Grace Georgiana 39
Tone, Jonathan 22, 24, 25
Tone, Maria 19, 20, 21, 23, 31, 34, 37
Tone, Mary 19, 22, 24–30, 33
Tone, Margaret 19, 22
Tone, Martha *see* Matilda Tone
Tone, Matilda 12, *14*, 15–39
altercation with brother 23
America with William 34
arrival in Hamburg to news of failed rebellion

in Cork 30
Atlantic crossing to join her husband 30
bids farewell to William 37
births of children 19, 22, 23, 25
changes name from Martha to Matilda 18
death and burial 39
death of brother-in-law William 33
death of grandfather 23
death of second husband 38
death of sister-in-law and husband 33
death of Theobald Wolfe Tone 32
deaths of children 23, 34, 39
disowned by family 18
emigration to America 26–7
execution of brother-in-law Matthew 33
execution of Thomas Russell 34
first sighting of Theobald Wolfe Tone 16–7
Georgetown 37–9
grandfather withdraws financial support 18
husband leaves America for France 28
husband leaves to study in London 20

marriage to Theobald Wolfe Tone 17
marriage to Thomas Wilson 37
memoir 18, 23, 34, 36, 37
miscarriage in America 29
moves to Dublin on husband's return from London 21
moves to Kildare to live with Tones 19
moves to Paris with children 31
petitions Napoleon 36
petitions Talleyrand-Périgord 36–7
pregnancy and loss of child, 1796 28–9
publication of *Life of Wolfe Tone* 38
return to Kildare 24
reunited with husband in Holland 31
robbery at Tone house 19–20
St Germain to be near William 35–6
summer in Irishtown 22
Tone, Matthew 19, 31, 33
Tone, Peter 17, 19–24
Tone, Richard Griffith, 22, 23, 25
Tone, Theobald Wolfe 12, 15–39, 96
auditor of College

Historical Society 19
bankruptcy of father 22
capture off coast of Donegal 32
Catholic Committee job 24
death 32
deaths of sister and uncle 25
discord with James Napper Tandy 31
emigration to America 26–7
failure of Bantry Bay expedition 29–30
failure of father's business 17
failure of second attempt at Irish invasion 31
first sighting of Martha Witherington 16–7
founding member of Society of United Irishmen 23–4
graduation from Trinity 19
implicated when Reverend William Jackson arrested 25
leaves America for France 28
leaves home to study at London's Inns of Court 20
meets Napoleon 31
moves family back to Kildare 24

persuades Martha to change name to Matilda 18
robbery at Tone house 19–20
sets up home in Dublin with support of grandfather-in-law 21
Thomas Russell joins Tones in Irishtown 22
wedding 17
Tone, William (brother of Theobald Wolfe) 20, 22, 23, 33
Tone, William (son of Matilda and Theobald Wolfe) 23, 24, 25, 29, 30, 31, 33–9
Tower, Reverend Frederick 147
Townsend, Reverend Chambrè Corker 93
Townsend, Horace (father of Charlotte Shaw) 95–9, 107
Townsend, Reverend Horatio (Horace) 93
Townsend, Mary Susanna, née Kirby see Mary Susanna Payne-Townshend
Townsend, Mary Stewart see Mary Stewart Payne-Townshend 95
Townsend, Willie 97, 100
Tralee, County Kerry 42, 44–8
Trebitsch, Siegfried 108–9

Trevelyan, Charles 103
Trinity College, Dublin 16, 19–20, 39, 70, 94, 118, 246
Tucker, Harry 213, 214, 215
Tuohy, Doctor 175
Tuohy, Patrick 175
Twain, Mark 80, 111

U

Ulster Volunteer Force 173
United Irishmen, Society of 16, 23–4, 26, 28, 31

V

Vacquerie, Charles 78
Vane-Tempest Stewart, Charles, sixth Marquess of Londonderry 147, 150, 155, 159
Vane-Tempest-Stewart, Theresa, Marchioness of Londonderry 147, 148, 150, 152, 153, 157–8, 160
Victoria, Princess (1868–1935) 127
Victoria, Queen 121, 165

W

Walker, Mrs Hall 159
Wallas, Graham 103
War of Independence, Irish 12, 179, 228
Washington, George 28
Waterford, Lady see Blanche Elizabeth

Adelaide Beresford (née Somerset), Marchioness of Waterford
Waterford, Lord see John Henry de la Poer Beresford, fifth Marquess of Waterford
Waters, Father 167
Webb, Beatrice, née Potter 102–3, 104, 105, *113*
Webb, Sidney 102, 103, 104, 105, *113*, 114
Westminster, London 123, 212, 215, 219
Parliament 48, 59, 147
Whistler, James McNeill 75
Whyte's Auctioneers 189
Wicklow 204, 208, 244
Wilde, Constance *64*, 65–91, *85*
acts in *Helen of Troy* 80
'At Home's in Tite Street 79–80
attends Lady Wilde's Saturday salons 71
attends *The Importance of Being Earnest* with Oscar and Bosie 86
birth 66
births of sons 79, 80
changes name from Wilde to Holland 87
death 91
death of father 67
death of grandfather 77
divorce 87, 88, 89
edits the Rational Dress

Society gazette 81
engagement to Oscar
74–6
enrolment at St John's
Wood School of Art 72
failing marriage 84–6
fall downstairs 86
financial support of
Oscar 90
first meeting with Oscar
70–71
honeymoon in Paris 77
interest in mesmerism 68
introduction to Bosie 84
involvement in fashion
68, 78, 79, 81–2, 85, 91
involvement in politics
81–2, 84, 91
involvement in
spirituality 82–3
mother's cruelty 67
moves to Germany 88–9
moves to Italy 88
moves to Lancaster Gate
69
operations in Genoa 88,
90–1
Oscar imprisoned facing
charges of indecency 86
Oscar's release from
prison 90
warning from Otho of
rumours about Oscar 74
proposal from Stanhope
Hemphill 70
publication of children's
book 81

relationship with Richard
Claude Belt 69–70
remarriage of mother
67–9
reunited with Oscar after
American tour 73
secret engagement to
Alec Shand 70
sends sons to Europe 87
visit to Delgatie Castle
72–3
visits to Oscar in jail 87–8
warning from Otho of
rumours about Oscar 74
wedding 65, 76–7
Wilde, Cyril *see* Cyril
Holland
Wilde, Isola 80
Wilde, Lady Jane 65, 66,
67, 70, 71, 73, 79, 80,
83, 88
Wilde, Oscar 13, 65, 66, 67,
68, 70–91, *85*, 159, 246
American lecture tours
71, 72, 73, 75
commissioned to write
The Duchess of Padua 73
death of Constance 81
edits *The Lady's World: A
Magazine of Fashion and
Society* 80–1
father's rape trial 67
failure of *Vera* in New
York
final separation from
Bosie 90
imprisonment facing

charges of indecency 86
introduces Constance to
Bosie 84
libel suit against Marquis
of Queensbury 86
Monte Carlo with Bosie
86
Naples with Bosie 90
premiere of *Vera or The
Nihilists* 71
publication of *The Happy
Prince and Other Tales* 81
release from prison 90
reunited with Constance
after American tour 73
signs Deed of Separation,
giving up his parental
rights 89
talks at the Gaiety
Theatre, Dublin 74
*The Importance of Being
Earnest* at St James's
Theatre, London 86
*The Picture of Dorian
Gray* 83, 84
wedding 65
Wilde, Sir William (father of
Oscar) 65, 67, 70
Wilde, William (Willie)
(brother of Oscar) 66,
70, 71, 88
Wilde, Vyvyan *see* Vyvyan
Holland
William of Orange 35
Wilson, Edward Adrian 128,
135
Wilson, Henry 65

INDEX

Wilson, Oriana (Ory) 128
Wilson, Thomas 37, 38
Wilson, Thomas George 70
Witherington, Catherine 16
Witherington, Edward 17, 18, 23
Witherington, Harriet 32–3
Witherington, Kate 18–9, 33
Witherington, Martha *see* Matilda Tone
Witherington, William 16
Woods, Dr Moira 260
Wordsworth, William 87
Worsley, Frank 141
Wriedt, Etta 216
Wright, Sir Almroth 110

Y

Yeats, Anne Butler 227, 228, *230*, 234, 235, 236–7
Yeats, Cottie 226, 236
Yeats, Georgie 'George' 12, 209–37, *210, 229, 230*
   American tour with WB 228–9, *229*
   birth 211
   births of children 227, 230
   death 237
   death of WB 234
   enrols in Heatherly School of Art 214
   father's death 212
   final holiday to Italy 236
   first experiment at automatic writing 224–5
   interest in spiritual matters, 215–21, 224–5, 234
   introduction to Maud and Iseult Gonne 222
   introduction to WB 214
   involvement in drama 232
   Ireland to meet Yeats siblings 226
   later life 235–7
   meets father-in-law 228–9
   miscarriages 232
   Order of the Golden Dawn 213, 218, 219, 220
   parents' separation 212
   remarriage of mother 214
   renovation of Thoor Ballylee 226, 231
   repatriation of WB's remains to Sligo 236
   school 211, 212
   Voluntary Aid Detachment Programme 219
   wedding 223
   works at hospital on Berkeley Square, London 219–21
Yeats, Jack B 203, 209, 226, 236
Yeats, John Butler 209, 214, 226, 227, 228, 229
Yeats, Lily 226, 227, 228, 233
Yeats, Lolly 226–8, 233
Yeats, Michael 230, *230*, 234, 236
Yeats, William Butler 11, 12, 82, 109, 171, 209, 211, 214–36, *229, 230*
   American tour with George 228–9, *229*
   appointed to Senate 231
   automatic writing 224–6
   awarded Nobel Prize for Literature 232
   death 234
   depression on honeymoon 223–4
   first night at Thoor Ballylee 231
   introduction to George 214
   love affairs in later life 233, 234
   proposal to George 221–2
   purchase of Thoor Ballylee 220–21
   relationship with Maud and Iseult Gonne 217, 220–27, 235
   release of *The Tower* 232
   wedding 223
Young, Edward Hilton 135
Young, Louisa 128

PICTURE CREDITS

The author and publisher thank the following for permission to use illustrative material: pp. 40, 64, 85, 116, 151, 166, 229, 358 Alamy; pp. 92 (National Trust Photographic Library/John Hammond), 194, 230 (© Brian Seed) credit Bridgeman Images; p. 199 Centre for the Study of Irish Art, National Gallery of Ireland Collection, IE NGI/IA/CLA2/1/3/2/2;

p. 188 © Estate of Margaret Clarke, National Gallery of Ireland Collection, NGI.2007.71; pp. 113, 158 Library of Congress; p. 14 National Library of Ireland, NL vtls000792813_001; pp. 142, 156 © St Margaret's Churchyard. Text credit: quote from *My Life with Brendan* by Beatrice Behan by kind permission of the Behan estate and publisher. *If any involuntary infringement of copyright has occurred, sincere apologies are offered, and the owners of such copyright are requested to contact the publisher.*

BOLD, BRILLIANT AND BAD

IRISH WOMEN FROM HISTORY

MARIAN BRODERICK

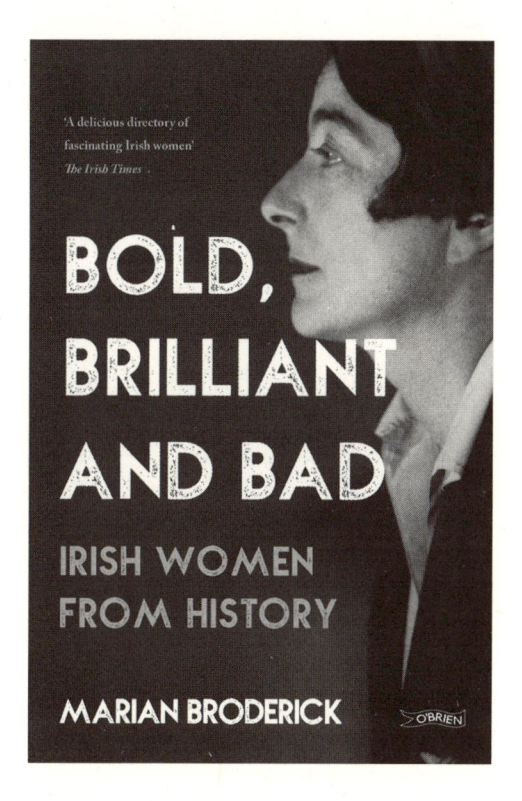

'A delicious directory of fascinating Irish women'
The Irish Times

'Astonishing, true-life stories … [An] eye-opening anthology of audacious dames! Highly recommended.'
Midwest Book Review

Bold, Brilliant & Bad brings together the stories of over 120 amazing Irish women from every county in Ireland. From creative craftswomen to singing sensations, poets to sporting champions. From Lilian Bland to Maeve Binchy, and from Anne O'Brien to Professor Sheila Tinney, these women paved the way for the future and made massive changes in their various fields.

Meet the women from history who went against the grain and challenged the expectations of the world. They were and are a force to be reckoned with.

*'Broderick's prose is simple and accessible, and her fascination
with her two favourite subjects – Irish history and women's studies –
jumps out from every page'*
Sunday Business Post

In times when women were expected to marry and have children, they travelled the world and sought out adventures; in times when women were expected to be seen and not heard, they spoke out in loud voices against oppression; in times when women were expected to have no interest in politics, literature, art, or the outside world, they used every creative means available to give expression to their thoughts, ideas and beliefs.
In a series of succinct and often amusing biographies, Marian Broderick tells the life stories of these exceptional Irish women.

obrien.ie